Protocols of the Elders of Sodom

By the same author

Protocols of the Elders of Sodom

And Other Essays

---◆---

TARIQ ALI

VERSO
London • New York

First published by Verso 2009
© Tariq Ali 2009
All rights reserved

The moral rights of the author have been asserted

1 3 5 7 9 10 8 6 4 2

Verso
UK: 6 Meard Street, London W1F 0EG
US: 20 Jay Street, Suite 1010, Brooklyn, NY 11201
www.versobooks.com

Verso is the imprint of New Left Books

ISBN-13: 978-1-84467-367-4

British Library Cataloguing in Publication Data
A catalogue record for this book is available from the British Library

Library of Congress Cataloging-in-Publication Data
A catalog record for this book is available from the Library of Congress

Typeset by Hewer Text UK Ltd, Edinburgh
Printed in the US by Maple Vail

For Peter Gowan and Philippa Collins

Sancho Panzas and Don Quixotes
And, alas, some Lots from Sodom
Are sampling the deadly juice.
Aphrodites rise from the foam,
Helens shimmer in the mirrors,
And the time of madness nears.

Anna Akhmatova

CONTENTS

PREFACE

What these essays share in common is a refusal to downgrade politics and history in favour of academic 'discourse', the general trend of which has, over the last three decades, been mind-numbing. Aijaz Ahmed, in particular, has written sharply on the impact of postmodernism on discussions of literature and culture as a whole. The same three decades also produced a single and dominant narrative in the form of global capitalism, policed by the economic, political and ideological instruments of the Washington Consensus. This ensemble of relations, in which campus postmodernism played a significant part by encouraging blindness, was severely disrupted by the Wall Street crash of 2008. The events of 9/11 and the subsequent occupations of Afghanistan and Iraq had already made it difficult to completely ignore history. The wave of rebellions and the resulting electoral triumphs for the Left in South America, with Paraguay and El Salvador as its latest, were a clear indication that politics was in a process of recomposition. Now political economy, too, has returned with a vengeance. This has revived an interest in ideas long considered unfashionable or even moribund. A good time, I thought, to publish these essays in book form. The first three were written especially for this volume. Others have appeared in various publications but mainly the *New Left Review* and the *London Review of Books*. Some were published in the *Guardian*, the *Times Literary Supplement* and the *Nation*. Three conversations—Rushdie, Vargas Llosa and Juan Goytisolo—

1

took place at the Institute of Contemporary Arts in London. They have been severely edited. Pedants interested in the complete versions can find them in the archives of the Tate Modern. Thanks to all at Verso in London and New York, and especially Lorna Scott-Fox, for ensuring they were publishable and produced on time.

Tariq Ali
April 2009

Part One

POLITICS AND LITERATURE

1

PROTOCOLS OF THE ELDERS OF SODOM

There are two crimes that would merit death – murder and sodomy. For either of these crimes I would wish to confine the criminal till an opportunity offered to deliver him as a prisoner to the natives of New Zealand, and let them eat him. The dread of this will operate much longer than the fear of death.

Arthur Phillip, first Governor of the
convict colony at Sydney Cove, 1788–92

'Politics in a work of literature', Stendhal famously wrote, 'is like a pistol-shot in the middle of a concert, something loud and vulgar, and yet a thing to which it is not possible to refuse one's attention.' The sentence should not be taken literally. His own work was scented with gunpowder. This most authoritative and political of post-revolutionary French novelists was both justifying his own work and mocking critics and purists who erected an artificial wall to seal off politics from literature.[1] Sometimes even the most aesthetic of novelists find it difficult to restrain themselves from firing a few shots. Proust used a silencer.

Re-read decades later, the books one has loved always contain a few surprises. A first reading is determined by the composition of one's life at

---

1   Till recently, it was difficult to get away with this in France. While many of its media and celebrity 'intellectuals' embalmed themselves under Anglo-Saxon dustsheets, France remains the most politically unpredictable country in Europe – as its President acknowledged in 2008 when confronted with an economic disaster that destroyed the Washington Consensus.

the time. The same is true of subsequent readings. Aspects of *In Search of Lost Time*, long forgotten in the night of time, come to the fore again in the twenty-first century. Literature is sometimes veiled, but it never exists in a world separate from that in which the writer lives, dreams, thinks and writes. The apartness cultivated by some is usually a matter of form. And even the most apolitical or nihilist writers, whether they recognize it or not, are adopting a political stance. It is one of the things that gives fiction its meaning and social significance.

A few paragraphs that I missed thirty years ago, on reading Scott Moncrieff's translation of *Cities of the Plain,* appear startling in the new translation by John Sturrock, which both reverts to the original title, *Sodom and Gomorrah,* and also reinstates sentences and meanings left out of earlier English-language editions, presumably for reasons of delicacy. What I had totally missed in my earlier reading was his linking of Zionism and Sodomism. But more important than the translation is the realization that comes with a second reading: this is not simply a profound account of an extremely frivolous world. It goes much deeper, to become a novel of social, political and sexual crises, of artistic movements and, in its own way, of soldiers and wars. The prodigious love of detail was necessary to the unveiling of an entire world.

The basis of Proust's emotional insecurity was his concealed homosexuality, at least as long as his mother was alive. This guilty desire and how it played in the salons and boulevards became a complete obsession, inducing much self-hatred, at least on the literary level. The famed 'inverts', their habits and manners were all carefully observed and reported but, as the excellent George Painter biography reveals, much of what was laid on the protruding posterior of poor Baron Charlus was, in fact, based on the writer's own intimate experiences. Yet even he, the most painstakingly literary of novelists, could not ignore the explosion that shook France in the shape of the Dreyfus Affair. It divided French society; it provoked an eruption of violent anti-Semitism that affected life in the Faubourg Saint-

Germain. This much any reader can glean from even a cursory first reading of the novel.

Casual anti-Semitism was, of course, common at the time and thrived in every class location. Despite his Jewish mother, Proust was not immune to its influence and was, as in the case of homosexuality, extremely anxious to distance himself from the stereotype so that nothing could threaten his full integration into French society – something that he desperately craved. All assimilation usually requires an escape from some previous ethnic, religious or political identity.

It was this desire to conform and please his upper-class friends that explains some of the more regrettable passages in the book, such as an unpleasant description of Swann – a character based on a person whom Proust greatly admired, and from whom he learnt a great deal regarding the social etiquette necessary to penetrate the prized salons of the Faubourg.

He writes of how 'Swann's Punchinello nose, absorbed for long years into an agreeable face, now seemed enormous, tumid, crimson, the nose of an old Hebrew rather than a dilettante Valois' and then speculates that 'perhaps, too, in these last days, the physical type that characterizes his race was becoming more pronounced in him, at the same time as a sense of moral solidarity with the rest of the Jews, a solidarity that Swann seems to have forgotten throughout his life, and which, one after another, his mortal illness, the Dreyfus case and the anti-Semitic propagandas had reawakened . . .'

Here too, as in the sections on homosexuality, Proust was partially writing about himself. He felt threatened by the wave of anti-Semitism that swept through the Faubourg. The Dreyfus Affair polarized France into two open factions: a predominantly anti-Semitic and monarchist Right, and a cosmopolitan Republican Left.[2] Proust, shocked and disgusted by the

---

2 In 1895, Alfred Dreyfus, a Jewish army officer, was falsely accused of espionage and stripped of his rank in a disgraceful public ceremony, while a right-wing mob chanted 'Death to the Jews'.

talk he overheard in fashionable salons, understood – probably for the first time – how deep-rooted this prejudice was in the upper reaches of French society (and though he portrayed the Prince and the Duc de Guermantes as Dreyfusards, they were a token minority).

Anti-Jewish prejudices were not confined to Proust's friends. The mass anti-Semitism that he witnessed in France had a deep impact on Theodor Herzl, who later became the founding father of the Zionist movement. In Paris at the time, as a correspondent for the *Neue Freie Presse*, a liberal Viennese daily, Herzl was shaken by the scale and character of the racism, and the violence that was never far from the surface. Until then Herzl had been sceptical of Zionism. A couple of years before the Dreyfus Affair erupted, he had written in the course of a book review:

> The good Jew Daniel wants to recover his lost homeland and to gather anew his dispersed brothers . . . But in fact such a Jew should know that he would not be doing his kith and kin a service by restoring them to their historic homeland . . . And if indeed the Jews did go back, they would discover the very next day that they do not have a great deal in common. They have been rooted for centuries in new lands, denationalized, differentiated, and the slight resemblance which still distinguishes them is due only to the oppression which they have had to undergo everywhere.[3]

The ordeal of poor, innocent Captain Dreyfus drove Herzl to rethink this position. Or so he wrote. Proust, while not as actively engaged in the campaign as his fellow writer Emile Zola, was likewise an unapologetic Dreyfusard. The sea-mists of Baalbec had evaporated. He now found himself

---

3   In the opening chapter of his illuminating and stimulating work, *The Returns of Zionism*, London and New York: Verso, 2008, Gabriel Piterberg challenges Herzl's account and suggests that the use of the Dreyfus Affair as something that pushed him in the other direction is itself a cleverly constructed myth.

swept along by a turbulent and controversial political campaign, which forced him to reflect on this and related matters in a way he had not done before.

Though he was never sympathetic to early Zionism, Proust was quick to detect an analogy. From biblical Israel his thoughts flew to biblical Sodom and Gomorrah, depicted as dens of vice. He felt that God should have entrusted to a homosexual the task of determining who was permitted to leave the city before it was destroyed – since only such a person could have recognized the fake heterosexuals, and effectively policed the supposed final solution to 'inversion':

> He would not have been led benevolently to lower the flaming sword or temper the sanctions by the excuses, 'Father of six children, I have two mistresses, etc.' He would have answered: 'Yes, and your wife suffers the torments of jealousy. But even if these women were not chosen by you in Gomorrah [according to Proust and the poet Alfred de Vigny, a lesbian sanctuary], you spend your nights with a keeper of flocks from Hebron.' And he would immediately have made him retrace his steps towards the town about to be destroyed by the rain of fire and brimstone.

In the same passage, the novelist warns that the descendants of those who lied to escape from Sodom now populate the world and 'form in every country a colony at once Oriental, cultivated, musical and slanderous, which has charming virtues and unbearable defects.' Proust is concerned that these 'inverts' might organize themselves and for that reason he 'wanted provisionally to forestall the fatal error that would consist, just as a Zionist movement has been encouraged, in creating a sodomist movement and in rebuilding Sodom.'[4]

I disagree.

The year 2008 marked the sixtieth birthday of the state of Israel, an entity that brazenly justifies its existence and territorial expansion by citing

---

4   Marcel Proust, *Sodom and Gomorrah,* trans. John Sturrock, London: Penguin Classics, 2002, 34–36.

the political geography of the first magical-realist text, also known as the Old Testament – a view uncritically accepted by the governing elites of the Western world, whose Christian forebears regarded Jews primarily as Christ-killers. Is it not therefore time now for other tribes whose tribulations have also been recorded in the same five books to claim what is rightfully theirs? Why should the sauce for the Zionist gander be denied to the Sodomist goose? The Old Testament is seen by some as the family history of the Jewish tribes (for challenging this view in the seventeenth century and claiming that the stories were fairy tales, Baruch Spinoza was excommunicated by the Amsterdam Synagogue), but for the citizens of Sodom and Gomorrah it is nothing more or less than slander, an elder version of what we could describe as the Protocols of the Elders of Sodom: a false account of the destruction of tribal groups that resisted Abrahamic hegemony.

Another painful biblical anniversary was the year 2008. Three and a half thousand years ago, or perhaps four and a half (does it matter?), the cities of the plain, Sodom and Gomorrah, were destroyed by fire and brimstone. The account in the Old Testament is straightforward. A pair of comely male angels were despatched to Sodom to supervise the evacuation of non-homosexuals – amongst whom the most prominent was Abraham's estranged nephew, the gatekeeper Lot and his family – before the wrath of heaven descended on the wicked city and its Gomorran twin. Genesis 19 describes the events preceding the destruction of Sodom thus:

> And the two messengers came into Sodom at evening, when Lot was sitting at the gate of Sodom. And Lot saw, and he rose to greet them and bowed, with his face to the ground. And he said, 'O please, my lords, turn aside to your servant's house to spend the night, and bathe your feet, and you can set off early on your way.' And they said, 'No. We will spend the night in the square.' And he pressed them hard, and they turned aside to him and came into his house, and he prepared them a

feast and baked flatbread, and they ate. They had not yet lain down when the men of the city, the men of Sodom, surrounded the house, from lads to elders, every last man of them. And they called out to Lot and said, 'Where are the men who came to you tonight? Bring them out to us so that we may know them!' And Lot went out to them at the entrance, closing the door behind them, and he said, 'Please, my brothers, do no harm. Look, I have two daughters who have known no man. Let me bring them out to you and do to them whatever you want. Only to these men do nothing, for have they not come under the shadow of my roof beam?' And they said, 'Step aside' . . .[5]

There is no historical evidence whatsoever to suggest that the destruction was accelerated because the burghers of Sodom, informed that two comely young male spies had entered the town, surrounded Lot's dwelling and threatened to gang-rape the angels, but let us take it at face value. In fact, either the angels were being slyly provocative by first suggesting that they would sleep in the public square, or they knew that the propaganda against the Sodomites was false, and so did not feel threatened. Lot's generous offer of his virgin daughters in lieu of the angels was contemptuously rejected by the angry crowd, but why did he make the offer, if he knew they were all gay?

What is far more likely is that in a period when inter-tribal wars were common, the Sodomites were suspicious (correctly so) of Lot, knowing he was in league with their enemies; for that reason, they wanted to see and question the strangers in the house for themselves. It was a perfectly reasonable demand. The angels, acting on orders, refused to permit any inspection and instead hastened the final solution to the 'Sodom question' by bringing forward the fire and brimstone. Even old Abraham had muttered that perhaps the punishment was disproportionate to the crime, but he was overruled by Yahweh.

5 *The Five Books of Moses,* trans. Robert Alter, New York: W. W. Norton & Co., 2004, 91–97.

There has been speculation that the Sodomites were, in fact, members of the Essenian sect, which according to the ancient Jewish historian, Josephus, was the purest of them all in terms of celibacy and self-restraint. Flavius Josephus, born Joseph ben Matthias in Palestine in 37 AD, the year of Caligula's accession, served in the Roman occupation army, became Governor of Galilee, took an heiress as his second wife and settled down to writing history. He produced his account of the wars roughly at the same time as the gospels were being drafted by Matthew and Mark. The opening paragraph of the chapter titled 'Jewish Sects' provides a fascinating glimpse of tribal life, and a few clues as to the primitive communist beliefs of the Sodomites, or Essenes:

> Among the Jews there are three schools of thought, whose adherents are called Pharisees, Sadducees, and Essenes respectively. The Essenes profess a severer discipline: they are Jews by birth and are peculiarly attached to each other. They eschew pleasure-seeking as a vice and regard temperance and mastery of the passions as a virtue. Scorning wedlock, they select other men's children while still pliable and teachable, and fashion them after their own pattern – not that they wish to do away with marriage as a means of continuing the race, but they are afraid of the promiscuity of women and convinced that none of the sex remains faithful to one man. Contemptuous of wealth . . . their rule is that novices admitted to the sect must surrender their property to the order so that among them all neither humiliating poverty nor excessive wealth is ever seen, but each man's possessions go into the pool and as with brothers their entire property belongs to them all . . . Men to supervise the community's affairs are elected by a show of hands.[6]

Naturally, Josephus does not exclude the possibility that the Essenes tolerated or even encouraged homosexuality. Having spent some time in Rome, this might even have struck him as a modern and civilized way of life.

6 Josephus, *The Jewish War*, trans. G. A. Williamson, London: Penguin, 1959, 125.

However, the authors of the Old Testament retain only the version espoused by Abraham and his successors, according to which the angels, acting on behalf of God and his chosen people, saved Lot and his family together with a tiny minority of heterosexuals, warning them that they must leave evil behind them for ever and on no account look back at the fire and brimstone devouring their city. Witnesses can be dangerous. Lot's wife (like Orpheus in Greek mythology) disobeyed the divine injunction and was turned into a pillar of salt, which doubtless crumbled in time to further pollute the ecology of the Dead Sea.

We are told that Lot, not entirely unhappy with the transubstantiation of his wife into salt, retired to a cave in the hills with his virgin daughters, who ignoring the incest taboo got their father drunk and proceeded to have sexual intercourse with him. In the words of Genesis (19: 31–36):

And Lot came up from Zoar and settled in the high country, his two daughters together with him . . . and he dwelt in a certain cave, he and his two daughters. And the elder said to the younger, 'Our father is old, and there is no man on earth to come to bed with us like the way of all earth. Come, let us give our father wine to drink and let us lie with him, so that we may keep alive seed from our father.' And they gave their father wine to drink that night, and the elder came and lay with her father, and he knew not when she lay down or when she arose. And on the next day the older said to the younger, 'Look, last night I lay with my father. Let us give him wine to drink tonight as well, and come, lie with him, so that we may keep alive seed from our father.' And on that night as well they gave their father wine to drink, and the younger arose and lay with him, and he knew not when she lay down or when she arose. And the two daughters of Lot conceived by their father. And the elder bore a son and called his name Moab; he is the father of Moab of our days. And the younger as well bore a son and called his name Ben-Ammi; he is the father of the Ammonites of our days.

Lot, drowsy with wine, was largely out of it, but rape is certainly not implied. The girls, however, were extremely active. Why did they do what they did? Could frustrated broodiness have been compounded by a desire for revenge? They couldn't have been too pleased at being offered as a sacrifice to the citizens of Sodom, even if they knew they were in no danger from such men. Did Lot regard what they did to him as a punishment? Genesis is tantalizingly silent on these matters, making further speculation pointless. However, one is forced to deduce from what is written that fornication must have been frequent, since both girls produced healthy sons and grandsons: Ammon and Moab, the eponymous founders of tribes that later refused to accept Canaanite (orthodox Jewish) discipline. Why do the authors of Genesis slander Lot so viciously? It could only have been the result of violent factional disputes with Jacob over land and sheep, from which Lot emerged the loser; and history, as we well know, is usually written on behalf of the victors.

Did Lot ever regret his folly in not defying his uncle? Might he not have been better off had he aligned himself with the citizens of Sodom and Gomorrah, warning them of their impending doom and enabling the entire population to escape the fire and brimstone. It might have made Proust unhappy many centuries later, but Lot's place in history, as the José Martí of Sodom, would have been assured forever. Who remembers him now, apart from biblical scholars?

The Gospels are less strident on this issue. If we are to believe Morton Smith, the late Professor of ancient history at Columbia University, there may be a reason for this mildness. According to Smith and accepted by many scholars, a clandestine edition of St Mark's Gospel had been in existence for some time after the death of Christ: Smith had discovered a reference to it in a document dating back to 200AD. The author was a respected Church ideologue, Clement of Alexandria, and the document now in Smith's possession had lain undiscovered in an ancient monastery close to Jerusalem. According to this source, a Gnostic second-century sect known as the Carpocratians had circulated and used the secret gospel to good effect. They accepted Jesus as a prophet worthy of divine honour, but also studied the works of Pythagoras, Plato and Aristotle. They used material from the secret gospel of Mark to argue that Jesus had proclaimed the end of all laws and prohibitions, and told his followers that they were free: they could even win salvation through acts of which it had been hitherto difficult to speak, given the Old Testament strictures.

Clement, unsurprisingly, was extremely critical of Carpocrates and his sect and their 'unspeakable teachings'. He cited a passage from the secret gospel according to which Jesus, having raised a wealthy teenager from the dead in Bethany, became over-friendly with him. Writes Clement, quoting from the gospel: 'after six days Jesus told him what to do and in the evening the youth came to him, wearing a linen cloth over his naked body. And he remained with him that night, for Jesus taught him the mystery of the Kingdom of God. And thence, arising, he returned to the other side of the Jordan.' Possibly he lived in a village not far from where the Essenes once ruled, close to the ruins of ancient Sodom. In another passage, the Carpocratians suggested that when the Roman guards came to arrest him in Gethsemane, Jesus was naked with another man. It is difficult to dodge the implications. They saw nothing wrong in this, and may well have been the first Christian gay liberation group in history. Orthodoxy denounced them at the time (Irenaeus's comments were particularly harsh), but that is not surprising.

The world continues to echo with cries against homosexuals. Dormant prejudices are regularly revived. In a scathing and witty 1981 essay, 'Pink Triangle and Yellow Star', Gore Vidal excoriated the neocon author of a homophobic diatribe. In an essay titled 'Boys on the Beach', published in *Commentary*, Midge Decter had used language not dissimilar to that used against Jews, and currently against Muslims. Vidal wrote:

For sheer vim and vigor, 'The Boys on the Beach' outdoes its implicit model, *The Protocols of the Elders of Zion* . . . [S]ince homosexualists choose to be the way they are out of idle hatefulness, it has been a mistake to allow them out of the closet to the extent that they have. But now they are out (which most are not), they will have no choice but to face up to their essential hatefulness and abnormality and so be driven to kill themselves with promiscuity, drugs, S&M and suicide . . . Not even the authors of *The Protocols of the Elders of Zion* ever suggested that the Jews, who were so hateful to them, were also hateful to themselves. So Decter has managed to go one step further . . . she is indeed a virtuoso of hate, and thus do pogroms begin . . .

Twenty-seven years later, the President of Iran declared on a visit to the United States that since homosexuals do not exist in his country, they could not be persecuted – a blatant falsehood. For even he must know that his regime has not succeeded in exterminating them, despite several executions soon after the clerical triumph of thirty years ago. In December 2008, the Bavarian Pope Benedict declared that saving humanity from the depredations of homosexual or transsexual behaviour was just as important as saving the environment. In other words, climate change and sex change were equally disastrous. His stooges in the Vatican announced simultaneously that the UN resolution decriminalizing homosexuality had gone too far. These are only two examples, but could easily be multiplied by a few hundred others.

The history of the last three centuries, to go no further back, is one of persistent and systemic persecution of homosexuals within the Christian world. Islam accepted the Old Testament's analysis and prescriptions with few amendments. Hardly surprising, given that the same author produced both works.[7]

7 Despite this there were relatively few punishments in the world of Islam for most of its existence. Khomeini's executioners were busy, and a few hundred homosexuals were executed in the first years after the clerical triumph. Foucault, a supporter of the Ayatollah, never wrote on this aspect of his social policies.

The persecution of homosexuals during the Third Reich was not on the same scale as the judeocide, but even so, 50,000 homosexuals were sent to Nazi prisons and concentration camps. It is foolish to ignore the existence of prisoners forced to wear the pink triangle, or underplay the repression merely because some of the commandants and guards were of the same orientation. A delegation of predominantly American gay activists visiting Jerusalem in 1994, to pay homage to the victims in the Holocaust Memorial Museum, were harassed by Jewish survivors, some of whom had to be restrained from physically attacking the delegates.[8]

The fact is that the Sodom Question will not go away. The establishment of a Sodomstaat (the State of Sodom or Sodomistan) in the area close to the Dead Sea where the cities first existed has become an urgent necessity. Those who agree with this proposal should, without further delay, call an international conference to organize the 'Lovers of Sodom'.[9] The founding slogan of the new movement is already inscribed in the geography of the Sodomstaat: 'A sea without waves, for a people tired of cruising'. Glory awaits those who fight unselfishly for the cause. It doesn't require too much steam to lift the lid of an old-fashioned kettle, and I hope that this plea from a righteous heterosexual will be taken seriously, and not rejected by the po-faced charlatans of gravity.

The arguments that will be used are already familiar. Supporters of the Sodomstaat will hear many homilies to the effect that gay people should not create new distinctions and divisions, but rather strive to erase the old ones. It is not up to them. They have been waiting a long time. Despite the gains

---

8 One man shouted, 'My grandfather was killed for refusing to have sexual relations with the camp commandant. You are desecrating this place . . .' (*Jerusalem Post*, 30 May 1994). What if it had been his grandmother? Would all heterosexuals have been forbidden entry as well?

9 Were my old friend Derek Jarman still with us (see p. 256) I'm confident he would have seized the moment.

made during the 1960s, and, soon after, the beginning of Gay Pride marches in cities all over the world, gay people continue to be attacked, their bars firebombed, their way of life denounced from pulpit and platform. Extreme religious fundamentalists of every hue demand castration, prison and capital punishment. If this is universal brotherhood, the only solution is the State of Sodom.

To avoid being told that this is a utopian dream, and pre-empt accusations of frivolity by the charlatans of gravity, I will refrain from mapping the political contours or draft constitution of the future Republic of Sodom – alternatively, the Confederation of Sodom-Gomorrah, or possibly Sodomistan. These are decisions that must be taken by the Lovers of Sodom and affiliated groups.

A few cogs, however, are offered to set up the machine that is so desperately needed:

(a) The social composition of the state envisaged above will be such that ethnic domination by any one group will be virtually impossible, but to forestall all possibilities (such as the arrival of criminals masquerading as homosexuals from Russia), the constitution should explicitly prohibit the domination of the country by any single ethnic group. Ethnic political groupings should also be disallowed. The founders of the state will belong to all nations, cultures, peoples and tribes.

(b) Unlike other creations based on biblical history there will be no need to create an SDF (Sodom Defence Force). A popular militia will be sufficient for local needs.

(c) However, given the state of the world, the creation of an American Sodom Public Interest Committee (ASPIC) in the United States, where support for the new nation will be huge, does not require much explanation. It will be needed to prevent attacks on us by reactionary, heterosexist, patriarchal states and kingdoms. And we also need regular subsidies. Initially, ASPIC should buy up a hundred members of Congress plus a dozen Senators, and gain the support of professors in distinguished law schools (always useful for bullying and threatening opponents). Once the new state is established ASPIC must, of course, try for a majority and even run to win the White House, which has, since the tenancy of Abraham Lincoln, never been occupied by a Sodomist.

(d) Many gay people who have never been persecuted or vilified and who live in comfortable circumstances will oppose this idea. That is their right, and no pressure should be put on them. No pro-Sodom groups should engage in creating a climate of fear in the heterosexual world. Everything must be voluntary. That alone will provide the movement with an aura of moral superiority. The State of Sodom will not force people to leave their country and migrate en masse. One hundred thousand will suffice to set up a basic infrastructure, and these could be supplied by the United States, India and China alone – though a more representative group will be necessary to prevent ethnic domination. Besides, there are many righteous heterosexuals who might prefer to live in Sodom and Gomorrah. They should be welcomed with open hearts.

(e) As to the economic character of the state, the decision must be made democratically by its citizens; but one old formula would surely befit the new republic, on both the personal and the politico-economic level: 'From each according to his ability, to each according to his need.'

February 2009

2

CERVANTES IN HIS TIME AND OURS

'I believe that too', responded Sancho, 'and I'd like your grace to tell me why is it that Spaniards, when they're about to go into battle, invoke that St James the Moor-Slayer and say: "St James, and close Spain!" By some chance is Spain open so that it's necessary to close her, or what ceremony is that?'

Contrary to Mikhail Bulgakov, manuscripts sometimes do burn, but, more importantly, the masterpieces in which they are put to the flame always have a time and a date. In contrast to academic fashions, great works of literature are rarely, if ever, created in isolation. Nor can they be fully understood outside their given context. They are a reflection of life within a social, political and historical environment. This applies as much to Cervantes and Shakespeare as it does to Joyce and Proust, Tolstoy and Vasily Grossman. And it is true of historical novels as well. The past is interpreted by the needs of the present.

Miguel de Cervantes's *Don Quixote* has deservedly been called a universal novel, even the first modern novel produced in Europe, but it was and could only have been written in the Spain of Philip II, a century after the triumph of the *Reconquista* and when the country was beset with crises of every sort. The triumphalism generated by 1492 had long worn off. The history that was the backdrop to the masterwork is dramatic. We shall return to it after a modern detour.

In 2005, to mark the 400th anniversary of the publication of *Don Quixote*, the Venezuelan government printed a million copies of the classic for free distribution to a million households in their own country; it funded 70,000 copies in English for its Caribbean neighbours, and 5,000 in French for Haiti. A quixotic act? I don't think so. More an indication that there are a few political leaders still around who take culture quite seriously, genuinely enjoying the challenge it offers and viewing it as something apart from commerce. When asked if he thought that the million copies would all be read, President Hugo Chávez retorted that what was important was to have them in a million households, to become the property of future generations.

What a joy it must be to read this book in Spanish. Those of us not adequately versed in the language have no option but to grit their teeth and seek refuge in the translation. I was in my late teens when I first read the book. Far too young, alas, to understand what had been written and incapable of reading beyond the words. I enjoyed the cruel jokes, sided with the wrong people, laughed in the wrong places, totally ignored the tragic landscape and skipped a great deal. In other words, I never really read the book. The two principals I regarded with utter contempt, perhaps – no, definitely – because they were far too chaste.[1]

I cannot remember the name of the translator and when, early in 2009, I tried to recover the book in my late father's library in Lahore, it had disappeared. Might I have understood it better if the introduction (was there one?) had made some attempt to contextualize the work? I doubt it. I'm convinced that this is a novel that should be read by people later in life, perhaps after they have reached thirty, preferably even later.

The new 980-page English version published to commemorate the anniversary has turned out to be a soul-saver. Edith Grossman's modern

---

1   I had no problems with the *Decameron* by Boccaccio, which I devoured eagerly at roughly the same time and which was much more to my taste, a sad confirmation that it was probably the lack of sex that put me off Cervantes.

translation is exquisite. Her version, and one knows this instinctively, is much more in sympathy with the original than all the tedious attempts that sought to 'improve' the text and ended up as archaic and virtually unreadable. Some translators are haunted by earlier translations. Not Edith Grossman. Her footnote references are spare, but a treat, and of real use to any serious reader. The only spoiler in the book is Harold Bloom. It is a limiting and lazy introduction that he has written. It does not contain a single sentence that might help the reader contextualize the world that produced Cervantes and in which he struggled against adversities of every sort. Bloom could have done a little homework. The attempted profundity of his first two sentences is revealing: 'What is the true object of Don Quixote's quest? I find that unanswerable.'

Why? Did he even attempt to search for an answer? It would have meant immersing himself for a few weeks in Spanish history. It's obvious he has never read Américo Castro or Juan Goytisolo or Miguel Asín, but was he too lazy even to glance at a biography of Cervantes published by a fellow-countryman, William Byron, in 1978? It would appear so, which is a pity, as it would have helped him a great deal. Instead we are told of the impact the novel had on Melville among others and reminded that Nabokov found the cruelty repellent, amid trivial details of a similar sort that might be handy for compilers of middlebrow crossword puzzles, but are useless to a reader who wants to know more about the novelist and the culture that spawned him.

Bloom's problem is his lack of humility. He can't bring himself to confess that the drama contained in *Don Quixote* is enacted within a historical frame too large for his comprehension. Without that knowledge, it is impossible to discern the fragments that offer clues to the object of Cervantes's quest. For Bloom the realm of meaning is confined to literature alone – and the Western canon at that – but this is totally insufficient to understand the novel. Cervantes, like the rest of the population in the region, is a creature of the tragic drama that constituted the history of the peninsula in the fifteenth and sixteenth centuries.

These were times when the very act of living had become a colossal effort for the poor. The silver ingots from South America only exacerbated the structural economic crisis. Inflation was rampant, there was mass hunger in Andalusia, bubonic plague in Castile, brutal repression of vagrants everywhere (reminiscent of how a crisis-racked Catholic Italy is treating gypsies and other minorities today), corruptions of church and empire, against a background of growing depopulation and a severe crisis in agriculture. The decay of Spanish society was visible at the time to most of its inhabitants. The French historian Pierre Vilar, writing in 1956, was correct to stress this historical context against those who were beginning to reduce history to 'a discontinuous series of singular totalities':

> It is often said that it would be pointless to search in Cervantes for an interpretation of the 'decadence' of his country, 'because he could not have foreseen it'. This is to have a singular disregard for chronology. For if the word *crisis* rightly describes the passage from an ascending conjuncture to one of collapse, it is surely between 1598 and 1620, between the 'grandeur' and the 'decadence', that we must situate the decisive *crisis* of Spanish power, and much more surely still, the first great crisis of confidence for the Spaniards. Well: the two parts of *Don Quixote* are dated 1605 and 1615.[2]

And there was always the ever-present Inquisition. For these were also times when the torment of individuals attached to a defeated civilization had become unbearable. How to keep calm while evil, like polluted rain, covers all in darkness? It is all around them. Injustice flourishes as never before. Spanish Muslim rebellions in the Alpujarras are the harbingers of guerrilla wars and resistance in centuries yet to come. Critical thought is abolished. A secret police spies on suspect citizens and a vicious censorship

2   Pierre Vilar, 'The Age of Don Quixote', *New Left Review* 1: 68, July–August 1971.

is imposed by State and Church . . . Juan Goytisolo has argued that all the features of the modern totalitarian state had already been configured in post-1492 Spain. It's difficult to disagree.

Philip II had unilaterally annulled the agreements reached by his forebears with the Moriscos, as the Spanish Muslims were known at the time. The few rights they had left were withdrawn, and a humiliating code of conduct was imposed: it became a crime to read, write or speak Arabic, and to visit the public baths, which would soon be destroyed throughout Spain (cleanliness being considered by the Church as a licentious Moorish habit), while the use of Morisco surnames or the wearing of Morisco clothes was also banned. A whole people were thus criminalized. They were the enemy within, soon to be converted, expelled or killed.

This was the Spain into which Cervantes was born in September or October, 1547 (in the town of Alcalá de Henares, to which his family had moved from Córdoba). It is this that explains the writing of a book so rich in fantasy, imagination, poetry, mysticism, satire, joy and grief, as well as a degree of political and psychological perception that is astonishing. As I have already suggested, Spain during the sixteenth and early seventeenth century was a deeply fractured society, racked by turbulence of a very special sort. The Catholic Church had spearheaded a long campaign – the *Reconquista* – to ethnically cleanse the Iberian peninsula of alien influences. In 1492, several hundred years after a tiny Arab force had fought and defeated the Visigoths and established a political and cultural hegemony over the peninsula, the last Muslim kingdom of Granada fell to the Catholic Kings, Ferdinand and Isabella. Almost simultaneously, Columbus 'discovered' the New World. The two events became intertwined in many Christian minds as a show of divine support for the Catholic Church and retribution against the Muslims and Jews, who should be driven into the sea.

This was Spain after the fall of Granada in 1492, the final victory of the 'Reconquest' – but it turned out to be not quite as final as had been thought. As church bells rang everywhere to mark the triumph, an edict signed by the monarchs expelling all Jews from Spain unless they converted was posted on church doors in most cities. A century later, the Muslims would suffer the same fate: there were too many to expel in 1492, and the state feared a prolonged armed conflict.

During the eight hundred years of Muslim rule, the period between the tenth and fifteenth centuries was marked by the co-existence of three cultures: Islamic, Christian and Judaic. In pre-Islamic Spain the Visigoths had maintained a primitive dictatorship, with draconian anti-Semitic laws: 'Let them not keep their Passover, let them not be married under their own law, let them not be circumcised'. Any children born to them had to be baptized, failing which the Jew who fathered them would 'receive a hundred lashes, and let his head be shorn, and let him be cast out of the land, and let his goods come into the hands of the king.' This last sentence was probably what meant the most to the Visigoth nobility. Looting was second nature to them.

Small wonder then that the Jews eagerly supported the creation of al-Andalus and loyally served the Caliphs of Córdoba and subsequent Muslim rulers in the peninsula, often rising to high positions. It was these five hundred years that provided Hispanic society with a definitive structure, from which it could not fully escape, even after the *Reconquista*. The Spanish historian Américo Castro has written of this period that:

> It is not possible to break up this history into stagnant pools, or to divide it off into parallel, synchronous currents, because each one of the three groups was a part of the circumstances projected by the other two. Nor could we capture this reality merely by gathering together data and events, or by objectifying it as a 'cultural phenomenon'. We must try to feel the projection of the lives of the ones with the lives of the others. For this and nothing else is what their history was. Facts, ideas, and all the rest are inseparable from the lives with which they are integrated . . . At

the end of the fifteenth century, Spain was ruled by a single belief . . . It is thus that I conceive the creation and ruination of Hispanic tolerance, entirely outside the framework of the European Middle Ages. Between the savage Visigothic laws of the *Fuero Juzgo* against the Jews (seventh century) and Alphonse the Learned's mild laws relating to them there are five hundred years of Islam.[3]

That was then. One fear of the Church was that Catholicism might be the loser if the unique synthesis of al-Andalus continued to exist for another hundred years. In 1492, they began to pull down the entire edifice. Muslims and Jews reluctant to leave their homeland had no other option except a conversion to Christianity, only to be burnt at the stake for heresy when the Inquisition determined that a conversion was not genuine. While I was researching *Shadows of the Pomegranate Tree*, the first novel of my 'Islam Quintet', I came across some heart-rending trial proceedings of Muslim converts, one of which concerned a troubadour named Mahomad Jaffrey, *aka* Juan de Granada. He could never fully discard his Muslim identity and, as a result, was tried and sentenced to death.

Under Philip II, the entire peninsula was in the grip of Catholic monarchs, flanked by zealous prelates and obsessed with preventing 'New Christians' (recent converts) from becoming part of the Empire in the New World. Catholic, monocultural Spain was determined that the single Christian identity forged by means of torture, blood and the burning of books and people should be extended to all Europe. They were determined to ethnically cleanse Spain of its past.

The sixteenth century marked the meteoric rise of Spain as an imperial power. Having forcibly evicted two rival cultures, the new Spain wanted to restore Catholic hegemony within Christianity. Protestant England had to be crushed. Subversive Lutheran ideas from Germany had to be kept

3 Américo Castro, *The Structure of Spanish History*, Princeton: Princeton University Press, 1954.

out of the Low Countries. France had to be pushed to deal firmly with the Huguenot vermin. Philip II would use his power without scruple, and the Church would justify every atrocity on the grounds that the unanimously desired end – a paradisiacal Kingdom of God on earth – justified all the means used. Any measure adopted in this good cause was automatically virtuous. Religious and political fundamentalisms share this feature in common. The victims have to contend with the hard silence of justice.

Not that the Spanish Muslims passively accepted the new order. They fought back and defended their historical rights to their lands and their villages. There were three important rebellions in Granada and countless incidents of non-cooperation, expressions of anger (hurling excrement at the Holy Sacrament) and even the odd act of terror. After their defeat in the Second Granadan war of 1568–70, the Church suggested that since the New World was being rapidly depopulated (the *indios* were dying like flies of the diseases imported from Europe), it might be an idea to replace them with Moriscos. This was vetoed by the palace. The King was horrified, 'for after all', he said, 'they are Spaniards like ourselves.' What might have happened had half a million Spanish Muslims been despatched to shore up the Spanish Empire? We can but imagine.

Philip II was an effective, if paranoid, monarch. He saw rebellions everywhere, and almost triggered one in Catalonia by imagining that Protestant subversives were mounting an insurrection against him. He was hostile to compromises with either Muslims or Protestants, on the grounds that tolerance was a sign of weakness and would only encourage apostasy. Dissidents in Flanders attempting to free their country were treated with the same severity as 'heretics' at home. A couple of centuries later, Friedrich Schiller would see in Philip II a character who epitomized everything that was wrong in Europe and embodied the anti-Enlightenment. In *Don Carlos*, the German poet highlighted the instrumentalization of religion, making of it little more than the handmaiden of political tyranny:

KING (*after a pause*)
My son is meditating treason.

GRAND INQUISITOR

                                                    Well!
And what do you resolve?

KING

                              On all, or nothing.

GRAND INQUISITOR
What mean you by this all?

KING

                                        He must escape,
Or die.

GRAND INQUISITOR
Well, sire! decide.

KING

                                    And can you not
Establish some new creed to justify
The bloody murder of one's only son?

GRAND INQUISITOR
To appease eternal justice God's own Son
Expired upon the cross.

Whoever wrote that the wise man laughs with fear and trembling must have been thinking of sixteenth-century Spain. Laughter in Cervantes is never innocent. It is usually linked to fear and cruelty, which for him was symbolic of the transition, from three cultures to one, that he was experiencing. The dominant culture in terms of language and learning had for more than half a millennium been Arabic. Ultimately it gave way to Castilian, but here too the traces would never disappear. As the second part of the novel nears the end, Cervantes has the Knight explaining this fact to his squire, who does not understand the use of the word *albogues*, as in 'Well, and what if in the midst of all this music albogues should resound!':

> 'What are albogues?' asked Sancho, 'I've never heard of them or seen them in my life.'
>
> 'Albogues', responded Don Quixote, 'are something like brass candlesticks, and when you hit one with the other along the empty or hollow side, it makes a sound that is not unpleasant, though it may not be very beautiful or harmonious, and it goes well with the rustic nature of pipes and timbrels; this word *albogues* is Moorish, as are all those in our Castilian tongue that begin with *al*, for example: *almohaza, almorzar, alhombra, alguacil, alhucema, almacén, alcancía,* and other similar words . . . I have told you this in passing because it came to mind when I happened to mention albogues'.[4]

There is nothing in these stories that is told 'in passing'. The treasure chest is full of fine-cut diamonds. Everything has been carefully considered before the commitment to paper. It could not have been otherwise during the Inquisition. What intrigues is what he thought could not go into the book at all, and here the tragedy of his own people must have been paramount in his mind, even in the midst of composition.

---

4 Miguel de Cervantes, *Don Quixote*, trans. Edith Grossman, New York: Harper Collins, 2003, pp. 900–901.

Ferdinand and Isabella celebrated the conquest of Muslim Granada in 1492 by expelling the Jews. The choice given to the Jewish community was simple; convert or get out. Many decided to leave. In most cases they sought and were granted refuge in the lands of the Ottoman Empire.[5] Till the end of the twentieth century, scholars had to travel to Istanbul to hear *ladino* being spoken as it was in medieval Spain. (The old community has died out, and since the rise of Turkish Islamism many of their descendants have left for other lands, including Israel.)

Others, understandably reluctant to be uprooted, were prepared to sacrifice their past for their children's future. They became *conversos* and stayed on as New Christians, their loyalty ever suspect. Some belonging to merchant families, or the Jewish physicians who served the court and the nobility, rose to high positions in the land – on occasion proving their loyalty to the Church with a vengeance that stunned former co-religionists.

Tomás de Torquemada was one such. He became the first Grand Inquisitor, and a living example of the adage that the fanaticism of the convert knows no bounds. From a *converso* family, he became a byword for cruelty. Torquemada authorized the burning of at least 2,000 Jewish 'heretics' – Jews who had converted to Christianity but whose motives were considered suspect, and who had been spied on and reported to the Inquisition. The real figure was probably three times higher. Statistics vary. The contemporary *Catholic Encyclopaedia*, while graciously accepting that the Inquisition sometimes went too far, nonetheless justifies the terror it unleashed by blatant untruths:

At that time the purity of the Catholic Faith in Spain was in great danger from the numerous Marranos[6] and Moriscos, who, for material considerations, became sham converts from Judaism and Islam to

---

5   A shipload even arrived in Cochin, on the Kerala coast in Southern India, and was given refuge and land in perpetuity to build a synagogue and homes for themselves by the Maharaja of Cochin-Travancore. The synagogue is situated in Jew Street and beautifully preserved.
6   The word 'marranos', used to describe Jewish converts, means 'swine'.

Christianity. The Marranos committed serious outrages against Christianity and endeavoured to Judaize the whole of Spain. . . . In 1483 the Pope appointed Torquemada, who had been an assistant inquisitor since 11 February 1482, Grand Inquisitor of Castile, and on 17 October extended his jurisdiction over Aragon.

The terror of the Inquisition was implemented by its own secret police, the Holy Brotherhood. The aim was to eradicate free speculative thought and establish a single Christian identity for Europe through wholesale ethnic cleansing.[7] It was not enough for Jewish silversmiths in Majorca to convert. They had to prove it by sitting outside their shops on the Jewish Sabbath, ostentatiously eating pork.

All the circumstantial evidence points to the fact that Cervantes belonged to a family of Jewish *conversos*, a *mala casta* for life. There is no documentary evidence because such families took care to destroy every trace (as Jews would again do under the Third Reich), so that when they applied to the relevant tribunal for a certificate testifying that they were Old Christians, no incriminatory material could be produced. Nonetheless Cervantes was denied permission to go to the New World on a number of occasions. He did get the 'certificate of purity' and, as a result, obtained a menial job at the home of a church dignitary in Rome. Back in La Mancha, however, it was generally known that he was of Jewish origin and his literary rivals, Lope de Vega for one, used this against him during heated exchanges. There is the odd clue in the masterwork as well.

One of the many conceits Cervantes deploys in the novel is that he never wrote it in the first place. He found a Moorish manuscript in the bazaar

7   In Sicily, Frederick II (extremely well versed in Arab and Muslim culture) had appeased his nobles and the Church by cleansing in slightly more humane fashion. Muslims who refused to convert were packed into boats and given a city of their own on the Italian mainland. Soon after Frederick's death they were attacked and massacred. A fictional account of this is contained in the concluding pages of my novel, *A Sultan in Palermo*, London and New York: Verso, 2000.

in Toledo. It was written in Arabic, and all he did was to hire a translator. Thus at the very beginning of the work, Cervantes is stressing the special features that helped to shape Spanish identity:

> One day when I was in the Alcaná market in Toledo, a boy came by to sell some notebooks and old papers to a silk merchant; as I am very fond of reading, even torn papers in the streets, I was moved by my natural inclination to pick up one of the volumes the boy was selling, and I saw that it was written in characters I knew to be Arabic. And since I recognized but could not read them, I looked around to see if some Morisco who knew Castilian, and could read them for me, was in the vicinity, and it was not very difficult to find this kind of interpreter, for even if I had sought a speaker of a better and older language, I would have found him.[8]

The older language is, of course, Hebrew and the sentence does offer a clue to Cervantes's origins. The title of the manuscript was 'History of Don Quixote de la Mancha, written by Cide Hamete Benengeli, Arab historian.' The Muslim theme is strong in the book. How could it not be, given the Morisco 'problem' at home and the final solution being mooted in Church and Palace? In ironic mode Cervantes mocks the prevalent orthodoxy, by suggesting that the Hispanic Muslim author of the novel has underplayed the virtues of Quixote, since Muslims are 'very prone to telling falsehoods'. So if there are any complaints, the 'fault lies with the dog who was its author'. And historians, he continues in the same passage, 'must and ought to be exact, truthful and absolutely free of passions, for neither interest, fear, rancor, nor affection should make them deviate from the path of the truth, whose mother is history, the rival of time, repository of great deeds, witness to the past, example and adviser to the present, and forewarning to the future.'

8   *Don Quixote*, p. 67.

Add to all this Cervantes's participation in the Battle of Lepanto where the Catholic coalition defeated the Ottomans, his subsequent spell in an Algerian prison and his experiences in the Maghreb. These events took place against the backdrop of a sixteenth-century Catholic obsession regarding the Ottoman threat to its hegemony in Western Christendom, already challenged from within by the Reformation.

Protestant heretics were welcomed by the Ottomans and given refuge and money. Juan Goytisolo has compared Philip II's fear of the Ottomans to twentieth-century anti-Communism during the Cold War:

> The Great Turk both attracted and intimidated Christian nations by way of a cultural and ideological coherency which, above and beyond its armed might, offered its enemies a possible and potentially dangerous alternative. Like the Soviet Union [1917–90], the Ottoman Empire was the object of analyses, portraits, novels, fiction, fantasy and denunciation . . . In this huge collection of works, the testimony of captives, fugitives, spies and renegades looms large . . . A master of the arts of insinuation, ambiguity and irony, Cervantes takes great pleasure in subtly eroding the reader's most deep-seated convictions and impelling him towards terrain sown with uncertainty and enigmas . . .

How else could one interpret the presence in the novel of the fictional Morisco, Ricote, a rural shopkeeper who, after the final solution that saw half a million Moriscos expelled from Spain in 1609 and depopulated many areas of the country (especially around Valencia), was granted asylum in Lutheran Germany? Cervantes, often keen to stress his loyalty to the regime, was sufficiently shaken by the expulsions to cast caution aside and allow his heart to dictate directly to the quill. The result is a moving exchange between Sancho Panza and Ricote, who once lived in Sancho's village; he has returned secretly from exile to collect hidden valuables, but more importantly, to breathe the air and feel the sun of Spain. Even this demanded to be written carefully, and Cervantes included a few get-out clauses lest an intelligent Inquisitor should read the book too closely. He does so between the lines:

> Ricote, without slipping at all into his Moorish language, said these words in pure Castilian:
>
> 'You know very well, O Sancho Panza, my neighbor and friend, how the proclamation and edict that His Majesty issued against those of my race brought terror and fear to all of us; at least, I was so affected, I think that even before the time granted to us for leaving Spain had expired, I was already imagining that the harsh penalty had been inflicted on me and my children. And so I arranged as a prudent man, I think, and as one who knows that by a certain date the house where he lives will be taken away . . .
>
> 'In short, it was just and reasonable for us to be chastised with the punishment of exile: lenient and mild according to some, but for us it was the most terrible one we could have received. No matter where we are, we weep for Spain, for, after all, we were born here and it is our native country; nowhere do we find the haven our misfortune longs for, and in Barbary and all the places in Africa where we hoped to be received, welcomed and taken in, that is where they most offend and mistreat us . . . the greatest desire in almost all of us is to return to Spain; most of those, and there are many of them, who know the language as well as I do, abandon their wives and children and return, so great is the love they have for Spain; and now I know and feel the truth of the saying that it is sweet to love one's country . . .'[9]

Dostoevsky, who compared the novel to the Bible, slightly misread Cervantes. His Quixote is a reborn Christ, embodying all good against all evil. The novel is far too heteroclite for any such reading. The great Russian literary critic Bakhtin wrote very little on Cervantes. Did he see the work as an assault on all religious dogmas and did that put him off?

9 *Don Quixote*, p. 813

Difficult to say. But what Bakhtin wrote on Dostoevsky's novels applies even more to the Spanish masterpiece:

> A plurality of independent and unmerged voices and consciousnesses, a genuine polyphony of fully valid voices is in fact the chief characteristic of Dostoevsky's novels. What unfolds in his works is not a multitude of characters and fates in a single objective world, illuminated by a single authorial consciousness; rather a plurality of consciousnesses, with equal rights and each with its own world, combine but are not merged in the unity of the event.

Yes, Cervantes permits a hundred flowers to bloom in the novel. It is polyphonous; but a tiny mystery remains. What is the real object of his anger? Leaving aside the story-within-a-story model inherited from Arab culture, what lies at the heart of this amazing epic? Considerable space is devoted, in the first part of the novel, to rubbishing and even burning the works of third-rate romantic writers obsessed with the age of chivalry. What is all this about? I suspect they are a substitute for something that he cannot write about, except in the most oblique fashion. The whole of Chapter 6 (First Part) is devoted to purging Don Quixote's library while the knight is asleep. The books that are burnt in the style of the Inquisition are third-rate works of chivalry, a medieval Mills and Boon. A priest helps to select those destined for the fire, saying of the first book of chivalry that: 'all the rest found their origin and inspiration here, and so it seems to me that as the proponent of the doctrine of so harmful a sect, we should, without any excuses, condemn it to the flames.' The barber who is helping the priest suggests that perhaps the book should be spared, since it is the original. The priest reluctantly agrees. A few paragraphs later, a book derived from the one that has been pardoned is briskly consigned to the flames, the priest insisting that 'the mercy shown the father will not help the son.' The use of a priest is designed to mask the real target of

Cervantes's venom. Could he not be saying that the Old Testament will be spared, but all else burnt?

That he loathed injustice is evident in the freeing of the slaves, and from the episode of Sancho's imagined Governorship of an inland *ínsula* – a practical joke played on the loyal squire by bored aristocrats. It certainly makes them laugh in the novel, though not the reader. Cervantes is suggesting that the joke is on the perpetrators.

That he intensely disliked dogma is made clear on many occasions, as when Don Quixote, lance raised, charges at a bunch of penitents and priests perceived as the enemy, or in numerous ironic asides and dialogic exchanges with Sancho Panza. At one point in the novel Sancho announces that if his only virtue lay in his loyalty to the Roman Catholic Church and his hatred for the Jews, that alone would be sufficient to save him a place in history. Or take the following, from the opening of Chapter 27 of the Second Part, where Cervantes's fictitious Moorish author is back in action:

> Cide Hamete, the chronicler of this great history, begins this chapter with the words *I swear as a Catholic Christian* . . .; to which his translator says that Cide Hamete swearing as a Catholic Christian when he was a Moor, which he undoubtedly was, meant only that just as the Catholic Christian, when he swears, swears or should swear the truth, and tell the truth in everything he says, so too he was telling the truth, as if he were swearing as a Catholic Christian, when he wrote about Don Quixote . . .[10]

Could it be that it is Catholicism, as practised in a new, purified Spain, that is the absent centre of the novel around which everything else is constructed? The traditionalists will not like this interpretation, but it is there waiting to be gleaned from virtually every chapter. Clever old

10   *Don Quixote*, p. 637.

Bakhtin, I think, understood this and kept well clear of the book as a result. Unlike Dostoevsky, he knew what the book meant.

After the knight's death, the author writes the first sentence of the last paragraph: 'For me alone was Don Quixote born, and I for him; he knew how to act and I to write . . .'

We know the acts well. Phrases describing certain aspects of them have entered everyday usage, 'tilting at windmills', for example. By identifying his writing with such actions, I think Cervantes is trying to tell us something. Don't think, he is saying, that when I charged in the direction of my literary windmills at the very beginning of the novel, I was unaware of what I was doing. It had to be done like that, because of the times in which he lived. That is what makes him so courageous and so contemporary. He wrote in his time, but for all time. What he wrote was intended to forewarn the generations to come.

January 2009

3

WAR AND PEACE, LIFE AND FATE

Growing up in a Communist household in a non-Communist country after the Second World War meant being part of and sharing a common cultural experience with a cohort that spanned every continent. A 'red diaper baby' is how my US equivalents describe themselves, and their kitchens and living rooms were also littered with copies of *Soviet Weekly*, *Soviet Literature*, *Masses and Mainstream*, *Labour Monthly*, *For a Lasting Peace*, *For a People's Democracy*, etc. The last-mentioned magazine was a short-lived affair. Versions of these were available in all the major languages and many minor ones.

This was the result of the universal appeal of the 1917 Russian Revolution for our parents' generation. One consequence was a global diffusion of Russian culture: music of every sort, art forms including the dreaded ballet but also the more interesting *gopak* and, of course, literature, glorious literature that became part of the education of red-diaper households throughout the planet. Ours in Lahore was no different and in later years it was always fun comparing notes with Turkish, Chinese and South American friends who had undergone similar experiences.

Thus Russian literary classics occupied several shelves in my father's study. I was never told to read them, which is probably why I did. Though I was, at the age of six or seven, compelled to memorize the Urdu and English translations of a Pushkin poem (all about freedom and how the heavy, hanging chains of Siberia would fall) and recite it at a meeting of the Progressive Writers' Association in the presence of many of our greatest poets and critics – one of whom had no doubt translated the poem in question. It was lovely being patronized and having my cheeks affectionately pulled so that they felt bruised long afterwards. In later years I wondered whether any of the comrades had realized that the Pushkin poem applied even more to the gulags of the Stalinist period. I doubt it.

This put me off Pushkin for many years to come, but when I found him again he remained a friend for ever. 'To Siberia', the poem I had read, was written to honour the Decembrists: 'Your heavy chains will fall, / Your prisons crumble – and freedom / Will greet you joyfully at the gate, / And your brothers will place a sword into your hands'.

For years I puzzled over the ending in *Onegin*. How was it that Pushkin had given the last word to a woman? Her rejection of a man she had once loved was an extremely unconventional and bold way to end an epic poem in the eighteenth century. Or so I thought. Much later I discovered that the poet, too, was uneasy about ending his work with a man humiliated. He then thought to end on a more heroic note: a chastened Onegin breaking with his world for ever, and deciding to become a Decembrist. The few stanzas Pushkin showed his friends were regarded as too incendiary for publication. Some of the Decembrists were friends of the poet – which could explain why, on one of the pages in the manuscript of the poem, he had drawn a gibbet with five Decembrist corpses hanging from it. The suppressed verses included references to the Tsar as a 'weak and devious ruler', a 'bald fop and enemy of honest toil', 'accidentally warmed by glory'. But the others were destroyed. Had he not died in a foolish and meaningless duel, the poet would undoubtedly have reconstructed the burnt verses for posterity.

Russian writers under the Tsar and much later, during the Stalinist years, usually wrote under the watchful, wolves' eyes of the censor and the commissar. A great deal slipped through nonetheless. Little has been said, however, about the similarities between the dogma of Socialist Realism under Stalin and its parent social-realism under the Tsar.

In the latter case it was not the censor but the critic who insisted that certain essential norms be upheld. The much-celebrated Russian literary critic Belinsky was a monster whose review could kill a book instantly, but never the author. (In Stalin's time, a bad review could trigger imprisonment and death.) At least Belinsky loved literature. The same could not be said for many of his colleagues. Before affixing their seal of critical approval to a story, play, poem or novel, they had to be convinced of its pedagogical content. Did it raise popular consciousness? If not, the only solution was the critical guillotine. The opposition of the social-realist critics to Tsarist tyranny was magnificent, but the way they dealt with literature revealed a simplistic fanaticism on their part. Mercifully they could apply no judicial sanctions.

In *Three Years*, an 1895 novella, Anton Chekhov brilliantly encapsulated this entire debate in the form of a literary discussion held at the house of a wealthy intellectual:

> 'A work of literature cannot be significant or useful unless its basic idea contains some meaningful social task,' Konstantin was saying, looking at Yartsev angrily. 'If the book protests against serfdom or if the author indicts high society and its trivial ways, then it is a significant and useful piece of writing. But as for those novels and tales where it's oh and ah and why she fell in love with him, but he fell out of love with her, – such books I say are meaningless, and to hell with them.'
>
> 'I quite agree with you, Konstantin Ivanych,' said Yulia Sergeyevna. 'One writer describes a lovers' tryst, another describes infidelity, a third – a reunion after separation. Can't they find any other subjects? There are, after all, many people who are ill, unhappy, worn out by poverty, who must be disgusted to have to read about such things.'
>
> Laptev was disturbed to hear his wife, a young woman of not quite

twenty-two, speak of love so seriously and coldly. He could guess why this was so.

'If poetry does not solve the problems that you consider important,' said Yartsev, 'why don't you try books on technology, the police and financial law, or read scientific essays? Why should *Romeo and Juliet* have to deal with academic freedom or with sanitary conditions in prison, instead of with love, when you can find any number of articles and handbooks on these other subjects?'

'But look here, you exaggerate!' Konstantin interrupted him. 'We are not speaking of such giants as Shakespeare or Goethe. We speak of scores of talented and average writers who would be of much more use were they to leave love alone, and take up indoctrinating the masses with knowledge and humanitarian ideas.'

This was Chekhov's response to the ferocious attacks on his own work by populist critics. Alexander Skabichevsky had referred to the writer as a 'literary clown' who would perish in some obscure gutter, unmourned and forgotten. Perhaps this was why Bulgakov satirized Skabichevsky in *The Master and Margarita*, or perhaps because he had many Soviet-style equivalents. Despite the Tsarist censors and the populist critics there was a strong and vital tradition of pre-Revolutionary literature. A set of lively literary magazines had managed to function despite the Tsarist censor, and the works of Pushkin, Lermontov, Gogol, Dostoevsky, Saltykov-Shchedrin, Chekhov, Turgenev, Tolstoy and Ostrovsky were read as widely as literacy permitted.

The first decade after the Revolution witnessed fierce cultural debates, but without disruption of literary continuity. Both Lenin and Trotsky opposed the notion of 'proletarian art' and the first People's Commissar for Education, A. V. Lunacharsky, was a gifted cultural critic for whom modern Russian literature was born with Pushkin. While the notion of proletarian culture had its devotees, it was not state policy in the twenties. Trotsky argued that all talk of 'proletarian literature' was meaningless and pernicious. Its defenders 'falsify perspectives, they violate proportions, they distort standards and they cultivate the arrogance of small circles which is most dangerous.'

The Soviet avant-garde fought back, insisting that a new class was in power and their art was the result, even though the roots of constructivism, the most exciting development in art, predated the revolution – a harbinger of that eruption. Trotsky replied that 'a new class does not begin to create all of culture from the beginning, but enters into possession of the past, assorts it, touches it up, rearranges it, and builds on it further. If there were no such utilization of the "second-hand wardrobe" of the ages, historic processes would have no progress at all.'

Soviet writers endeavouring to produce works during the Terror achieved little of real merit. Socialist Realist painters did better, and could sometimes be more subversive. One such painting depicts Lenin in heroic mode, addressing a small group of workers. On closer examination we see that one worker is fast asleep. The writers resorted to allegory (Bulgakov), or to mediocre morality-tales devoid of any real conflict. There were some advantages: with rapidly expanding literacy there emerged a discerning readership which devoured the classics that were always kept in print by the State Publishing Houses.

In the late fifties, the period described as 'the thaw', the country's most highly regarded literary magazine, *Novy Mir*, published Alexander Solzhenitsyn's first novel, *One Day in the Life of Ivan Denisovich*, depicting the life of a political prisoner. It became an overnight sensation, startling the Politburo, which made sure that the thaw was halted. Boris Pasternak's novel *Dr Zhivago* was banned (a circumstance that won him the Nobel Prize for Literature) and Solzhenitsyn's later works, *The First Circle* and *Cancer Ward*, were subjected to similar treatment. The manuscripts were smuggled abroad and appeared in several languages, making a nonsense of the censorship. The 'Enemies of the People' never die.

In the eighties two other writers, who have remained my favourites, were published abroad: Andrey Platonov and Vasily Grossman. Platonov, born in 1899, was the son of a metal worker employed on the railways. His early education focused on engineering, but his literary skills rapidly became evident and since he belonged to a solid working-class family he was, at the age of twenty, despatched by the Voronezh Union of Proletarian Writers to the founding conference of the All-Russian Union of Proletarian Writers in 1920. Asked in a questionnaire to identify which literary trend he subscribed to, Platonov responded accurately: 'None. I have my own.'

In 1929, Platonov travelled extensively in the countryside and wrote a sharp satire on Stalinist collectivization, *For Future Use: A Poor Peasant's Chronicle*. Every publisher rejected it, on exactly the same grounds: they felt that the tone was 'mistaken'. A literary magazine, *Red Virgin Soil,* edited by the loyalist writer Alexander Fadeyev, astonished Platonov by agreeing to publish the work. According to the last edition of the Soviet Writers' Encyclopaedia, this is what then happened:

> While editing the story, Fadeyev had underlined the passages he thought should be excised for political reasons. The typographers, however, misunderstood Fadeyev's markings; and, instead of being deleted, the politically suspect passages appeared in the journal in bold-face type. This made Stalin's job much easier when the journal turned up on his desk. The tale infuriated Stalin, who labelled it a 'kulak's chronicle' and branded the author as 'scum' (*svoloch*). A special session of the Politburo was called to condemn Fadeyev's journal for publishing Platonov's 'kulak and anti-Soviet story'. Knowing which way the wind was blowing, Fadeyev quickly changed direction and published an article condemning the story which he himself had approved. He called Platonov a 'class enemy' and a 'kulak agent' in disguise.

I doubt that the typographers 'misunderstood' Fadeyev's instructions. The typographers were amongst the most politically conscious workers, before and after the Revolution. Everything suggests that they understood only too well what Fadeyev was up to, and decided to teach the hack a lesson.

Platonov's three major novels were written in an experimental mode strongly influenced by modernism. *The Juvenile Sea* was written in 1934 and published in 1986; *The Foundation Pit* was written in 1930 and published in 1987; and *Chevengur*, rejected by the Federatsiya Publishing House in 1929, was published in February 1988. The rejection of *Chevengur* upset Platonov the most. He sent the manuscript and a note to Maxim Gorky: 'They are not publishing it . . . saying that the book will be understood as a counter-revolutionary one. But I worked having absolutely different feelings . . .' Gorky understood, but could not help. Nobody could.

The manuscript survived, but Platonov's teenage son was arrested and kept as a hostage in terrible conditions for three years, during which he contracted tuberculosis. He died soon after his release. Platonov was right: *Chevengur* is a revolutionary novel that depicts the menace behind the collectivization plans and sees the total bureaucratization of the state machine as a disaster, a social peril threatening the Revolution. This process is described as a cancerous growth. Platonov predicts that it will distort, stifle and kill all living organisms.

In the novel, Chevengur is a small town with exactly eleven Bolsheviks, who believe they have already established communism. They are simple souls who think that communism comes when you've literally abolished the bourgeoisie. It is not the ownership of land and factories that is the problem, but individuals. Power is in their hands. Shoot the bourgeois dogs and then the half-bourgeois and then the quarter-bourgeois and then . . .? And then the sun will on its own compel the grain to shoot out of the ground. There is a startling depiction of the execution of landlords and half-bourgeois: 'a slow steam came out of the heads of the bourgeois, and afterwards oozed out some raw substance which looked like candle wax . . .' It is all very hard work. Platonov's Chevengurians then decide 'to wash the floor in the empty houses. To make them decent for tomorrow's proletariat.' The writer's attitude to the eleven Bolsheviks is remarkably sympathetic. They're the victims of history, products of illiteracy and serfdom stretching back centuries, children of absolutism. The novel sometimes reads like the literary equivalent of Gramsci's essay 'The Revolution Against *Capital*' in which the premature Revolution was a 'biological necessity' without which the Russian people would have been at the mercy of wolves.

The Communist leader of Chevengur instinctively understands the need for a Stalin:

> The only thing which reassured Chepurnoi was the fact that there is a secret place far away, somewhere near Moscow, as Prokofy found out on the map, it is called Kremlin. Lenin is sitting there with the lamp and thinking, he is not sleeping but writing. What is he writing there about? In fact, Chevengur already exists and it's time for Lenin to stop writing and to unite with the proletariat and to live . . .

It's hardly surprising that the novel was perceived as a ferocious attack on the ideology of the Soviet bureaucracy in 1929. Stalinism, the author is telling us, is the socialism of fools and primitives. Platonov died early, in 1951, infected by the same tuberculosis that killed his son.

Vasily Grossman belongs to a slightly later period. Born in the Ukraine in 1905, he studied chemistry at Moscow University and after graduating worked in the Donbass mines as a safety engineer. A short story, 'In the Town of Berdichev', attracted the attention of Maxim Gorky. Grossman started writing novels and stories in the Socialist Realist vein. They were unexceptional, but demonstrated real literary skills. In 1933 he moved to Moscow, where Gorky became a patron. As a more or less loyal Communist, Grossman was stunned when that same year his cousin and close friend, Nadhezda Almas, was arrested as a supporter of the Trotskyist opposition.

Both of them had known and liked the oppositionist Victor Serge. Many in that circle were arrested, though Serge was allowed to leave the Soviet Union in 1936.

Grossman himself was interrogated by the secret police, but as a formality. He was left alone. His cousin was exiled. Nadya was lucky to escape. Much of what Grossman had learnt about the Left Opposition came from her and others in her group. He was to make good use of it in *Life and Fate*, the masterpiece that he began to compose shortly after the Second World War.

It has become fashionable over the last three decades to underplay the Communism of those who later broke with the system. Grossman was a staunch Communist, but he did not allow this to cloud his judgement on several matters. Even when it was impolitic to do so, he often blurted out the truth. The Party's confidence in him is indisputable. How else could he have become a special correspondent of the Army newspaper, *Red Star*, sending back regular dispatches from the Eastern Front? He witnessed at first hand the two decisive battles of the Second World War – Stalingrad and Kursk – that broke the spinal chord of the Third Reich, making the final victory inevitable.

As the Red Army began to advance, Grossman discovered the circumstances of his mother's death and that of other Jews. He was racked by guilt for the rest of his life. Had his wife not objected, he would have brought his mother to the safety of Moscow. Together with Ilya Ehrenburg, he began to write the 'Black Book' detailing the judeocide. In the wake of Stalin's senile, anti-Semitic outbursts that led to the purge of Jews from the party and its apparatuses, Grossman broke definitively with the regime. He could not stomach any more.

Life and Fate grew out of all these experiences, with the siege of Stalingrad at its centre. The besieged city in the midst of a savage and pitiless war became Grossman's metaphor for the twentieth century.

Unlike Pasternak and Solzhenitsyn, the author of *Life and Fate* was an insider. He knew how the Stalinist system worked, and all his bitterness and anger during the immediate postwar period made him forget why he had become a Communist in the first place. It is the officers and men who live in 'House No 6/1' for whom the author reveals a real sympathy. These men fight for the Soviet Union while disregarding the Commissars attached to the troops. They fight because they possess independent minds and a fiercely critical spirit. They are the only heroes in a novel dominated by the stupidity and brutality of Stalinism and fascism.[1] All are former members of the oppositions destroyed by Stalin, the survivors of Atlantis. This is Grossman's homage to those who warned where things were headed as far back as 1924. In a conversation with a Commissar, an inmate from House No 6/1 says:

'I can't make head or tail of what's going on in there,' said Soshkin, 'they all seem terrified of this Grekov, but he just pretends to be one of the lads. They all go to sleep in a heap on the floor, Grekov included, and they call him Vanya. Forgive me for saying so, but it's more like some kind of Paris Commune than a military unit.'

The divisional commissar took a serious view of all this. He ordered Pivovarov to obtain detailed information about the situation in House 6/1 and to give Grekov a good talking-to then and there. At the same time he wrote reports to the member of the Military Soviet and to the head of the Army Political Section, informing them of the alarming state of affairs, both morally and politically, in house 6/1.

Life and Fate is loosely modelled on Tolstoy's *War and Peace*. Both authors indulge their own (often semi-coherent) views on history and philosophy

---

1 Something he could never equate during the war itself became much easier in the novel. After all, if there were no difference between the Soviet Union and the Third Reich, why bother to take sides at all? Grossman knew that despite the anti-Semitic wave the Soviet Jews had organized their own resistance, which is why those who migrated to Israel do not feel they are the victims of a defeat as much as their co-religionists who survived the judeocide.

and, as a result, overload the narrative. Grossman's work would have been improved had he not imitated the Count in this respect. It can be extremely tedious.

There is however, one great difference between the two books, which makes *Life and Fate* a much better novel, even if one sometimes disagrees with the history that underpins the work. Grossman is in ultra–nihilist mood, hostile to almost everything Soviet. He denounces every single facet of Stalinism, with a wholesale loathing that must include a tiny element of self-hatred for having once been, however tangentially, part of the system.[2] Good and evil are absent categories as the plot weaves its way through the suppressed passions of everyday life in the Soviet Union under Stalin. In some ways this is a realist historical novel par excellence, movingly written and often understated, as in Chapter 24, when Yevgenia's attempts to get a permit to stay in Kuibyshev (a city now reverted to its original name of Samara, one of whose thoroughfares is named after her Old Bolshevik father) are frustrated by bureaucratic intransigence, inhumanity and fear. There is not a trace of melodrama in Grossman's description. This is daily life as it was for even the marginally more privileged citizens of the Soviet Union.

The difference between Grossman and Tolstoy is that the former actually experienced the war he later transformed into his literary masterpiece. Tolstoy had to reconstruct it all. Great care is required when reconstructing history in a novel. Real events and characters should not be distorted. If a 'great leader' is being portrayed there should be no fictional falsification apart from what can only be imagined and the bed–chamber, far from being one of Tolstoy's favourite places, was usually a site of pain.[3] Tolstoy's

---

2   Had he not died in 1960, he would have seen his novel serialized in the official literary magazine *October* in 1988 – a few years before the collapse of the Soviet Union.

3   Anthony Powell once remarked that *Anna Karenina* would have been a much better novel had the eponymous heroine married Vronsky and had an affair with Karenin. It would certainly not have required a change in the opening line: 'Happy families are all alike; every unhappy family is unhappy in its own way.'

reconstruction of Kutuzov is essentially ahistorical, resulting in one of the weakest heroes he has ever created. *War and Peace* vilifies Napoleon while placing the ultra-reactionary General Kutuzov on a plinth. The serf-owner represents the peasants of Mother Russia, just as the glorified slave-owning families in *Gone with the Wind* understand the needs of their slaves better than any abolitionist. It may be an unsettling analogy for Tolstoy fans, but worth a thought: Natasha as the Scarlett O'Hara of the war against Napoleon. And Kutuzov as the soul of eternal Russia:

> For Russian historians – strange and terrible to say – Napoleon, that most insignificant instrument of history, who never and nowhere, even in exile, displayed any human dignity – Napoleon is the object of admiration and enthusiasm; he is grand. While Kutuzov, a man who, from the beginning to the end of his activity in 1812, from Borodino to Vilno, while always being true to himself in all his acts and words, shows an example uncommon in history of self-denial and awareness in the present of the future significance of the event – Kutuzov seems to them something indefinite and pathetic ... And yet it is hard to imagine a historical figure whose activity was so invariably and constantly directed towards one and the same goal. It is hard to imagine a goal more worthy and more concurrent with the will of the whole people. . .

What on earth was the Count thinking of when he wrote these lines? Could it have been self-identification? Tolstoy morphed into Kutuzov as the saviour of all Russia, the great teacher, the guiding star of the people. Writers are sometimes prone to such fantasies. The often brilliantly-drawn, fictional characters on the periphery simply cannot compete with the General. The portrait of Napoleon is a travesty. Stendhal, who participated in the conflict, was also critical of Napoleon – but from a much more radical position.

Stalin and his heirs later mimicked the chauvinist thrust and tone of *War and Peace*. Grossman was not unaware of all this and in *Life and Fate* he mocked the use of Tolstoy during the Second World War. A Soviet General in Stalingrad is convinced that Tolstoy participated in the war against Napoleon and has to be corrected by a Commissar:

> Then Guryev held forth about how badly the war was reported in the newspapers.
>
> 'Those sons of bitches never see any action themselves. They just sit on the other side of the Volga and write their articles. If someone gives them a good dinner, then they write about him. They're certainly no Tolstoys. People have been reading *War and Peace* for a century and they'll go on reading it for another century. Why's that? Because Tolstoy's a soldier, because he took part in the war himself. That's how he knew who to write about.'
>
> 'Excuse me, comrade General,' said Krymov. 'Tolstoy didn't take part in the Patriotic War.'
>
> 'He didn't take part in it – what do you mean?'
>
> 'Just that', said Krymov. 'He didn't take part in it. He hadn't even been born at the time of the war with Napoleon.'
>
> 'He hadn't been born?' said Guryev. 'What do you mean? How on earth?'
>
> A furious argument developed – the first to have followed any of Krymov's lectures. To his surprise, the general flatly refused to believe him.

And later in the novel, Grossman returns to the subject:

> 'If you're going to talk like that,' said Sokolov, 'there'll be no room in the official canon for any of the literature of the last century.'
>
> 'Far from it,' said Madyarov. 'What about Tolstoy? He made poetry out of the idea of a people's war. And the state has just proclaimed a people's war. Tolstoy's idea coincides with the interests of the state. And so – as Karimov would say – the magic carpet is whisked in. Now we have Tolstoy on the radio, we have literary evenings devoted to Tolstoy,

his works are constantly being reprinted; he even gets quoted by our
leaders.'

Many years later, K. Damodoran, a leader of the Indian Communist Party,
returned to the subject in a lengthy conversation with me. His anger and
shock were still present as he recalled the following incident:

I remember visiting the Soviet Union again in 1962 for health reasons.
While in prison during 1940–5 I had managed to learn a bit of Russian,
enough to read *Pravda*, albeit at a snail's pace. The period I was in
Moscow coincided with some anniversary commemorating Napoleon's
failure to take Moscow and his subsequent retreat. The very fact that a
Tsarist victory was being celebrated was odd enough in itself, but what
compounded the error in my view was the lengthy diatribe against
Napoleon in the pages of *Pravda*. The nationalist fervour of the article was
horrifying to me. Of course Napoleon was a counter-revolutionary in
the context of the French revolution, but in a war with Tsarist absolutism
if one had to retrospectively take sides, it would be with Napoleon not
the Tsar.

After all he was carrying the bourgeois-democratic revolution, even
in a distorted and impure form, to the territories being conquered. The
whole of reactionary Europe was arraigned against him. If anything,
there is an analogy with the Red Army's sweep into Eastern Europe
at the conclusion of the Second World War and the abolition of the
capitalist mode of production. I was lying in the hospital reading this
article, and I did not have much else to do, so I decided to write a
letter to the editor of *Pravda* expressing my shock and dismay at the
reactionary nature of this article. After that I used to grab eagerly a copy
of *Pravda* every day to see whether or not it had been printed and every
day I was disappointed.

After a week I was visited by a member of the Central Committee of
the CPSU who ostensibly came to inquire about my health. And then
he informed me that he had read my letter to *Pravda*. I asked how he
had read it, if it had been addressed to the *Pravda* editor. He preferred

51

to ignore this question and proceeded to defend the *Pravda* assessment of Napoleon. I cut the discussion short by saying I would be happy to discuss with him or any other comrade in the columns of *Pravda*, but I would rather be spared a heavy-handed lecture in my hospital room. Of course all these things are symptomatic of a more serious disease, but this was the way in which my eyes were opened. If you want to you can learn a lot in the Soviet Union![4]

Tolstoy was planning to write a novel about the Decembrists, but changed his mind and wrote *War and Peace* instead, a schmaltzy soap opera, a costume romance enlivened by a few interesting characters, although not Andrey (the face of eternal nobility) and not Natasha, the Princess Di of Russian culture.[5] 'For a country to have a great writer is like having another government,' remarks a character from Solzhenitsyn's best novel, *The First Circle*. He couldn't have been thinking of the author of *War and Peace*.

Some of Tolstoy's other novels, in which he challenges established wisdoms, fit that description much better, even though the convoluted morality-tale aspect that comes into play can be off-putting. In *Resurrection*, for instance. Despite this the novel's intensity is gripping, because its targets are what many could identify with today: established religion. Tolstoy was excommunicated from the Russian Orthodox Church for writing this book. The passage below, a memorable pen-portrait of a leading church bureaucrat, helps to understand why:

> The position occupied by Toporov, involving as it did an incongruity of purpose, could only be held by a man who was dull and morally obtuse. Toporov possessed both these negative qualities. The incongruity of

4   *New Left Review* 1: 93, September–October 1975.
5   During a visit to Moscow in the 1980s I was a guest of the Writers' Union. My host informed me that the beautiful building had once been the home of a noble family on whom Tolstoy had based the Rostovs. I smiled.

the position he occupied was this. It was his duty to maintain, and to defend by external measures not excluding violence, that Church which, by its own declaration, was established by God himself and could not be shaken by the gates of Hell nor by any human effort. This divine and immutable God-established institution had to be sustained and defended by a human institution – the Holy Synod – managed by Toporov and his officials. Toporov did not see this incongruity, nor did he wish to see it, and he was therefore much concerned lest some Romish priest, some pastor, or some sectarian, should destroy that Church against which the gates of Hell could not prevail. Toporov, like all those who are quite destitute of the fundamental religious feeling which recognizes the equality and brotherhood of man, was fully convinced that the common people were creatures entirely different from himself, and that the people needed what he could very well do without; for at the bottom of his heart he believed in nothing, and found such a state very convenient and pleasant. Yet he feared lest the people might also come to such a state, and looked upon it as his sacred duty, as he called it, to save them from it. His position towards the religion he was upholding was the same as that of the poultry keeper towards carrion he feeds his fowl on: carrion is very disgusting, but fowls like it and eat it, therefore it is right to feed fowls on carrion.

War and Peace was clearly an aberration. When later he wrote his anti-colonial novella, *Hadji Murad*, Tolstoy's rage is wonderful to behold. Chapter 15 in particular delivers a withering portrait of Nicholas I and a highly concentrated denunciation of the corruptions of the autocratic order:

Nicholas sat at the table in a black coat with shoulder-straps but no epaulets, his enormous body – of which the overgrown stomach was tightly laced in – was thrown back, and he gazed at the newcomers with fixed, lifeless eyes. His long, pale face, with its enormous receding forehead between the tufts of hair which were brushed forward and skilfully joined to the wig that covered his bald patch, was specially cold and stony that day. His eyes, always dim, looked duller than usual; the compressed lips under his upturned moustaches, and his freshly shaven cheeks – on which symmetrical sausage-shaped bits of whiskers had been left – supported by the high collar, and his chin which also pressed upon it, gave to his face a dissatisfied and even irate expression.

. . . though convinced that he had acted properly, some kind of unpleasant aftertaste remained behind, and to stifle that feeling he began to dwell on a thought that always tranquilized him – the thought of his own greatness.

'Evidently the plan devised by your Majesty begins to bear fruit,' said Chernyshov.

This approval of his strategic talents was particularly pleasant to Nicholas, because, though he prided himself on those talents, at the bottom of his heart he knew that they did not really exist; and he now desired to hear more detailed praise of himself.

[After decreeing, with spelling mistakes, that a Pole should be condemned to run the gauntlet of 1,000 men twelve times:] Nicholas knew that twelve thousand strokes with the regulation rods were not only certain death with torture, but were a superfluous cruelty, for five thousand strokes were sufficient to kill the strongest man. But it pleased him to be ruthlessly cruel, and it also pleased him to think that we have abolished capital punishment in Russia.

[On entering a reception hall where 100 subjects await:] He came out to them with a lifeless look in his eyes, his chest expanded, his stomach bulging out above and below its bandages; and feeling everybody's gaze tremulously and obsequiously fixed upon him, he assumed an even more triumphant air . . . Having received all the New Year congratulations, he passed on to church. God, through his servants the priests, greeted and praised Nicholas just as worldly people did; and weary as he was of these greetings and praises, Nicholas duly accepted them. All this was as it should be, because the welfare and happiness of the whole world depended on him; and though the matter wearied him, he still did not refuse the universe his assistance.

Passages like these would have done wonders for Kutuzov as well as *War and Peace*.

4

THE WORLDS OF ANTHONY POWELL

Come Dancing

I was touched at being asked by the Wallace Collection and the Anthony Powell Society to deliver the inaugural annual lecture.[1] First because they clearly rejected the thought that someone holding my views might be an incongruous choice, but secondly, and much more importantly, because we need to get away from the blinkered view that regards *A Dance to the Music of Time* as a novel that can only be enjoyed by 'toffs' or readers of the *Daily Telegraph*, not that the two are identical these days by any means. It is, however, a prejudice that has dogged Powell's great novel sequence for far too long and I think it's high time it was discarded. I'm always surprised when I mention these books to young men or women; they look at me in bewilderment. It's not that they don't like them. They've never heard of Powell. Could it be a result of the provincialization and marketization of the cultural life of this country, or the fact the people read less these days? I'm not sure, and in some ways speculation is pointless. How many would read Shakespeare were he not an eternal icon of official culture: a necessary part of the school curriculum, with a state-subsidized theatre dedicated to his plays?

1   This is an abridged and edited version of the inaugural lecture given in January 2008.

56

What is on offer to those coming for the first time to the twelve novels that constitute the *Dance* is not the nuances of class snobbery, but a fictional reflection on the social history of five crucial decades of the last century, beginning with the end of the First World War and ending with the turbulence of the sixties. History, culture, comedy and the interrelationship of each to the other form the centrepieces of this novel. What we have on offer is the work of an extremely intelligent novelist and moreover one who, unlike many of his peers, was deeply steeped in European culture.

And it was his knowledge of that culture – not just his admiration for Proust which is well known, but his fondness for Stendhal – that undoubtedly affected his own work. I was very struck by his liking for Stendhal (my own favourite French novelist), because it reveals a literary openness that is admirable. Despite his own conservative political opinions, he could appreciate the work of a writer whose worldview was far removed from his own, not to say pretty far-left for those times and ours. And the Stendhal that Powell likes the most is the *Life of Henri Brulard*, a thinly disguised autobiography that pours bucketfuls of scorn on French conservatism. His favourite year, Stendhal calmly informs the reader in a footnote, is not 1789 (the beginning of the Revolution), but 1793 . . . the year the French King and Queen were beheaded. The 'ultras', as he refers to the supporters of the ancien régime and its latter-day successors, include his own father and the local priests, who have betrayed every single ideal that he, Stendhal, believes in – it is a very spirited and lively piece of writing. Powell's favourite novel, he tells us time and time again, is Dostoevsky's *The Devils* (or *The Possessed*). All this is a far cry from the style of the *Dance*. Neither Proust nor Stendhal, leave alone Dostoevsky, influenced the way Powell wrote, just as Proust was not influenced by his favourite literary work: the *Thousand and One Nights*.

Powell was, in some ways, the most European of English writers and that is why it is worth repeating that the literary project that became *A Dance to the Music of Time* has no equivalent in English letters: there is nothing that's comparable to this project. The *Dance* can better be seen in the same framework as Proust or Musil. Powell, while of a younger generation than both, is nonetheless not so far removed from them. Proust grew up during the Belle Epoque; Robert Musil fought in the First World War. Anthony Powell was born in 1905, but was still haunted, in some ways, by the memories of that war — he came from a military family, he knew military people, he knew that a whole generation had been wiped out by that war, and he served, himself, in the Second World War. There is a moving passage in *The Military Philosophers*, when the narrator in uniform is going through Normandy, and suddenly:

'Just spell out the name of that place we stopped over last night, Major Jenkins,' said Cobb. [I've always wondered whether this was a name inspired by Richard Cobb, who was one of the history tutors at Balliol College, Oxford.]

'C-A-B-O-U-R-G, sir.' As I uttered the last letter, scales fell from my eyes. Everything was transformed. It all came back, like the tea-soaked madeleine itself, in a torrent of memory. Cabourg — we had just driven out of Cabourg, out of Proust's Balbec. Only a few minutes before, I'd been standing on the esplanade along which, wearing her polo cap and accompanied by the little band of girls he had supposed the mistresses of professional bicyclists, Albertine had strolled into Marcel's life. Through the high windows of the Grand Hotel's dining room, conveying to those without the sensation of staring into an aquarium, was to be seen Saint-Loup, at the same table Bloch, mendaciously claiming acquaintance with the Swanns. A little farther along the promenade was the casino, its walls still displaying tattered playbills just like the one Charlus, wearing his black straw hat, had pretended to examine, after an attempt at long range to assess the narrator's physical attractions and possibilities.

There's actually a very funny scene, earlier on, where the narrator finds himself under the table during a bombing raid with General Liddiment, who asks, 'What do you think of Trollope?' to which the reply comes, 'Not very much.' They then turn to a discussion of what he really likes, and while this is taking place he's holding a copy of *Swann's Way* that he was reading before the bombs fell.

Despite the generational gap between Proust, Musil and Powell, their literary projects, while different in style, content and preoccupations (Proust and ambivalent sexuality, Musil's Kakania) are nonetheless analogous in terms of scale and ambition. The problems each confronts in developing their writing styles before the masterworks make an interesting comparison. Compare, for instance, the word experiments of Robert Musil to Anthony Powell. The early short stories penned by the Austrian are brisk and entertaining, but very different in style from *The Man Without Qualities*. Powell's early novels are very witty and in his first fiction, *Afternoon Men*, for instance, you can see the seeds of the *Dance*. The dialogue between Atwater and Lola at a sordid bohemian party is incredibly funny, containing the minimalism that would later be transformed into a unique craft by Beckett and Pinter. You can see the way he was working. But the break comes not so much in terms of subject matter or literary temperament, but in the style. Whereas the early novels were written in a self-consciously selective mode, by the time he began to write the *Dance* – a project that took him twenty-five years to complete – his style had changed. No doubt his immersion in Burton's *Anatomy of Melancholy*, and the impact of working on a book on John Aubrey had something to do with it. We await Hilary Spurling's biography to learn a lot more on these subjects. But by the time the *Dance* commences, the style is almost antique, baroque – and that actually lifts the comedy to a far higher level than one finds in the early novels. And that is what makes the *Dance* such a fine work of literature.

Powell was lucky. He was a survivor. His European counterparts never finished their work. Proust died relatively young, at fifty-one, and the complete *In Search of Lost Time* had to be published posthumously, the author's proofreading and rewrites still incomplete. Musil's pencil of creation snapped with him: *The Man Without Qualities* remained an unfinished masterpiece. Powell was well aware of all this, and was determined to finish his work. The *Dance* took him twenty-five years to write. He said himself he brought it to a close when he did because he understood the dangers of going on for too long. Also times had changed. His own political sympathies had always been on the Right, but his bohemian friends (and Orwell) tended to veer towards the Left. By the time he concluded the *Dance* with *Hearing Secret Harmonies*, all this had changed. The book is dedicated to Robert Conquest. Charlotte Street in the late sixties was no longer a bohemian haunt. Bertorelli's had become the regular meeting place of a virulently anti-Left, cold-warrior group of writers, who like Conquest supported the wars in Indo-China. This, in my view, adversely affected the tone and structure of the last novel.

When did I first *Dance*? It was either 1979 or 1980. I was travelling from London to Mexico to attend a left-wing conference with Perry Anderson. He was sitting next to me and re-reading some volumes from the *Dance* throughout the flight (it's an eleven-hour hop). One of them was definitely *Casanova's Chinese Restaurant*. At one point his laughter became so infectious that an American passenger came up to him and said: 'Hey, guy, what's that you're reading? It must be really funny.' My friend held up the book briefly, said, 'It certainly is' and carried on as before.

My own reading matter was comparatively dull, which made me envious. Several months later, back in Britain, I bought the whole collection with Mark Boxer's amazing covers and read the entire work. Sometimes one hears people explaining how they started off with *A Question of Upbringing* when it first came out and stopped there, because they had no idea how this could go on and become what it became. They didn't like that first one and never read the rest. I loved the first one, but it was useful to have them all stacked up on the bedside table, so that the reading could be systematic and continuous. I'm sure that's the reason the *Dance* had such an immediate impact on me.

Some years ago I encountered one of our leading literary critics at an Xmas party, and the following conversation took place:

'What do you think of the *Dance*?'

'Oh, you've read it?'

'Yes, I have.'

'Well, I didn't like it. You obviously did?'

'I did, but why didn't you?

'Closed world.'

That's all he would say and I resisted asking whether he had actually read it all. I confess I've only read the *Dance* twice, but a closed world it definitely is not. It contains the most entertaining accounts of bohemian life in London from 1920 to 1958, decades during which Anthony Powell not only mingled with that world, but often enjoyed it more than coming-out parties in Belgravia. And one of his jottings in the *Notebook* is apposite: 'You can't be a creative artist if you are in any restrictive sense an intellectual snob.'

What then is the central theme of this novel? It is creativity – the actual act of production. Of literature, of books, of paintings, of music; that is what most of the central characters in the novel are engaged in for the whole of their lives. Moreland composes, Barnby paints, X Trapnel writes, Quiggin, Members and Maclintick criticize, and the narrator publishes books and then becomes a writer. What excites the novelist is music and painting, literature and criticism. And it's this creativity together with the comedy of everyday life that sustains the *Dance*. The comedy, it needs to be reiterated, is on a very high level.

If the exploration of artistic creation is one of the great themes of the *Dance*, it is also remarkable for its astonishing characterizations. To Charlus in the Proust epic; to Diotima and Ulrich in *The Man Without Qualities*, must be added Widmerpool and, I think, Pamela Flitton in the *Dance*. The late Lord Longford often claimed that Widmerpool was based on him. There's an entertaining entry in one of the journals where Powell is at a college reunion at Oxford and runs into Denis Healey. The former Labour deputy leader greets him like a long-lost friend, and then: 'I've always wanted to ask you this: did you base Widmerpool on Edward Heath?' The first time one finishes reading the *Dance*, there is a natural curiosity to discover who particular characters could have been based on. It can become an obsession, like trainspotting, and should be resisted.

Anthony Powell has written somewhere that no character in fiction is ever based on any other single character, they are always composites: different aspects of people you've met are sometimes synthesized in one particular creation. This is even more true of him than of Proust, as we know from George Painter's excellent biography: many of the 'vices' that he ascribes to Charlus are actually his own; and the person on whom he most based Charlus, an aristocratic popinjay named Montesquieu, certainly understood what was going on and said to a friend: 'Perhaps I should now change my name to Montproust.' Widmerpool is, in some ways, a more inspired creation than Charlus, a universal character. After all, thrusting mediocrity rises to the surface in almost every sphere. Virtually every European government (including Gordon Brown's collection of deadbeats) is packed with Widmerpools – and not just in Europe. Yet another reason to complain at the total transformation of Widmerpool in the last volume where he is taken out of character, made into a grotesque and killed. Powell's *Notebook* reveals he had another ending in mind: Widmerpool disappearing into the mist from whence he had emerged, much more in keeping with the dance of life and death.

The *Dance* is set over five decades and coincidence plays an important part in the characters' many encounters. How many times, since I've read the books, I've run into someone not seen for twenty years or so and muttered inwardly 'It's the *Dance*' − and it is. Yet structured as art, the coincidences also build up into the greater patterning of the dance. Friendship is another crucially important theme. There are moving passages in the novel about friendship, what it means, and how important it is, and what you feel when you lose a friend − usually, but not always, during the war. That leaves a deep impact, so that the friends who survived become even more important and when they behave badly, it is very hurtful.

In his literature, his memoirs and the journals, Powell can be witty, waspish, patronizing and even vicious, but not malicious; that is not something you get from his work. He writes about many people generously − some would say too generously. So what is to be said about some of the recent remarks that have been made about him, seven years after his death? They are related to the question of friendship. V. S. Naipaul was regarded as a friend. The Powell journals are full of him. Too full. Naipaul's latest book, not his best by any means, probably his worst, also contains an essay on Powell. Now, what surprised me about that was not what passes for literary criticism. That is not a problem. To each her own. What is astonishing is his claim − I assume it must be true − that he had never read the *Dance* in all the years that he was a close friend of Anthony and Violet Powell, visiting them regularly and often playing the court jester by mouthing remarks about race and class that were being discouraged in polite society. If he hadn't read the *Dance*, why not? You don't have to like a friend's work, but surely to read it is obligatory. Be that as it may, let's accept that he didn't read the books but must have pretended that he had at numerous gatherings. He then says that when he did read them, after

Powell's death, he was struck by the fact that he didn't like them, that they were overrated, with no narrative worth speaking of, and so forth. This was then followed by tittle-tattle picked up from X and Y who also dislike the novels and the man. It was the unpleasantness of the tone that surprised me – even if he hadn't read the books when Powell was alive, what caused him suddenly to sit up now and urinate on his friend's grave? I know that getting the Nobel Prize can have a strange effect on people, but one always hopes they rise above it. So the ill will remains a bit of a mystery.

Or does it? In *Books Do Furnish a Room*, the novelist X Trapnel, besotted with Lady Pamela and dominated by her, is slowly losing his grip: 'In the street his incoherent, distracted state of mind was much more apparent. He was certainly in a bad way. All the talk about writing, its flow not greatly different from the termination of any evening in his company, was just a question of putting off the evil hour of having to face his own personal problems.'

Or to put it another way, as the great eighteenth-century Chinese novelist, Cao Xueqin wrote:

> Truth becomes fiction, when the fiction's true
> Real becomes not-real where the unreal's real.

2008

Crotchets from the Music of Time

This is a peculiar book.[2] It consists of fragments, random and discontinuous scribblings, 'erratic juxtapositions' of names, book titles, aphorisms, situations, quotations, plot outlines – 'Two men share a flat, one reads the other's diary, it becomes a vice'; 'A is having an affair with B's wife, and tries to teach her habits of punctuality, so that B too shall profit in some way from the situation' – and many entertaining one-liners: 'The eponymous nourishment of the Earl of Sandwich'; 'We thought of the FO, or the BBC. You know there is no exam for the latter'; 'Some women seem to imagine that one has nothing better to do than to sit up all night listening to anecdotes about their first husband'; 'She wrote badly, even for a lesbian novelist.' The overall tone is relaxed. The jottings are witty and light in style. Reflections of a literary, political, military, or personal nature are absent. The brief introduction provided by the author tells us very little.

Begun in 1930, when Anthony Powell was twenty-five years old, this notebook – so the internal evidence suggests – continued throughout the war years and long after he had finished choreographing and crafting *A Dance to the Music of Time*.

No dates are attached to the entries, strengthening the impression that *A Writer's Notebook* was never intended for publication. Its appearance is timely nonetheless, and will greatly amuse Powellites of every stripe. It contains many anticipations of the masterwork whose fiftieth anniversary is being marked this year with a conference at Eton.

This choice of location is somewhat unfortunate (the museum in Manchester Square where the Wallace Collection is housed would have been far more appropriate), pandering as it does to a blinkered view that dismisses all twelve volumes of the *Dance* as being nothing more nor less than

2   Anthony Powell, *A Writer's Notebook*, London: Heinemann, 2001.

an account of the whims and prejudices of a particular group of 'toffs' – and the nuances of class snobbery – rather than a truly virtuoso performance. It is the interrelationship of history, culture and comedy that makes the *Dance*.

The changes in focus and subject, from a coming-out ball in Belgravia to a bohemian assembly in seedy Fitzrovia and thence to a desolate Welsh-dominated army camp in Northern Ireland, are both rapid and exhilarating, the descriptions vivid and funny. The time span covers half a century, and in this period the material processes of life – being born, working, drinking, dining, quarrelling, falling in love, producing children and dying – affect people in different ways. The portraits of writers, painters, dons, musicians, left-wing intellectuals, army officers, literary critics, businessmen, bohemian women, mystics and fading aristocrats are so varied and vigorous that, when social barriers are breached and characters from different walks of life appear in a single scene, the result is hugely diverting. The psychology, behaviour, morals, dress, manners, language and customs of the men and women in the *Dance* spring from social requirements. Chance throws them together. History and the laws of the heart do the rest.

A Powellism from the *Notebook*: 'You can't be a creative artist if you are in any restrictive sense an intellectual snob.' A return to the text, necessitated by the emergence of the *Notebook*, was even more joyful. A second reading of a novel can in some ways be much more fruitful. Since the narrative no longer holds any mysteries, the architecture of the work can be appreciated more fully. It is not the lives of 'toffs' that drive the novel forward. At its heart is the creative process itself.

Moreland composes, Mona poses, Barnby paints, X Trapnel writes, Jenkins thinks, Quiggin, Members and Maclintick criticize. In the garb of the narrator, Powell reflects on a linguistic problem: 'Intricacies of social life make English habits unyielding to simplification, while understatement and irony – in which all classes of this island converse – upset the normal emphasis of reported speech.' But: 'Understatement, too, had its own banality . . . it could encourage evasion of unpalatable facts.'

The *Dance* remains a work of literature without equal in modern English letters. The only projects equivalent in scope were crafted during the first decades of the last century in Paris and Vienna. Proust, Musil and Powell all shared an aversion to cultural Fordism. They could not write to please. Commercial gain was subordinated to a passionate seriousness and a strong belief in their respective literary projects. Despite the differences in tone and style, one can easily imagine a George Grosz sketch in which three self-absorbed characters – Charlus, Diotima and Widmerpool – are captured peering eagerly into the same trough.

The *Notebook* is littered with names. These include choices made by other novelists which stimulated Powell's curiosity. There is a note of triumph in the following entry: 'Chatterley a name in Surtees. ? Lawrence got it from there. cf. "Game Keepers", Mr Romford's Hounds, Chapter 1, page 161.' And irritation: 'Henry James's inability to invent good proper names, and his country house names particularly inept.' Powell himself took names very seriously, often searching as far afield as the Domesday Book to find a name that could be matched to a character.

This fixation is very visible in the *Dance*. Thus the narrator: 'The name "Sunny Farebrother" struck me as almost redundant in its suggestion of clear-cut straightforward masculinity.' Or again, Widmerpool to narrator: 'I thought it might be you, Jenkins. Only yours is such a common name that I could not be sure.'

Rosie Manasch's surname is derived from the Baron Manasch with whom Swann fought a duel in the Proust epic. But what about the freelance violinist Carolo, who plays the Wigmore Hall in *Casanova's Chinese Restaurant*? Just as we are wondering whether this was concocted in an Italian restaurant after a concert and is a cross between Caruso and Barolo, we are casually informed that the name is a pure fantasy and that his real name is 'Wilson or Wilkinson or Parker – a surname felt to ring too much of plain common sense'. And what of the name Widmerpool, which makes its first appearance from Anthony Powell in the *Notebook*? The *Journals*

1982–86 reveal that he lifted it from Lucy Hutchinson's account of the English Civil War: Widmerpool was one of Cromwell's captains.

One can only hope that Captain Widmerpool of the New Model Army, unlike his fictional reincarnation, agreed with the Protector's maxim to the effect that 'A man never rises so high as when he does not know where he is going.'

While on the subject of the monster, a confession is in order. After reading the *Dance* again, another impression was confirmed. I was not convinced by the final volume. Widmerpool's evolution seemed to be out of character. If in the immediate post-war period the author's political inclinations were to the Right, he tended to veer to a leftish bohemianism socially. The dedication of *Hearing Secret Harmonies* to Robert Conquest suggests a change in orientation.

Was the unconvincing transformation of Widmerpool into a Dickensian grotesque, and his awful death, the literary outcome of this shift? The *Notebook* offers a clue on p. 110: 'The whole series ends with Jenkins looking out of a window at the men working in a street from a room in which some incident has been taking place. Possibly Widmerpool walking away, as he walked in out of the fog.'

Well, exactly. This would have encouraged readers to imagine different futures for Widmerpool. I could see him becoming a founder member of the SDP. And then one day, thinking himself unobserved, he bends down to tie a shoelace in the lobby of the House of Lords and finds himself being whacked on the bottom with a folded copy of the *Daily Telegraph*. As he looks up and realizes it is the Prime Minister herself in a jovial mood, a look of adoration disfigures his face.

Subsequent to this life-enhancing event, he changes allegiances once again, becoming a much-sought-after platform speaker for the Poujadist wing of the old party. And as he approaches his ninety-eighth birthday in January 2001, his face is once again flashed on the TV screens. He is the oldest millionaire supplier of soft money to the New Labour apparatus . . .

2001

5

THE PRIME OF SIR SALMAN RUSHDIE

Midnight's Children and After

Midnight's Children has been widely acclaimed as a literary tour de force. It has won plaudits for its author, Salman Rushdie, from critics throughout the Anglo-Saxon world and has been awarded the prestigious Booker Prize. Rushdie has been compared, at different times, to Günter Grass and Gabriel García Márquez, whose influences, openly acknowledged, are evident in *Midnight's Children*. Saleem Sinai, the semi-autobiographical narrator and central figure in the book, has clear affinities with Oskar in *The Tin Drum*; and it would not be difficult to find the Latin American equivalents of the sub-continent's generals in *Autumn of the Patriarch*. However, these analogies are not of prime significance. Danzig/Gdansk and Macondo are not Bombay.

Rushdie's work provokes comparisons not only with Grass or Márquez, but with other writers who have made India their subject. The reason this has not been done so far is because English critics and commentators have tended to downplay the politics of *Midnight's Children*. Whether this is the result of guilt, embarrassment, ignorance or a combination of all three is a matter for speculation. What is beyond doubt is that Rushdie's novel is centrally an attack on clearly identifiable targets: the indigenous ruling classes in South Asia. His book is not simply a pleasing mosaic of everyday life in the South Asian sub-continent. It is a devastating political indictment of those who rule these countries and, by implication, of those who placed them in their present positions of power and privilege. In that sense it is fair to say that the publication of *Midnight's Children* marks an important turning point in the relatively short life span of Indo-English literature.

It is important to briefly recall the evolution of this rather unusual literary tradition. The thirties and forties were crucially important decades in India as elsewhere. The rising tide of nationalism, the growth of the Communist Party and the birth of militant trade unionism produced a ferment in the country's intelligentsia. The formation of the Anti-Fascist League of Writers and the Progressive Writers Association (both bodies were essentially CPI front organizations) helped to channel the anger of writers, poets and playwrights in leftist directions. The foremost exponent of Socialist Realism in the English language was the Indian novelist Mulk Raj Anand, who deliberately confined his scope to writing about those who were well below the lowest rung of the social ladder. The Coolie and The Untouchable are emblematic of his politico-literary project.

Further south in Madras, R. K. Narayan was beginning to produce novels that were the polar opposite of Anand's. Narayan wrote semi-mystical social comedies of village life in Southern India, whose cumulative impact was to idealize Hinduism and the Indian village. His formula appealed to only a limited layer of Indians, but was extremely popular with English civil servants. (He remains to this day a great favourite of V. S. Naipaul. One can see why.) It was only after 1960 that the new Indian novel emerged on the scene.

It is essential at this point to comment briefly on what surely must be considered the main forebear of *Midnight's Children*. I refer to the series of four novels by Paul Scott commonly known as *The Raj Quartet* and currently being filmed in India by Granada TV. In literary and political inclination, Paul Scott (who died prematurely of cancer in 1977) was far removed from

Salman Rushdie. Yet his novels are one of the most evocative accounts of the last decades of British colonialism in India. Scott succeeds in depicting the nuances of imperialist strategy far better than most political tracts, and in the process he helps to explain how the British managed to rule India for so long without facing a generalized revolt. He portrays the marriage between the colonial administration and the indigenous landed gentry with a rare subtlety and sensitivity. His representation of colonial racism and of the peculiarities of the English racist have direct relevance to the domestic racism of Britain today.

The ideological heritage of the Raj has often been talked about, but rarely analysed in detail. Imperialism wove a powerful web which sought to imprison the consciousness of those whom it oppressed. It instilled a self-hatred based on race and colour that redoubled the discriminations of caste society. The natives were 'taught' to regard white skin as a mark of superiority. True, this was not simply a case of ideological aggression. White 'superiority' was backed up not simply by Kipling – the 'hireling minstrel' of British imperialism – and the hordes of missionaries who descended on the colonies like parasites, but by material strength and privileges. When sections of the oppressed did challenge this myth, they were ruthlessly put down. Scott's quartet of novels facilitates our knowledge of colonial racism, but shies away from discussing its illegitimate offspring: even today in India the Northerners regard the Southerners as inferior because of their slightly darker complexion. Moreover this phenomenon is largely restricted to three distinct, though interrelated, layers of South-Asian society: the ruling classes, the civil service and the army. All three are direct descendants of the Raj. This deformation is the extreme opposite of Anglo-American racism, widespread amongst the underprivileged layers of the white population and cynically exploited by a heartless governing class.

The very process of 'midnight' (India and Pakistan obtained their independence at the stroke of midnight, hence the title of Rushdie's novel) was determined by a concordat between the departing colonial power and the two nationalist parties. (It is worth noting that both the Indian National Congress and the Muslim League were set up on the initiative of Englishmen.) Thus a reading of Scott is useful if one wishes to explore the parentage of 'midnight's children'.

'Reality', writes Salman Rushdie in his book, 'can have metaphorical content. A thousand and one children were born; there were a thousand and one possibilities which had never been present in one place at one time before; and there were a thousand and one dead ends. Midnight's children can be made to represent many things, according to your point of view: they can be seen as the last throw of everything antiquated and retrogressive in our myth-ridden nation, whose defeat was entirely desirable in the context of a modernizing twentieth-century economy; or as the true hope of freedom, which is now forever extinguished . . .'

Before commenting on the accuracy or otherwise of this counterposition, it is worth drawing attention to the two-part structure of the novel. The first half is essentially a recreation of the past. Grandfather Aadam Aziz returns home after studying medicine and Lenin's *What Is to Be Done?* at Heidelberg. He leaves behind a German lover and companion, Ilse Lubin, and is soon embroiled in a traditional arranged marriage to the daughter of a rural notable. His first glimpse of this bride-to-be is through a hole in a sheet. Ilse comes to visit him in India, hears of his new love and drowns herself in the still waters of Srinagar's Dal Lake in Kashmir. Here, at the very start of the novel, is a symbolic rendering of a theme that will recur: modernization is fighting a losing battle.

Father Ahmed Sinai is the protagonist of another symbolic event. We see him purchasing an Englishman's mansion in fashionable Bombay, in an area previously reserved for the 'pink conquerors'. This image stays with us throughout the novel: the houses, offices, uniforms, attitudes, style and manners of the Raj are being usurped by a new ruling class. This class has grown up in the shadow of the colonialists, permitted to observe its betters from a distance; now cosseted, now rejected, it is ready and waiting to step into the shoes of its former rulers. Even its most urbane and cultured spokesmen speak an unfamiliar jargon. 'Long years ago', declares a tearful Jawaharlal Nehru as the clock chimes the twelfth stroke of midnight on 15 August 1947, 'we made a tryst with destiny . . .' His sentiments are comprehensible to the poorest and humblest citizen, but the language in which he chooses to communicate with the masses is English. In neighbouring Pakistan, M. A. Jinnah addresses hundreds of thousands of illiterate peasants, many of them unversed even in Urdu and confined to speaking their own dialects – in English! As time passes, the veneer of what has been learnt from the English civil servant wears distressingly thin, and then disappears altogether. Rushdie's description of this important transition period is acute and, at times, comic, if lacking in the power and anger of the novel's second part.

The perspectives of Rushdie's 'history' are sometimes questionable. Saleem Sinai's grandfather Aziz is implacably hostile to separatist Muslim politics, and hence to the new confessional state being established in Karachi. The family will not migrate, at least not while the old man is alive. Yet the Partition episode is almost muted in *Midnight's Children*. The personal conflicts and political contradictions that traumatized the bulk of middle-class families in towns that were to remain a part of India have been movingly represented in the Indian film *Garam Hava* (*Hot Winds*). The torment and occasional crossing of the communal divide on behalf of trapped friends has been depicted by the Indian writer and journalist, Khushwant Singh, in his novel *Train to Pakistan*. The anguish of Partition was best described by the first poem of a sixteen-year-old Sikh girl written in 1947. Now one of India's foremost poets, Amrita Pritam appealed then to the memory of the great Sufi epic poet of the late eighteenth century, Waris Shah. As Sikhs and Muslims slaughtered each other indiscriminately, Pritam wrote:

> I say to Waris Shah today, O speak up from your grave
> And from the Book of Love unfurl a new and different page
> When one daughter of the Punjab wept
> You wrote a myriad dirges
> Today a million tearful daughters
> Are calling out to you:
> 'Arise, you healer of innermost pain
> Look now at your Punjab:
> The forests are littered with corpses
> And blood flows down the Chenab.

Again, Rushdie chooses to concentrate on the familiar and much-written-about massacre at Jallianwalla Bagh in Amritsar in 1919. This was undoubtedly a major event in the history of the Raj, but not as significant in other ways as the Moplah uprising in Malabar in 1921, or the unprecedented Naval Mutiny (and the accompanying General Strike) that shook the authorities in 1946. Of course *Midnight's Children* is a novel, not a history proper. But it is a novel that self-consciously explores the rich seam of sub-continental history, and its selectivity is not irrelevant. The second part of the novel is far more coherent. Its literary directness and political force confront the reader with a powerful vision.

Saleem Sinai is a growing man in the late fifties and sixties, and fully mature in the seventies. He can thus observe at first hand three crucially important sequences: the military coup in Pakistan in 1958, the struggle for Bangladesh in 1971 and the Indian State of Emergency in 1976. The Sinai family's emigration to Pakistan transforms them all. Saleem's sister is affectionately known in Bombay as the Brass Monkey, a person full of mischief and independence. In Pakistan she turns into a pure and pristine Muslim, a singer who regales the nation with patriotic hymns during the 1965 clashes with India. A key character in this phase of the novel is the self-serving Muslim army officer, Zulfiqar. In the first half he is witnessed as an unctuous subordinate of Brigadier Dodson, who marries Aunt Emerald and realizes that his commercial future lies in Pakistan. By the second half the young major has become a 'Punchinello-faced general', plotting with fellow-generals at his dinner table to usurp political power in 1958:

> General Zulfiqar described troop movements; I moved pepperpots symbolically while he spoke. In the clutches of the active-metaphorical mode of connection, I shifted salt-cellars and bowls of chutney: this mustard-jar is Company A occupying Head Post Office; there are two pepperpots surrounding a serving spoon, which means Company B has seized the airport. With the fate of my nation in my hands, I shifted condiments and cutlery, capturing empty biriani-dishes with water glasses, stationing salt-cellars, on guard, around water jugs. And when General Zulfiqar stopped talking, the march of the table-service also came to an end. Ayub Khan seemed to settle down in his chair; was the wink he gave to me just my imagination? At any rate the Commander-in-Chief said, 'Very good, Zulfiqar; good show.' A few weeks later the real pepperpots had taken over the country.

Zulfiqar is, in many ways, Rushdie's most inspired creation. A Pakistani version of Ronald Merrick in Paul Scott's *Raj Quartet*, he is an archetypal, relatively privileged, middle-class Muslim refugee from India. His chosen profession is the army. Years of loyalty to his British superiors are now transferred to his new Punjabi bosses in Pakistan. (Like most officers of his generation he is shallow in the extreme, probably regarding the *Reader's Digest* as incisive and *Time* magazine as far too intellectual.) He is crude, calculating, corrupt and callous. His servility to his superior officers verges on self-parody. His son Zafar is a great disappointment. The lad still wets his bed. Urinary disorders are, of course, unmanly – an attribute General Zulfiqar extends to all Hindus. Rushdie's delineation of a Pakistan run by generals and fed daily on the poison of communal and national chauvinism – interspersed with vignettes portraying feudal rulers of decrepit states, mothers who 'eavesdrop on the daughter's dreams', childhood love, youthful fantasies and the effect of alcohol – constitutes one of the most powerful passages in the book.

The position of Zulfiqar as a central actor on Rushdie's stage symbolizes the elements of continuity and discontinuity in the period preceding and following 1947. It is this sort of army officer who will organize and push through atrocities on a grand scale. Rushdie's account of the Pakistani invasion of East Bengal is unique in Indo-English literature. It is a portrayal not simply of wicked individuals (though there are plenty of these), but of the collective frenzy of a desperately frightened ruling class: the training of special commando units to kill Bengalis, the constant use of semi-fascist communal imagery, all designed to justify and facilitate the task of murdering Bengali intellectuals and workers. The Bengalis were not 'proper Muslims'. They were relatively recent converts from Hinduism, declared many a Punjabi military maniac in 1970–71. Rape was justified on the grounds that 'we were going to plant genuine Muslim seeds in those black Bengali bitches'. (I still remember these words being quoted to me by a young army officer who, to his credit, was so disgusted that he left the army and subsequently the country.)

Reading *Midnight's Children* brought back many old memories. I can still recall the amazement of my Bengali friends and comrades when in March 1969 at a public meeting in Dacca University I argued that there was no hope for any meaningful autonomy, and that they should aim for a 'Lal Bangla' (Red Bengal). In private, I told many disbelieving Bengalis that the army would engage in large-scale massacres rather than concede their demands. Many of those with whom I argued are now dead. Some died on the first day of the Pakistani military offensive, here described by Rushdie:

Midnight, March 25, 1971: past the University, which was being shelled, the buddha led troops to Sheikh Mujib's lair. Students and lecturers came running out of hostels; they were greeted by bullets, and Merchurichrome stained the lawns ... And while we drove through the city streets, Shaheed looked out of windows and saw things that weren't-couldn't-have-been true: soldiers entering women's hostels without knocking; women dragged into the street, were also entered, and again nobody troubled to knock ... When thought becomes excessively painful, action is the finest remedy ... Dog-soldiers strain at the leash, and then, released, leap joyously to their work. O wolfhound chases of undesirables! O prolific seizings of professors and poets! O unfortunate shot-while-resisting arrests of Awami Leaguers and fashion correspondents! Dogs of war cry havoc in the city ... Farooq Shaheed Ayooba take turns at vomiting as their nostrils are assailed by the stench of burning slums ... No undesirable is safe tonight; no hiding-place impregnable. Bloodhounds track the fleeing enemies of national unity; wolfhounds, not to be outdone, sink fierce teeth into their prey ...

Zulfiqar must be punished for his crimes. His death will be violent, an act of catharsis rather than a political finale. The instrument chosen to despatch the old General is his own son, Zafar, who on discovering that his father is a corrupt scoundrel in league with smugglers, kills him. The act is carried out not in a fit of rage, but calmly, its perpetrator displaying (presumably to everyone's surprise) hitherto hidden reserves. But Zulfiqar's death does not by any means indicate that the travails of 'midnight's children' are over. They will be politically crippled, physically sterilized or vasectomized and be subjected to numerous other indignities by the Widow during her notorious State of Emergency. They will cast her out but her octogenarian replacement ('an ancient dotard who ate cashews and pistachios and daily took a "glass of his own water"') surrounded by his own gangsters will not prove much better. The Left is seen by Rushdie as a 'Magicians' Ghetto' where

> the prestidigitators, the pullers of rabbits from hats, aligned themselves firmly behind Mr Dange's Moscow-line official CPI which supported Gandhi throughout the Emergency; the contortionists, however, began to lean more towards the left and the slanting intricacies of the Chinese-oriented wing. Fire-eaters and sword-swallowers applauded the guerrilla tactics of the Naxalite movement; while mesmerists and walkers-on-hot-coals espoused Namboodripad's manifesto (neither Muscovite nor Pekinese) and deplored the Naxalites' violence. There were Trotskyist tendencies amongst card-sharpers, and even a Communism-through-the-ballot-box movement amongst the moderate members of the ventriloquist section. I had entered a milieu in which, while religious and regionalist bigotry were wholly absent, our ancient national gift for fissiparousness had found new outlets.

If Rushdie had travelled a bit further south he would have been able to pay tribute to another Widow with her own State of Emergency, who destroyed the flower of Ceylonese youth in an orgy of violence. His conclusion would have been further reinforced: 'Midnight has many children; the offspring of Independence were not all human. Violence, corruption, poverty, generals, chaos, greed and pepperpots . . .' But is that all? Is South Asia then mystically fated to lurch from one disaster to the next? Or will 'something' happen and, if so, what will it consist of? Are we seeing the end of all hope, as is sometimes implied in the text?

There is undoubtedly a streak of pessimism and nihilism in the book. In a fascinating self-analysis Rushdie has recently denied the charge, arguing eloquently that his views do not coincide with those of the narrator. He admits that the 'story of Saleem does indeed lead him to despair. But the story is told in a manner designed to echo, as closely as my abilities allowed, the Indian talent for non-stop self-regeneration. This is why the narrative constantly throws up new stories, why it "teems". The form – multitudinous, hinting at the infinite possibilities of the country – is the optimistic counterweight to Saleem's personal tragedy. I do not think that a book written in such a manner can really be called a despairing work.'[1]

Perhaps, but this argument is not totally convincing. In the first place the tension between form and content is not as effective as Rushdie seems to imply. The new stories and sub-stories reinforce each other, and the overpowering impression towards the end is of despair. As for the notion of 'non-stop self-regeneration': what does it mean, if anything? Has village life been characterized by 'non-stop self-regeneration' over the past six centuries? Or is the term meant to imply the possibilities of a new awakening in terms of political consciousness? In that case one can agree, but the problem is not totally solved. The response to the novel in South Asia has been on a number of levels. In the salons of Islamabad, Lahore and Karachi (and no doubt Bombay and Delhi and Calcutta), it has been a central focus of gossip. Who is General Zulfiqar? The fact that the character is partially a pastiche of the now retired General Shahid Hamid has not, of course, escaped anyone, including the original himself. The social snobbery, exaggerated politeness and all the airs and graces associated with Aunt Emerald are still much in evidence and, so I'm told, the characters in question have not been particularly amused by the literary efforts of the reprobate Rushdie.

1 Salman Rushdie, 'Imaginary Homelands', *London Review of Books*, 7–20 October 1982.

On a deeper level, as Rushdie himself acknowledges, the charge is one of pessimism. Many South-Asian friends have told me that 'the book has nothing good to say about anything in our part of the world'. It has been pointed out, in response, that the book says nothing that Indians or Pakistanis do not say to each other in private. The feeling of helplessness is much stronger in Pakistan, Bangladesh and India today than it is in *Midnight's Children*. The tragic fate of the Bangladeshi masses, the triumph of the iron heel in Pakistan, the inability of the CPM (Communist Party of India (Marxist)) regime in Calcutta to satisfy even the minutest aspirations of its followers – all this has vindicated Rushdie's approach to a certain extent. *Midnight's Children* is a novel in the tradition of radical-democratic humanism. It goes no further, but as such it is a work of immense importance.

There is, however, a rational kernel in the objections registered by some socialists in the sub-continent. It is not so much the undoubted national nihilism that is a strong element in the work. It is that Rushdie, writing from the outside (as he himself explains), has been able to recreate his subject only partially. This has meant that many extremely rich aspects of the sub-continent's culture and politics are absent. As one example, we could refer to the amazing impact of poetry as a mass medium in South Asia. This is largely due to the fact that the majority of the people are still illiterate in their native languages (leave alone English), and consequently the novel or the short story have not replaced the public poetry-reading or *mushaira*. Poetry has been the dominant form of literary expression in the sub-continent for the last four hundred years. The ghazal – a short lyrical poem – dates back to the early Mughal courts of medieval India. It is often used to attack (sometimes savagely) the very institutions that permit its existence and, on occasion, the divine Creator as well. The ghazal has survived and is popular to this day, largely because it is written to be recited rather than read. Many of the sub-continent's poets, both before and after independence, have stood up and recited what politicians could or dare not say. Iqbal, Tagore, Nazrul Islam, Faiz Ahmed Faiz, Josh Malihabadi gave birth to a new tradition. They were followed by poets such as Sahir Ludhianvi (now dead) or Habib Jalib, still very much alive and imprisoned by every single regime in Pakistan, or Ahmed Saleem, the Punjabi minstrel who wrote poems for Bengal while Punjabi generals were embarking on a bloodbath.

One must not idealize our poets. They were and are capable of all sorts of human and political errors, but many of them refused to be silenced or bought. Neither political repression, nor old age, nor poverty, nor personal tragedy, nor rejection by literary policemen or imprisonment by real ones had the capacity of destroying their morale, their patience or their pens. Rushdie would, I'm sure, be deeply moved by Faiz's striking imagery in his poem on the rape of Bangladesh. He would be pleased to discover that the Taj Mahal was already the subject of a savagely Brechtian lyric by Sahir Ludhianvi in the thirties, which discussed aspects other than corridors stinking of urine (a common condition of public telephone boxes in contemporary Britain!). If one is after facts long obscured from public view, hidden from history, carefully concealed lest they excite newer and more dangerous passions, then one need only study the outpourings of South Asia's poets, from the highest to the lowest. It is this aspect which is missing from *Midnight's Children* and which annoys many who try to conceal their own despair by attacking that of others.

Since Rushdie wrote his book, the situation in the sub-continent has deteriorated further. The Saudi Arabians have organized an Islamic coup in Bangladesh, a country that was savaged in the name of Islam. General Zia in Pakistan could not have been created by a novelist. The affluent Afghan refugees who have increased the quantity of heroin produced in Pakistan a hundred times over are prospering, as are the two Generals who are their protectors. The nation is deprived of alcohol, but Islam does not forbid heroin! General Zulfiqar's crimes seem almost petty by comparison. It is impossible to read an Indian magazine or newspaper without encountering stories still more grotesque than those that adorn the pages of *Midnight's Children*. Increasingly the veterans of past struggles, old, not-so-old and young are beginning to ask the same question: 'Was our struggle in vain?' To some of them (mainly disillusioned Maoists) one can reply forcefully in the affirmative. The Naxalites were the product of a very real, rather than a literary, despair. Their politics were doomed to fail. The gods they worshipped proved unreal. But to the bulk of yesterday's warriors we have yet to reply. True, these answers cannot simply be provided through literary onslaughts or poetic metaphors, yet one must not underestimate the power of ideas. The poet, the filmmaker and the novelist could, I am convinced, play a much more crucial role than ever before.

Rushdie's novel will not reach the South Asian masses, but it will be read by an English-speaking intelligentsia (probably much larger than in Britain) and, in that sense, it is extremely welcome. The very fact that it is being discussed constitutes a unique tribute to its author. No other novel about India has had such an impact. But what answer do we give to the temporarily atomized intellectual, trade unionist, ex-Naxalite or rank-and-file member of the Communist Party of India (Marxist)? We could do worse than repeat the words of an old man in his Mexican exile, who had lived through the most massive defeats ever inflicted on the European working class, but refused to retreat intellectually. In a private letter to a friend who had written complaining that she was now utterly pessimistic, Trotsky replied: 'Indignation, anger, revulsion? Yes, even temporary weariness. All this is human, only too human. But I will not believe that you have succumbed to pessimism. This would be like passively and plaintively taking umbrage at history. How can one do that? "History must be taken as it is"; and when she allows herself such extraordinary and filthy outrages, one must fight her back with one's fists.'

General Zia, Salman Rushdie and the Donkeys

I hope that Salman Rushdie wins the Booker Prize once again. It will be richly deserved. His latest novel *Shame* is a more focused and powerful work than *Midnight's Children*. It shares all the strengths of the latter book, but has shed its weaknesses. The literal translation of Urdu phrases into Rushdie's elegant and sparkling English prose is incredibly funny. Yet, it is almost as if one's amusement is circumscribed. Rushdie forces it to co-exist with indignation. His directness has meant that laughter and anger are coeval – the inseparable emotional twins to come out of *Shame*. This is because the book is not about some imaginary homeland. It is, alas, only too real. *Shame* is a savage literary-political impeachment of contemporary Pakistan. Nor could it have been published at a better time. But this is not intended as a review of the book, rather of its subject. One just hopes that the English *literati* who review the work at length will not simply concentrate on the literary plumage, but will at least have a peep at the dying state that lies underneath.

General Zia-ul-Haq is busy killing people again. The victims on this occasion are the citizens of the southernmost province of Sind. Much to the army's surprise they are fighting back. The West has been alerted, but we can't have too much of a fuss. Zia-ul-Haq is one of the favourite dictators of the Pentagon and the British Foreign Office. Nor is the affection one-sided. The dictator recently surprised a Western journalist by a long soliloquy on the virtues of Madam Thatcher. She was his favourite world leader. He wished he could emulate her more, etc. In private, the journalist discerned a puppy-love. If Zia was not so repressed he could have joined the world's most exclusive club of men who find the lady sexually attractive. To the list of Anthony Powell, Sir Isaiah Berlin and Christopher Hitchens, we could have added General Zia-ul-Haq. At the moment, however, his thoughts are more on clinging on to power rather than the British Prime Minister.

The mystique of fear through which he has ruled for six years is now at an end. When he goes, the people will dance on the streets. It will be another eighteen months at most.

In Zia's hell-state, Truth often overshadows Fiction. In *Shame*, Rushdie creates the figure of Maulana Dawood, a twisted and decrepit mullah who curses Omar Khayyam, the illegitimate anti-hero/bystander or whatever, thus: 'Oh God! O scourging Lord! Bring down upon this human abomination thy sizzling mountain of fire!' Dawood's appeal is to the Creator, not to direct action. Just as Rushdie had finished his novel, the following incident took place in the supposedly cosmopolitan city of Karachi. A newborn baby was discovered outside a mosque. The mullah was informed, inspected the infant, but ordered that it remain untouched. The same day he preached a sermon on the evils of sex, illegitimacy, adultery, and the rest. All the iniquities of women were denounced. Then he brought the congregation outside and led the stoning of the infant, which died, because it was socially undesirable. Hence extermination was the only solution. A salutary lesson in Islamic justice. My own theory is that the mullah was probably the father of the baby, which is probably why it was left there in the first place. Mullahs in Pakistan are notorious rapists, their victims often being young boys. Stories of mullah-inflicted sexual oppression abound in town and country. That Zia has appointed them as the guardians of a diseased morality is, in a horrible way, quite apt.

In *Shame*, Rushdie's avenging angel is a female half-wit determined to wipe out her various oppressors. I am convinced that many Pakistani men, politically sympathetic to Rushdie's book, will find it difficult to grapple with this carefully-laid symbolism. Male domination is so pronounced that any attempt by males to understand their role is constantly drowned in a sea of rituals, socialization, double standards, political norms and religion that all reinforce gender oppression. Only a few weeks ago in the township of Sahiwal a young couple were arrested and charged with adultery and having an illegitimate child. The woman was blind. She was sentenced to three years imprisonment, fined 1,000 rupees and awarded fifteen lashes. The flogging was to be in public so that her shame acted as a deterrent. And the man? He was acquitted. Of course. The child was unharmed. We must be thankful for small mercies in Zia's Pakistan.

As in the novel, real life sometimes offers a diversion. In a society where human beings (especially women) are treated like animals, the opposite can also sometimes happen. A few weeks ago in the town of Umarkot, Zia's vigilant cops noticed some stray donkeys. They were unaccompanied and carried no burden on their scrawny backs. The policemen got suspicious. They arrested the donkeys, took them to prison and charged them under the Vagrancy Act. The law refused to free an ass: no lawyer could be found to file an application for bail. It was when the donkeys began to bray, defecate and urinate simultaneously that an Umarkot magistrate ordered their immediate release. This uniquely effective display of collective action by the imprisoned quadrupeds has won the admiration of many an ordinary citizen. Flogging, you see, is for blind women and recalcitrant politicos. Stoning is for babies. In the face of this originality, Salman Rushdie faces stiff competition.

Time Out
September 1983

A Conversation with Salman Rushdie About *Shame*

Tariq Ali: My butcher said to me this morning, I read that thing you wrote somewhere about *Shame*, and I bought it, because I'd read *Midnight's Children*. Well, this took me aback a bit, because, given the elitist literary scene in Britain, one doesn't normally expect one's butcher to discuss the latest cult novel with one as one's buying meat – and certainly not on a Tuesday morning. But he did. And I said, Well, what did you think of *Midnight's Children*? And he said, It freaked me out. And I said, Oh, good. I then said, And so you've bought *Shame*? He said, I've just started reading it – I don't think its opening is as sensational and dramatic as *Midnight's Children*, but, he said, I've just started it, so I'll tell you what I think when I've finished it. Now, this is a very tiny episode, of course, and I would not like to generalize from it and say that every butcher in Britain is reading a book about the butcher of Pakistan. But I think what is beginning to happen in Britain is that people, and Salman Rushdie is one of them, are beginning to write novels which are slowly crossing the old literary divisions, if you like, and are making this literature accessible and available to a very, very large cross section of the public, and this is something which we can only be pleased about – that in the days of televisions and videos and privatization, there is a reading public which continues to grow. So, I don't think introductions are in order – you all know that Salman Rushdie is the author of *Midnight's Children*, which won a top literary prize; you all know that he's written *Shame*, which is now being short-listed for the same literary prize this year, and that this book is, of course, not just a novel: it's a very, very powerful, profound political novel which discusses a particular society where the novel is in great demand, and clandestine, samizdat copies are no doubt crossing the frontier from India at a very rapid rate. It's something which people in this country find very difficult to imagine, but I'd just like to say at the beginning, before turning to Salman, that the size of the literary public, or the reading public for English-language literature in India is much larger than it is in Britain. So the impact which these novels have – and other novels, but these in particular because they're about that part of the world – on India is something very profound. And *Midnight's Children* was seen instantly in India as a political book, as a political novel – as *Shame* is. I'm very pleased to see that *Shame* is now seen by the literati in this country as a novel which is not totally removed from politics, but is a powerful political novel. *Midnight's Children* tended to be treated rather as a literary feat – which of course it was, but it wasn't just that; whereas in India it was almost the opposite, the way in which it was received.

Salman, you have not really lived in Pakistan as such – your early life was in India. Your family then, as you've said in numerous interviews, betrayed you and crossed the confessional frontiers, and went and settled in Pakistan, and so your trips to Pakistan were essentially on holidays from here. Well, how do you think it is that you've captured this society so accurately without ever having lived there?

Salman Rushdie: Well, for a start, not all the visits were that short. I've been there for six months at a time, sometimes, so that's long enough. It's *quite* long enough, actually. But also, it's a simpler society than India, for instance, because it's not plural. The thing that's odd about India is it's a great mixture, whereas Pakistan, by contrast, is one thing. I don't know, I mean, how I've captured it – I rather thought I was making it up. [LAUGHTER] I discovered with *Midnight's Children* also that the most bizarre elaborations, the most extraordinary flights of fantasy that you have, which you don't think can conceivably be true, turn out to be true. For instance, I made up a sequence in *Midnight's Children* about how, when Salim, the child, is born, and he's just come home, his mother and his ayah get very worried that the baby doesn't blink, you know, and eventually they blink him manually until he gets the hang of it. Now, this whole sequence, which I thought was a kind of absolute, absurd invention, was written in order to enable me to write the line that the first lesson of his life was that nobody could face the world with his eyes open all the time, you see? And then later, when my son was born, this Filipino nurse in University College Hospital came up to me and said, You mustn't be worried that the baby doesn't blink. [LAUGHTER] And I fell off my chair, because

I'd made this up. But, apparently, the blinking reflex takes some time to get going, and first-time parents can get worried.

TA: This brings one to the whole intricate and fascinating relationship between fiction and history. I've been asked by lots of people: is *Shame* accurate? Or is it so grotesquely exaggerated that it's completely distorting history? And I've said that, in many ways, General Zia is a far more consistent producer of fiction than Salman Rushdie. One episode which astounds people, but is a fact, reported in the Pakistani press – a herd of donkeys, unaccompanied, was careering across the high street of a tiny place called Umarkot, and some vigilant policemen arrested them. They were taken into a prison, locked up, and then they tried to get lawyers to bail them out. The lawyers said, We're not coming to free any asses. And the magistrate then was summoned, late at night when the donkeys were braying, urinating and defecating simultaneously, and ordered their immediate release. Now, this story did the rounds in Pakistan, and the donkeys became – I can't say the toast of the country, because toasts aren't allowed – but they became greatly admired. Now, if you had put that episode in *Shame*, people would have said, this is just crazy stuff.

SR: Yes . . . *Shame* is very mild understatement, it seems to me. We could swap anecdotes all night, but I think that the story about the village, you know, which walked into the sea, is worth telling in this context.

TA: That was amazing, yes.

SR: Again, I couldn't write it down without you disbelieving me. A girl in this village began to have visions, and the villagers agreed that she was a visionary. And she said one day that she had seen in a vision that the whole village had to go on a pilgrimage to Karbala, which is in Iraq, and is a sacred place. And they pointed out, being reasonable people, that Karbala was a long way away, that they were villagers – how were they going to get there? And she said, Oh, the vision instructed all the villagers to go to the seaside, and the waters would then open, you see, and they would walk across the sea-bed to Karbala. So, off they went – the whole village packed up and walked several hundred miles to the sea, went to this rather fashionable beach called

Hawks Bay where they all walked into the sea, and with I think about six or seven exceptions, everybody in the village drowned, including the girl– fortunately, I think, for her. It's a comic thing, but it's also an extraordinary image about depth of faith, you know . . . It then acquired two more ramifications, one of which was comic and one of which was not. The comic one was that the Pakistan government seriously considered – this indicates to you what the Pakistan government is like – it seriously considered bringing an action against these people for attempted illegal migration. [LAUGHTER] Eventually this was dropped. But the other thing, which was very strange, was that the villagers who survived swore – independently, without conferring – that they had seen the waters parting, and they had seen the rest of the village going to Karbala, and they had in some way been unworthy, and so the seas had closed on them. And it was pointed out to them that there were all these corpses, and they said, You can show us anything you like: we saw what we saw. And that's an extraordinary kind of parable, it seems to me, about Pakistan, and you couldn't invent that. So, if *Shame* were naturalistic, you wouldn't believe it.

I think I should explain again the political point of view from which the book is written. I think there's a danger in this book, that people who know about Pakistan will read it too directly as an allegory of Pakistan. But you can't translate the events of the book directly into the events of Pakistani life, and you can't say that all the characters are versions of actual characters. Arjumand Harappa, for instance, is not Benazir Bhutto; it doesn't work like that. And Benazir has, as far as I know, never been known as the Virgin Ironpants . . . actually her nickname, Pinky, is given to a different character in the book, just to confuse the innocent. But what I thought about Zia and Bhutto is that apart from the oddity of Bhutto's yes-man becoming his hangman, which struck me as an interesting thing to explore from the points of view of both men – the odd thing about them is that they are not tragic figures; they are not Othellos or Hamlets; you know, they are not flawed great men – they are goons, comedians, gangsters, clowns, they are very kind of low-life people. It is perhaps symptomatic not only of Pakistan but of the world that, at the moment, we have comedians in charge. That dictated a special kind of approach in a book. What I had to try and do was to write what in fact is a tragedy – because the situation is, I think, a tragedy; but it had to be written like a comedy, because the protagonists of the tragedy didn't deserve tragedy. This is what made the book both difficult and interesting to write, because these are comic grotesques who occupy a kind of tragic position in history that makes them worth writing about.

Question from the floor: *Actually, I'm very disappointed to hear that you do not consider Arjumand Harappa to be Benazir Bhutto. I think one of the great attractions of the book remains the fact that the major characters are related to real characters in Pakistan.*

SR: I knew that Iskander Harappa was a kind of version of Bhutto, and that if he had a daughter, that people would make that assumption, but she isn't – I think she's actually much *more* interesting than Benazir Bhutto! I tell you what I did. It's almost a commonplace that what every writer would do when he invents a fictional character is to use pieces of people that he knows. You quite often use so-and-so's eyebrows, and so-and-so's bad temper, and so-and-so's accent – whatever it might be. That's part of how you construct a fictional character. But somehow, when you use pieces of people in public life, that process is more perplexing. The Zia and Bhutto figures – Raza Hyder and Iskander Harappa – have so many echoes of Zia and Bhutto that I'm not going to deny them.

TA: You can't.

SR: No. Well, I *can*, but it wouldn't work, you see. [LAUGHTER] But you can't translate the rest of the book simply into their families. There is no family relationship, as far as I know, between Zia and Bhutto, whereas in the book the family relationship is very important; the book is, in a way, about kinship.

Q: *The ignorance of the English about their history and their oppression of India and Pakistan is perhaps second only to their ignorance of what they do in Ireland. And surely, by reading this fantastical, often very humorous view of a society, does it worry you, the response that can be evoked amongst people in this country?*

SR: Perhaps fortunately, it's very difficult for writers to know exactly how readers will read – and quite often people read in more interesting ways than you write; it is possible for readers to add to a text as well as to subtract from it. As Tariq was saying to begin with, I think there is a tendency here, and in America also, to underplay the reality of these books. It seems to me that the fantasy in what I write is a relatively minor element; or at least, it exists only to enable me to say certain things which I think to be real. I always get depressed when people talk about fantasy as being a kind of escape from reality, because it seems to me *not* to be an escape – when you do it properly, it becomes a way of making one's experience of the real world more intense. I do think it will be harder for the readers of *Shame* to ignore its political content than in the case of *Midnight's Children*, simply because the political content is more central here, more openly discussed.

TA: And one reason for that is because you introduce this literary device, which I think is very powerful, of just talking straight to the reader, and recounting actual incidents, like your dinner with a senior official from the Foreign Office who defends Zia, or the incidents which happen in the East End – the ghosts of how Sufiya Zinobia was constructed, which I think is very powerful, and makes it therefore difficult to retreat totally from what the book is trying to say.

SR: Yes, well, that's what it was for, you know. I thought that it was important to discuss my relationship with the material, and also the sources of the material; because the material is fairly explosive – and not only that, the story of Zia and Bhutto has enormous emotional involvement for many people, and I thought it was fair to discuss that, and to say, this is my point of view on the material. I also knew that it was what – if people were to dislike the book – they would dislike it for, because it's something that you're not supposed to do as the writer, to interject and talk about yourself in the middle of telling a story. But if it were an oral story – I mean, if I were sitting here and you were sitting there, and I was telling you the story of this book, it would be completely unproblematic for me every so often to interject my comments on the behaviour of a character, or the meaning of an incident, or what I thought of such-and-such thing, because, you know, in the oral narrative the story-teller and the tale are always mixed up in that way. But it's relatively rarely done in writing. And those were some of the hardest bits of the book to write.

TA: The other thing which comes across very strongly, I think, is the women in it. At the very opening of the book you have these three women locked up in a house in Quetta, and the claustrophobia which they must feel just hits you, and then throughout the book there are references. For instance, you have the choicest Punjabi abuses, vulgar abuses, which I think, sociologically, is absolutely fascinating. And then ultimately the main character, Sufiya Zinobia, a woman, becomes the exterminating angel. You've talked at other times about the repressed sexuality, which is very close to violence a lot of the time, in countries like Pakistan and the whole Muslim world, something which was brought out also in *Yol*, Yilmaz Güney's film. Have you had any specific responses to that?

SR: Not really. In fact, somebody – from *Marxism Today* – was very worried about the women in the book, and said how unpleasant I'd been about them. And this was *very* disturbing to me, because I thought they were kind of the heart of the book, really.

TA: I think they are.

SR: They took it over – and they became more important, really, than the Zia–Bhutto story; or rather the Zia–Bhutto story only became interesting when it was seen through the eyes of this panoply or galaxy of women around them, mothers and daughters and lovers and so forth. The women are in many cases weak characters and all that, but I think that the men are much nastier. In societies like that, women are obliged to form their own networks of support, their own ways of expressing solidarity, and so forth – that's really where these three mothers came from. It was a way of saying that here are these three girls who, as you say, have been locked up in this house, and they've had to find a way of handling that; and what they've done is to become this kind of three-headed being, this trinity. And the odd thing is that for a long time I didn't know whose mothers they were. I just thought, here's this idea that I can't ditch, you know, because it's too enjoyable. And they wouldn't fit – I kept trying them out on people:

I thought for a while that they might be the dictator's mothers, Raza's mothers; and I tried to write a passage in which they were his mothers, but they didn't like him at all – they didn't want him. So I had to scrap all that, and wait for them to find their child, and eventually they did, and then I had to rewrite the book to let them have him. But I was very fond of them. Because unlike *Midnight's Children*, in which I was making the characters do things the way I wanted them to – in this one, the characters did quite frequently refuse me their privilege, you know, and they would simply instruct me what I had to do with them. The mothers are one instance, but there's also the fact that I originally didn't think that the book would end in Pakistan – I also didn't think that Raza would necessarily die. In fact, I thought he'd end up in London. And I thought that he'd escape, and end up in a kind of flat in South Kensington – you know, with all the curtains always shut and the central heating turned on, and no pictures on the walls, and some bad furniture. And I actually wrote this entire chapter about Raza in exile, in the Gloucester Road; and I thought it was quite good, really. And then when I tried to fit this into the book, two things became clear: one was that he was refusing to leave the country. The book deals very much with the idea of the frontier, the frontier beyond which there is nothingness; and, having set up that idea, the characters then obeyed it, they said, we can't cross this frontier, because beyond the frontier is the void, and they only existed inside this frontier – so he wasn't going to leave. The other was that having set up the idea of Sufiya Zinobia's becoming this kind of nemesis, you just had to allow her to do it, really, and you couldn't duck that issue. And so I found that the logic of the characters that had grown, just dictated the book.

TA: I think the British Foreign Office will be very upset if she does do it, because those who've read the book know that the dictator comes to a very nasty end in a dumb waiter, all these knives coming out and getting him.

SR: Yes – he gets cut to pieces, really. Well, I had to do something, and, not being able to stage a revolution, I just knifed him! And that incident you were mentioning about the diplomat was, I thought, very chilling, really, because here was a complete chance encounter with a

British diplomat who's a career South Asian figure, knew the countries very well, spoke the languages, and I'd rather liked him. And then he started making this speech about how it was quite right for the British and American governments to support General Zia, for the sake of the stability of the region. And this is one of those conversations that you want to walk away from – you know, you tell yourself, nothing will be achieved by having this fight: go home! But you find yourself having the fight. And so I accused him of the usual stuff, I said, this is hypocrisy; and he said no, it isn't. It went on like this for quite some time, and the thing that was interesting was the behaviour of his wife, who was a pro, because twenty years of being a Foreign Office wife teaches you something. Every time he spoke, whatever he was saying, she would look very suspicious, there would be sharp intakes of breath, and she'd shake her head – never say anything. And as we were leaving the dining room, this lady drew me aside, and she said to me, Tell me, Salman, why don't people in Pakistan deal with General Zia in, you know, the usual way? So I said to her, What, you mean assassination?, and she said, Yes. And I thought this was a bizarre remark. And I then thought it was rather sinister, because what this was saying was that the West, when it intrudes on a society or a government or a political situation like Pakistan, leaves the people no option except assassination. What she was saying to me was that all roads are closed except the one of violence, so do what you have to do, and then it'll be fine. And then, of course, what happens is a violent takeover; then everybody says, Look at that country, it's so violent – violent, barbaric, semi-civilized, hasn't emerged from the dark ages, needs our controlling hand; so they put another guy in control, and the only way you can get rid of him is by killing him too. And it's even suggested to you that you might do this by the wives of diplomats at dinner parties. So I put it in the book, and I took her advice in a way in the book.

TA: There was a fascinating interview with Enoch Powell four or five years ago in which he was being interviewed on a radio programme, and they asked him, Mr Powell, you seem to be a fairly isolated figure now, but let's say you had a choice of any job – what job would you most like to do? And the interviewer was obviously trying to draw Powell out on what he would do if he were prime minister, home secretary, or whatever. And Powell turned on him, quick as a flash, and said, Oh, I don't think I have that choice – he said regretfully – but if I did I would like to be viceroy of India. He came out and said it! So the link with India – especially of a particular layer of British society, lower-middle-class British society – and, of course, upper-middle-class and upper-class society – is very, very close, and it's fascinating to see this big drift now towards nostalgia. *The Far Pavilions* being filmed, Paul Scott being serialized for Granada Television, and all these things which may be good, or not so good. But the real problem which exists in this country is, how do you tackle racism? It's forgotten now, because they've cut down immigration, so that no blacks are allowed into this country; people therefore imagine – that is, those people isolated from this – that the problem's over: it isn't over.

SR: I think that's true.

TA: The other thing which comes across in the book extremely sharply is the relationship between shame itself and violence. That's what makes the book very universal, actually, and I think it's the point you are making. Because shame isn't explicitly or specifically something confined to South Asia, or to the East; I mean, both Simone de Beauvoir and Sartre have written about what shame does to people: it makes them violent. So what you're talking about, though it's set in the East, is just as applicable to many, many countries of the West.

SR: Well, I thought it might be, you know; and I think there's a danger when you're writing a book, and you think, I am saying something of universal application, that you try and write the book in such a way as to show this is a universal problem; and then, usually, you write rather a bad book. So I thought I would leave that out of my thinking, and simply discuss it in the world which I was writing about; and then, you know, if people who read it saw applications in their own lives, then that would be good. But what was interesting about the relationship between shame and violence was that it worked both ways: it was not just that humiliation engendered violence, which it does, but also that violence engendered shame. This is almost a commonplace about women who are raped, people who are assaulted in the street: they quite often react not with anger, not with a desire for vengeance, but with a sense of feeling ashamed. And that's a very odd reaction, you know, that *they* should feel ashamed: what have they done? But it seemed that this was a two-way street, that violence led to shame and shame led to violence, and there was a kind of axis there, I thought. The book was written partly to explore that.

Q: *There is, presumably, in the actual Pakistan a religious fanaticism which I didn't find in the book.*

SR: Oh, didn't you? In that case I obviously should have done it somewhat more extremely. I have a mad mullah in my book, who is the General's best friend; that was one way of hinting at it. I thought I did talk about Raza as being somebody who has a close relationship with God, doesn't he – God rubs people out for him.

Q: *Perhaps I wasn't convinced by the mad mullah.*

TA: But the mad mullah is a very, very real character, you know. There are lots of them, and the things they are doing these days – I mean, this instance of ordering a newborn baby, illegitimate baby, to be stoned to death . . .

SR: Which they did, yes.

TA: . . . which they did in Karachi, a fairly cosmopolitan town . . .

SR: I'm sorry you didn't like the mad mullah – I was very fond of the mad mullah. Mullah Dawood, he's called – he's a nice man. When he goes to Islamabad he thinks he's gone to Makadi.

TA: He's actually a rather moderate mullah, compared to what really exists.

SR: Yes, yes! I have to keep repeating that this book is an *extreme* understatement of reality. I mean, the reality is so horrendous that you can't write it.

TA: There have been no religious motives in this big revolt which has taken place in Sind. You know the ordinary slogan shouted on the streets when the masses come out, *Nara-i-takbir Allah hu akbar*, 'God is great'. For the first time in decades, the central slogan chanted by these demonstrators in Sind, far from being this, was a parody of it: they said *Nara-i-Sind*, the slogan of Sind, *Jeeay Sind*, 'Long Live Sind', precisely to parody the religious slogan – so a change is happening before our eyes.

SR: But I do think that whoever takes over, whatever leaders, secular leaders, are found in Pakistan after the army is kicked out will have a very short space of time to build a secular state – founded on secular institutions, let's say. And if that attempt fails, then I think Pakistan really is in deep trouble.

Q: *I wondered how you saw Pakistan as a viable state. Does Pakistan actually have a future? Does it have an identity that defines it as a nation with a permanent existence, or does that identity depend on the links that it can create and develop with India?*

SR: Well, since Tariq's just written a book called *Can Pakistan Survive?*, I think . . .

TA: Well, it's too detailed to go into. I agree with what Salman said in replying to the previous question: that, when this dictatorship falls, the civilian politicians who are waiting in the wings have, in my opinion, three to four years to get their act together – and that means reconstructing the state from top to bottom; that means very, very radical, massive land reforms to break the grip of the landlords and the army or ex-army generals, who constitute a sizeable section of the landed gentry in that country. So they have their task cut out for them. If they can't do it, and the army returns again and this cycle is repeated, I think you will get a process of Balkanization taking place. And it's very, very interesting that according to all the reports one is getting from Pakistan now, during the upsurge in Sind, one of the most popular foreign leaders in Sind in particular – in Baluchistan as well – is not Reagan or Margaret Thatcher, or various other leaders of Western democracies; nor, as in the past, is it Colonel Gaddafi or Ayatollah Khomeini or the king of Saudi Arabia: the most popular leader is Mrs Gandhi, which is a very, very interesting phenomenon, given that Pakistanis have been brought up to hate India. Why? Because she's the only leader who stood up and said, Stop the killings! You are killing people for doing this, that and the other, and this is intolerable. It was actually quite a moderate statement, but had enormous repercussions as people said, She is the only one who's spoken on our behalf. This sometimes can lead to a substitutionism – maybe she'll come in and do our work for us, which is a danger, because that would be very bad. But on the other hand, I think that the old cement with which they used to completely stifle any self-expression in Pakistan no longer works, it's broken down.

SR: It's breaking down. I think there are some negative reasons why Pakistan might survive. One is geopolitics. It is very valuable to the West to have a buffer state between Russia and India. Russia, China and India all have – well, thanks to Afghanistan – all have a frontier with Pakistan, and that's one reason why the West will, it seems to me, seek to maintain a state of some kind there, which is not weak, and which is not a part of India. Then I think there is the simple horror of the prospect of reunification. The physical process of reunification with India, which would be . . . I mean, it is just appalling to contemplate what would happen in the Punjab. So those two things would make people work very hard to preserve some kind of state there. Also, I do think that Pakistan is decreasingly like India, you know, and I think there would be a big cultural problem. The cultures have grown apart quite dramatically, since Independence. To put it crudely, even in my generation, most of us have many contacts across the frontier; it's decreasingly true that people have no knowledge across the frontier. When I was in India this year, it was amazing how little Indians knew about everyday life in Pakistan, what it was like – and they were very anxious to know, but they really knew very little, except awful, cartoon stereotypes of what it was like there; and in Pakistan the same was true the other way round, and it seems to me the countries are growing very, very far apart, and that would make unification difficult. And also, the Balkanization option is difficult, simply because of whether those states could survive independently. I suppose, the long-term prognosis might be that the North-West Frontier falls into Afghanistan, Baluchistan falls into Iran, Punjab falls back into India, and what happens to the Sind? But I think that for those negative reasons, there is a certain impetus to keep some kind of state there. But Tariq's right – there are three or four years when it can be made to work or not; and if not, you know, I wouldn't like to be there.

Q: *What do you say, Salman, to the possibility of foreign intervention?*

SR: I don't think, myself, that that's a serious option, yet. Do you?

TA: No, I don't. I don't think the Russians are interested at all – all the indications are that they are desperately trying to negotiate a settlement to get out of Afghanistan. I don't think the Iranians are in any position, militarily or economically, to try and take on another part of the world. The Indian regime, for its own reasons, does not want a Balkanization in Pakistan, because they are very frightened that once this model spreads, it could impart an instability into the Indian federation, which has been relatively stable so far, as third world countries go. So no foreign power actually wants the dismemberment of Pakistan; if it comes about, it will come about because explosions from below, within Pakistan, can no longer be contained by this state. In other words, they'll be pushed towards it, and then the Indians, or whoever, might be forced to act to prevent the thing from exploding completely. Maybe we could end on a slightly upbeat note, and discuss bestiality, which also figures in this book. Again, it's not a particularly Eastern phenomenon, as that excellent film, *Padre Padrone*, made very clear – the film by the Taviani brothers. Yet, bestiality is in *Shame*, Salman, and there's no running away from it . . . the Baluchi guerrillas are made into lovers of sheep, and so on. Why did you put that in? Did you have any evidence?

SR: Yes, my sources amongst the Baluchi guerrillas indicate [LAUGHTER] that sex is a problem. I also make them into angels, it has to be said. I mean, the fact that they fornicate with sheep does not diminish them, to my mind. No, I was just writing about, you know, men alone, and what they might do. And I do think it is a problem, that people live up there for years and years and years, and it was just a way of dramatizing . . . I think it probably *is* also true, actually. It has to be – it's one of those things which, if you used your imagination about what it would be like to be on that mountain for those many years, the time would come when the sheep would seem attractive.

Q: *Tariq briefly mentioned the reviews in India being rather more polemical than the reviews here. Could you tell us a little bit more about the differences?*

SR: Well, with *Midnight's Children*, I think it was most extreme. In England, and to an extent in America, there was a kind of unwillingness to engage with the political part of the book. In India, it was the other way round – and still, in India, people don't treat it as a fantasy novel, they treat it as a historical novel.

Q: *And do you think the unwillingness here is to do with our unwillingness to have any politics within literature, or is it something which has to do with India and Pakistan?*

SR: No, I think it's to do with ignorance, for a start. I don't think that people know a lot about the politics that the book discusses, and so it's easier to ignore it and just read the book as a story. I don't want to make a big thing about this, because I quite enjoy the fact that the book is different things here and there, so that people who read it without knowledge of India see certain things in it, and people who read it with knowledge of India see slightly other things in it. But I remember, when Tariq's review of *Midnight's Children* appeared in *New Left Review*, I'd never met him at that time. And it was a political review. It wasn't entirely a favourable review – I remember being criticized for excluding Urdu poetry, for instance, from the book. [LAUGHTER] It's not often you have the chance to do this – to seize this opportunity! But, anyway, it was so satisfying to see that somebody had written politically about the book in England, that I was moved to write to him, and the rest is history. With this new book, as I say, because the politics is much more explicit, even the English reviewers have been obliged to recognize its existence. Although I've still heard people reviewing it say, Of course, you know, on its surface it *appears* to be a political novel, but *actually* one can ignore that, because that's not very important, and the important things are aesthetic, and here they are. So I think, you know, one can't prevent the English from being themselves.

1983

Postscript: The Fatwa and After

It was a strange coincidence in the middle of that summer. The day – 17 August 1988 – that a proof copy of *The Satanic Verses* landed on my desk, General Zia-ul-Haq's plane exploded in Pakistan killing him, a few fellow generals and the US Ambassador to Pakistan. He was a much-hated dictator inside a country that has had more than its fair share of them. I was at the time producing *The Bandung File*, a current affairs series for Channel 4. The commissioning editor, Farrukh Dhondy, was on the phone insisting we produce a special programme on the death of the dictator. The entire Bandung team was on the phone to Pakistan. I managed to get hold of Benazir Bhutto who told me she was having difficulties in restraining her followers from celebrating in public. Her own voice was trembling with nervous excitement. 'Insist on immediate general elections', was my advice at the time.

As if the death of one of the characters in *Shame* and a conversation with another wasn't enough for one day, there came a call from its author.

'What do you think?'

'It's amazing news,' I said. 'God knows who organized this one.'

There was a pause.

'I was actually asking what you thought of my book.'

I informed him that it had just arrived, that I had not even looked at it and we were immersed in producing a special programme. Then we briefly discussed Pakistan.

Events moved swiftly that year. I did not read the book till much later, on a flight to Pakistan soon after Benazir Bhutto was elected prime minister for the first time. I didn't think it was as good or as compact as *Shame*. Nor was it as skilfully edited as *Midnight's Children*. The naughty bits did not offend me. Reading the book was like entering a large, rambling mansion. Some of the rooms were well appointed, others a total mess. I had made notes on the plane for a friendly, if critical review, but was pre-empted by events.

When I arrived in Pakistan, local Islamists belonging to the Jamaat-i-Islami – upset at the death of the General whose patronage had seen them implanted on campuses, in the media and in the Army – had begun a campaign to destabilize the secular Ms Bhutto's government. This included burning copies of Rushdie's novel and attempts to storm the British Embassy. The police fired tear gas shells. Islamabad was tense. When I met Benazir we discussed the novel. 'Tell him to be careful,' she said. 'They're serious.' On a previous occasion she had asked me to explain why Rushdie had mocked her as the Virgin Ironpants in *Shame*. I suggested a letter to the *Times Literary Supplement* explaining why the characterization was unwarranted.

The first country to ban the book was India, where the Congress government did not wish to offend an important vote-bank. How times have changed. When I returned to Britain, local supporters of the Jamaat-i-Islami had been working overtime. They were busy burning the book in Bradford. One of the Jamaat's UK leaders, Iqbal Sacranie, mildly agitated, flushed but rapturous, defended the book-burning to the media in the name of the religious pain that had been caused, along with truth and virtue. His opponents described what had happened as false and evil. 'Hullabaloo over the *Satanic Verses*' was the title we gave the *Bandung File* response that was aired on Channel 4 in the weeks that followed.

It might have remained a local affair had not the late Ayatollah Khomeini decided to make it international. It was reported that the spiritual leader and inspirer of the Iranian Revolution was watching television when he saw scenes of the book being burnt. Since the book-burners were all bearded, the Ayatollah was curious as to what had made these Believers so angry. Till then Rushdie's novels, including *The Satanic Verses*, had been favourably reviewed or mentioned in the *Tehran Times*. An internal factional dispute among the clerics was brewing at the time, related to a fierce external rivalry with Saudi Arabia that had led to verbal and physical clashes between Shi'a pilgrims and Wahhabi police in Mecca. Riyadh and Tehran were spending a great deal of money in funding mosques in Europe. To reassert his leadership Khomeini decided to throw the novel into the mixture, without adequately studying the terrain he was now entering. It was the will of this individual that exacerbated the crisis. He would outflank the pro-Saudi Jamaat-i-Islami.

On 14 February 1989, he issued a fatwa sentencing Rushdie to death for apostasy, and calling on any 'good Muslim' to carry out the sentence. And this despite the fact that the Shi'a tradition itself has not been kind to the reputation of at least one of the wives of the Prophet. The decision was political, not religious. When we spoke on the phone that day Rushdie was stunned but buoyant: 'It's not every day that one makes history.' This was certainly true.

V. S. Naipaul mischievously referred to the fatwa as 'an extreme form of literary criticism' and I never did write my review. The novel had been wrenched out of literary space. It was a declaration of war. The writer had to be defended at all costs.[2] Rushdie went into hiding. He survived, becoming a global celebrity, something he relished with a childlike delight. How would all this affect his restless imagination? What would he write? How could he write in an environment resembling death row? Pre-fatwa,

---

2   Howard Brenton and I wrote a play dramatizing the crisis – *Iranian Nights* – in ten days. It was staged at the Royal Court Theatre, then under the charge of Max Stafford-Clark who was much more supportive than the boys running the National Theatre, even though he vetoed my original title: *A Mullah's Night Out*. Later I debated the mullahs at a special event organized by the Traverse Theatre in Edinburgh. The theatre was divided in two. On one side sat the busloads of supporters brought by the mullahs, on the other the defenders of Rushdie. When I asked if any of them had read the book not a single hand went up. It was a one-sided affair, alas, and my principal opponent did not help his cause by threatening to cut my tongue out after I had recited a few lines from the sceptic Muslim poet, the blind al-Ma'arri who lived in a village near Aleppo in 1087: *The inhabitants of the earth are of two sorts / Those with brains but no religion / And those with religion but no brains.*

a number of leftist critics had seriously questioned his credentials and subjected *Shame* to a merciless critique.[3] I did not agree with much of this, and in fact what was criticized as Rushdie's bleak and pessimistic view of Pakistan has unfortunately been vindicated by history. Nor did I regard that novel as misogynistic. The women were strong. Their oppression was highlighted.

Over the last two decades, however, and it is sad to write this, there has been a marked decline of imagination and the quality of writing. Even Salman Rushdie must realize that *The Ground Beneath Her Feet* is an excremental work. An aberration? He certainly did not write anything quite like that ever again. But something had changed. His new environment had begun to determine his consciousness. He enjoyed being surrounded by sycophants. His politics, too, underwent a big shift. In his prime he would have thought hard before covering his nakedness with the Stars and Stripes and posing for the cover of a French magazine, as he did after 9/11. Or accepting an invitation to the Bush White House, as he did after the Iraq war that had cost that country a million dead and five million displaced citizens. Overcoming a serious wobble, Rushdie had decided not to support this particular war, probably due to the influence of New York liberals who were much tougher than their British counterparts. The last two novels were effusively praised by his friends, but they read more like a sad attempt to mimic his earlier successes. This was difficult to achieve, since he was no longer the same person.

As for accepting a knighthood from Blair, the less said the better. New Labour's 'multiculturalism' was finely balanced. Iqbal Sacranie was also knighted. The book-burner and the author whose book was burnt, both honoured by the same corrupt and despicable regime. But there are reasons to be cheerful. Midnight's grandchildren in Pakistan have picked up the

---

3 *In Theory* by Aijaz Ahmed, London and New York: Verso, 1992, contained a stinging essay: 'Salman Rushdie's Shame'.

baton. Mohammed Hanif's *A Case of Exploding Mangoes* carries on from where *Shame* left off, and does so in a style and form peculiar to this author.

Daniyal Mueenuddin's stunning short stories evoke a country and a people usually missing in non-fictional descriptions of the country. Mohsin Hamid's *The Reluctant Fundamentalist* raises awkward questions and is infinitely superior to John Updike's novel on a similar theme. Younger US novelists have yet to tackle the terror inspired by their country. Nadeem Aslam's *The Wasted Vigil* is set in Afghanistan where the continuous occupation of the country – first by the Soviet Union, now by the United States and NATO – has helped to produce a malignant social order. The grandchildren are outdoing the grandfather. That is how it should be. For fiction, like history, reaches its peak when it can unravel the complexities of human life.

2009

6

THE ARGUMENTATIVE INDIAN:
A DISAGREEMENT WITH AMARTYA SEN

The sage of Bengal has pronounced. Pluralism, we are informed, has an ancient pedigree in Indian history. It is embedded in the oldest known texts of Hinduism and, like a river, has flowed through Indian history (including the Mughal period, when the country was under Muslim rule) till the arrival of the British in the eighteenth century. It is this cultural heritage, ignored and misinterpreted by colonialists and religious fanatics alike, that shapes Indian culture and goes a long way toward explaining the attachment of all social classes to modern democracy. The argumentative tradition 'has helped to make heterodoxy the natural state of affairs in India', exerting a profound influence on the country's politics and democracy, and conditioning the 'emergence of its secular priorities'. This view informs most of the thought-provoking essays in Amartya Sen's new book, a set of reflections on India written in a very different register from his other books on moral philosophy and poverty. It is designed not so much for the academy but as a public intervention in the country of his birth, to which he remains firmly attached despite the Nobel Prize and his latest posting at Harvard as a Boston Brahman.

Although the essays in *The Argumentative Indian*[1] were composed at different times, they have been successfully welded into a single volume.

1 Amartya Sen, *The Argumentative Indian: Writings on Indian History, Culture and Identity*, London: Allen Lane, 2005.

106

There is much to agree with here. Sen's lofty worldview remains staunchly secular and rationalist, as befits a scholar whose intellectual formation took place in Nehru's India, a historical time zone under constant attack today from Hindu nationalists on the one side and some of the more fashionable Indian luminaries of the US branch of the subaltern school of historians on the other. Unlike fellow Nobel laureate V. S. Naipaul, Sen does not see the entry of Islam into India as a dagger thrust in the heart of Indian civilization. On the contrary, he argues that the effect of Mughal rule was beneficial. This was undoubtedly the case on the dietary front: the historian Irfan Habib has shown how the average Indian peasant ate better and more often in this period than under the British.

Given the title of Sen's book, it would be churlish to prove him wrong by simply nodding in approval, as is so often the case in our wonderful sub-continent. What follows, then, from this argumentative Pakistani is the expression of a few doubts concerning his central thesis and the odd complaint with regard to some omissions.

Can the lineages of modern Indian democracy be traced back to the holy texts, as Sen suggests? And does the affection of ordinary citizens for democracy have any material (as opposed to mystical) links to the arguments once heard by Buddha or King Ashoka (273–32 BCE), let alone the Mughal emperor Akbar (1556–1605)?

It's true that disputes abound in the ancient Sanskrit epics. Their multiple tales are, as Sen puts it, 'engagingly full of dialogues, dilemmas and alternative perspectives', such as that of Javali, the notorious sceptic of the *Ramayana*, who explains in detail how 'the injunctions about the worship of gods, sacrifice, gifts and penance have been laid down in the *sastras* (scriptures) by clever people, just to rule over [other] people.' In codifying the rules for debate in the Buddhist councils, Ashoka demanded mutual respect among the various sects. While the Inquisition was sowing terror in Europe, Akbar, himself a Muslim, ruled that 'anyone is to be allowed to go over to a religion that pleases him'. The interreligious debates he organized in Agra included Hindus, Muslims, Christians, Parsees, Jains, Jews and the atheists of the Carvaka school, who argued that Brahmans had established ceremonies for the dead 'only as a means of livelihood' for themselves. Even the Vedic Song of Creation on the origins of the universe ends in radical doubt: 'Who really knows? Whence this creation has arisen – perhaps it formed itself, or perhaps it did not – the one who looks down on it, in the highest heaven, only he knows – or perhaps he does not know.'

Yet the scepticism voiced by some rulers and reflected in the ancient texts was usually, if not always, confined to the priestly elites. The model for the debates between scholars from different religions and sects that were organized by Akbar's court was little different from similar discussions a few centuries earlier in the camp of the Mongol leader, Genghis Khan (1162–1227). With this exception: Mongol soldiers were permitted to both listen and participate in the arguments. The Mughal courts in India were sealed off from public view: the courtiers listened and, no doubt, nodded when the emperor smiled appreciatively as a point was scored, but they did not speak. Only the emperor and a few of his close advisers posed questions. The tyranny of the few over the many – exercised through a ritual combination of coercion and religion – was never seriously challenged in India until the advent of capitalist colonization. Nobody spoke for the subalterns.

Unlike in ancient Greece, there were no city-based institutions where important issues could be debated, and the over-glorified village *panchayats*, or councils, were the domain of the privileged where the poor could only appear as supplicants. Ancient India produced an ugly caste system that led to early divisions and splits, but neither Brahmanism proper nor its wilder offshoots – Buddhism and Jainism – came even close to producing a political philosophy that could lay the basis for a popular or semi-popular assembly like those in ancient Greece, whose formal decrees always began with the invocation: 'The *demos* has decided.' The assemblies in Athens were barred to slaves, but they did include peasant proprietors and even some peasants who worked for others. Hence the debates between rich and poor; hence the fear of the multitude evinced by the wealthy; hence Solon's New Deal-ish boast: 'I stood covering both [rich and poor] with a strong shield, permitting neither to triumph unjustly over the other.' But even these traditions, while never forgotten, disappeared completely. The idea of democracy re-emerged in the debates that followed the English Revolution and found institutional form only after the American and French Revolutions.

Ancient India produced great poets, philosophers and playwrights, along with art forms, gods and goddesses to match anything on offer in Athens, but it did not give birth to an Aristotle. And nothing remotely resembling the Assembly in Athens or the Senate in Rome arose on the sub-continent. Surely this must reflect some deficiency. Despite arguments within the elite and some wonderful expressions of scepticism cited by Sen, the *demos* was kept under strict control throughout Indian history. Uprisings threatening the status quo were brutally crushed by Hindu and Muslim rulers alike. Superstition and irrationality were institutionalized via a network of priestly domination.

The resilience of Brahman traditions lay not in encouraging debate, but in the power of the iniquitous caste system that survives to this day and pervades the spirit of Indian democracy. One wishes that Sen, a long-standing critic of economic inequality, had given us his views on whether globalization was going to weaken or strengthen caste chauvinism in India. When in the third decade of the past century, the 'untouchable' leader Dr Ambedkar insisted that his caste not be considered Hindu so that they, like the Muslims, could demand separate electorates from the British rulers, he was sweetly rebuffed by Mahatma Gandhi, no doubt for the noblest of reasons. Hard-core confessional elements in the leadership of the ruling Congress Party were only too aware that without the 'low castes' being counted as Hindus, their overall weight in the population would be drastically reduced.

What of India's Muslims? The Mughal conquest of India created a strong centralized state, but there was not the embryo of a democratic consciousness, even in its most primitive, patrician form. The emperor was supreme. His subjects could plead for justice in his presence once a week, and if they were lucky they could be rewarded with a few coins and kind words. Interestingly enough, while all the existing texts of classical Greece and Rome were translated into Arabic during the eighth and ninth centuries, and while Islamic schools of philosophy, mathematics, astronomy and medicine flourished in Córdoba, Palermo and Baghdad, the one genuine innovation of the Greeks – the idea of democracy – did not travel. The caliph was both the spiritual and the temporal ruler, and any notion of an assembly of equals would have been seen as a godless challenge to Allah's vice-regent. The Mughal order in India was based on an alliance of the wealthy and the creation of a strong central bureaucracy, with rights over large tracts of land.

Sen is correct to stress the tolerance of the Mughals, particularly Akbar, toward the non-Muslim majority. The reasons for this policy, however, were not simply altruistic. The Muslim conquerors, like the British after them, knew that stable rule was dependent on securing the consent of crucial layers of the indigenous elites. This they did successfully, and even the last of the great Mughal emperors, the devout and narrow-minded Aurangzeb, presided over an imperial army led by an equal mix of Hindu and Muslim generals. When the British East India Company's army secured Bengal as a bridgehead in 1757 and made Calcutta the first capital of British India, it did so with a very small number of British officers, European weaponry and local recruits on a monthly wage. Like its Mughal predecessor, the Company was desperate for allies and often bought them in the marketplace. The Bengali Renaissance that produced the Nobel Prize-winning writer and poet Rabindranath Tagore, the film-maker Satyajit Ray, the Sens and numerous others was the result of a unique synthesis between local tradition and imperial modernity, based on a capitalist economy. Without capitalism there was no Indian modernity. Democracy in British India (as in Britain itself) came a century and a half later as a result of pressure from below on the part of a growing middle-class intelligentsia in Calcutta. 'What Bengal thinks today,' declared the reformer Ram Mohun Roy, 'India thinks tomorrow.'

That is why imperial ideologues, as well as colonial apologists like Rudyard Kipling, came to despise Bengal. The Bengalis, in their estimation, were effete intellectuals ill-equipped to fight, unlike the 'martial races' of the Punjab and North-West Frontier. Kipling's fiction is filled with crude stereotypes of the dark-skinned Bengali *babu* (clerk) as contrasted with the noble and fair-skinned Pathan, or the Rajput warrior. Better they were kept illiterate lest they become over-confident like the Bengalis.

Even supposing there was a strong 'argumentative' tradition in India 3,000 years ago, was this the frail aqueduct through which the democratic stream finally moved? Such is the argument of Sen and (in a more fashionable formulation) of postcolonial scholars who scornfully dismiss the suggestion that the British presence had anything to do with the spread of democratic ideas and the rise of Indian democracy. This is, in my view, a form of mysticism. We may not like it, but there is no denying the impact of 150 years of British rule in India, which brought capitalism to the country and overwhelmingly determined the nature and character of Indian institutions.

Sen accepts uncritically the historian Partha Chatterjee's argument that, in Chatterjee's words, the emergence of nationalism has created

its own domain of sovereignty within colonial society well before its battle with the imperial power. It does this by dividing the world of social institutions and practices into two domains – the material and the spiritual. The material is the domain of the 'outside', of the economy . . . of science and technology . . . where the West has proved its superiority . . . The spiritual, on the other hand, is an 'inner' domain bearing the 'essential' marks of cultural identity. The greater one's success in imitating Western skills in the material domain . . . the greater the need to preserve the distinctiveness of one's spiritual culture.

Here one discerns a retreat from the secular definition of nationhood espoused by Nehru and a slide into the murky domain of Hindu nationalism, albeit in an ultra-civilized fashion. In rejecting the heritage of Nehruvian socialism for its statism and affiliation with the urban middle class, 'left-wing' postcolonial historians like Chatterjee have eerily converged in their arguments with right-wing Hindu politicians, who insist that the content of Indian nationalism has always been spiritual, that is, religious, thus excluding India's large Muslim minority from the national community. (When the nationalist or Hindutva brigade in the United States mounted a disgraceful campaign, two years ago, against the Library of Congress decision to award a research fellowship to Romila Thapar, one of the most distinguished secular historians of ancient India, a majority of Indian historians on American campuses remained silent.) What is 'one's spiritual culture' and 'cultural identity' if not religion, even if lightly disguised as the Cow Protection League or the National Fund to Rebuild Mosques? Was it possible for nationalism to go in a more cosmopolitan than spiritual direction?

This raises the Gandhi question. Was it necessary for the Mahatma to use spiritual (Hindu) imagery and language to arouse the majority of the countryside from their torpor? Nehru and Tagore did not think so and argued heatedly with the old fox, but on this Gandhi would not budge. It was they who gave up, Tagore in despair and Nehru in the half-hope that the damage was reparable. But it wasn't, and it led ultimately to the fatal breach with secular Muslims, including Mohammad Ali Jinnah, the founder of Pakistan. That there were other straws in the nationalist breeze was revealed time and time again in the wave of strikes that paralyzed the country in late 1945 and then again in 1946, when Muslim, Hindu and Sikh naval ratings united against the British and seized the ships, raising the banner of revolution. This was the most significant mutiny in the history of the British Empire. On the advice of Jinnah and Gandhi, the sailors surrendered 'to India not the British'.

The attachment to the 'distinctiveness of one's spiritual culture' undoubtedly helped provoke the bloody partition of the sub-continent, but the institutions that provided the spinal cord of the new states owed little to spiritual traditions. They were British creations, and Parliament was not the only one. It certainly helped to unite India, but in neighbouring Pakistan it is the Army and, to a lesser extent, the Civil Service, both creations of the Raj, that have ruled the country. What happened to the 'argumentative' tradition here? Taxila, north of Islamabad, was, after all, the site of one of the world's first large (Buddhist) universities, centuries before the Christian Era. It is not that most Pakistanis did or do not like democracy. A new imperial power decreed that the Army was the most reliable guarantor of stability and order in the new country. Here Washington has been consistent. Only this year Condoleezza Rice, on a visit to Islamabad, praised General Musharraf and his regime – apparently secular and autocratic – as the model for the Muslim world. (Including Iraq?)

In India democracy has become embedded as the only acceptable form of rule, largely because of geography. If Pakistan split into two after an eleven-year military dictatorship from 1958 to 1969, what would an attempt to impose a military regime in India have done to that country? Created a three-way split? Or more fragments still? The regional elites realized that this would be an economic disaster, and the unity of India under a democratic umbrella became the common sense of the country. It is this combined with mass hostility to autocracy that explains the longevity of the democratic system, but one should not underestimate the power of turbo-propelled capitalism to weaken democracy in India just as it is doing in its heartlands. Indians may want democracy, but it is hardly a prerequisite for a dynamic capitalism. Europe demonstrated this during the first 300 years of capitalism; China does so today.

The essay on the giant of Bengali letters, Tagore (1861–1941), who died six years before India and his beloved Bengal were partitioned, is studded with gems. Sen knows Tagore's work well and his grandfather, a distinguished historian of Hinduism, worked with the great poet in Santiniketan – a progressive educational academy which provided the inspiration for Dartington Hall in England. Tagore's standing in the West has been subject to many fluctuations. His mystic-spiritual side appealed to many Westerners, including Ludwig Wittgenstein, but as Sen explains, this was only one side of the man. In Bengal and India he was the voice of reason, a cosmopolitan who encouraged the self-emancipation of the people and asked them to free themselves from both the Brahman and the British, to break the chains of caste and poverty. The dangers he saw for India were structural, not spiritual. As he wrote in 1939: 'It does not need a defeatist to feel deeply anxious about the future of millions who, with all their innate culture and their peaceful traditions, are being simultaneously subjected to hunger, disease, exploitations foreign and indigenous, and the seething discontents of communalism.'

Sen's reflections on Tagore, however, would have benefited from comparison with another great Indian poet: Muhammad Iqbal (1877–1938), who wrote in Urdu and Persian. Iqbal, too, was given to mysticism, but of the Sufi variety. Younger than Tagore, he was greatly influenced by Hegel and the German philosophical tradition and was a favourite of both Nehru and Jinnah. He, too, died before Partition. Tragically, he was immediately mummified by the new state of Pakistan, his message so distorted that he is seen by many in that country as a revivalist, which is far from the truth. Like Tagore, he loathed priest and mullah alike and celebrated reason and knowledge, as in this verse dividing God from Man:

> You created Night, I the Lamp
> You the earth, I the bowls
> You created wilderness, mountains and ravines
> I the flower beds, gardens and groves
> I make mirrors from stone
> I find antidotes in poison.

Both Tagore and Iqbal would have been dismayed at the direction taken by the modern leaders of the old sub-continent. Like Sen, both would have been alarmed by the nuclear turn and missiles with confessional names targeted by each side against the other. Even those who disagree with Sen or see him as a tame and toothless Bengal tiger will be compelled to engage with his arguments. That alone is sufficient reason to welcome the publication of this book.

2005

7

TWO CONVERSATIONS:
MARIO VARGAS LLOSA AND JUAN GOYTISOLO

Mario Vargas Llosa and *The Real Life of Alejandro Mayta*

Jason Wilson (chair): *The novel we're going to talk about concerns a minor Trotskyite revolutionary in Peru, who tries to start a revolution in the sierra and fails. Through a series of interviews and brilliantly crafted flashbacks, we as a reader get an image of the type of complexity that anybody has to face up to if they want to try to understand what has happened in recent history, and especially in Peru. However, it's also a novel about writing a novel. This means that it's both a compelling read, and a novel that raises many provocative issues: from the nature of political activity in South America to what one can say about recent history, to the writing of the novel itself, and, most interestingly, to a strange reversal that Mario has attempted here, and that deals with an age-old opposition between fiction and truth. In a sense, this novel continues a tradition that Mario has made his own in Latin American literature. I feel it's a combination of very carefully documented realism, and realistic effects – notably Mario's use of dialogue and the spoken voice – while at the same time, the fictions are not straight, realist novels, and the manipulation, at a technical level, of the reader creates another type of novel which, almost always successfully, traps the reader in the fiction. A fiction that proposes itself as a type of imaginative truth.*

Tariq Ali: I must say, when I was sent this novel, I was prepared, because of what one had heard about it – both on the gossip networks and how it had been greeted by the Left in Latin America – I was

116

prepared to hate it, I must confess that. So I started reading with a very prejudiced eye. And I was therefore surprised, in several ways. Firstly I found large parts of the novel very evocative of what life can be like, has been like, and will be like in small political groups of the Left, whether in Latin America or in parts of Europe, or even in parts of Asia. It makes me doubt the statement in the book which Mario makes, which is that all fiction is lies – well, on one level it's a cliché, of course, and yet all fiction is not lies. I think some of that life of a small left-wing group has been covered perfectly accurately. Some of the conversations had been recaptured very well, and I hope he'll tell us how he did that, because you can't just get that out of reading back-copies of small left-wing newspapers; you have to know some of the people who were involved. I must be honest, I didn't like it as much as his other novels, I don't think this is as good a book as *Aunt Julia and the Scriptwriter*, which is one of the great classic novels of this century. Partially, for me, the problem lies on the level of structure. There are three levels, or three structures in the novel. First, there's the overall futuristic situation, the external situation, which is a Peru torn by civil war – but it's not just a civil war; the civil war is a reflection of a more global conflict. You have the American marines backing the local oligarchy, and you have a Cuban–Bolivian expeditionary force backing the guerrillas, and this is set somewhere in the 1990s. Then you have the second level, which is the narrator as oral historian, going and recovering the history, the life of one guy. And in the last part the real Alejandro Mayta emerges, totally different from what people have said about him, or how he has been evoked – which on a literary level is very interesting, but I personally did not find it totally convincing. Now, I thought that the futuristic structure, to be perfectly frank, was unnecessary, because the situation in Peru itself today is pretty horrific without bringing in the expeditionary force of the Cubans and the Bolivians on one side and the Marines on the other. The implication is that you need foreign interference for these things to happen, whereas, this very year, communal graves have been uncovered . . . The thing which struck me the most, actually, is that the narrator, throughout the novel, is passive. He doesn't engage in big polemics himself, on one side or the other; when you come to the end of it the passivity is almost explained by the narrator actually becoming very cynical. I think essentially, on the basis of what the narrator himself is saying and on how it ends, it's a deeply cynical book, which poses other problems. And the last point, of course, is that it raises questions about Trotskyism, which are of interest.

The one thing I missed, actually, knowing the movement well from the inside, is that life in Trotskyist groups invariably consisted of discussing, not so much politics in your own country, but world politics. And *that* feel, you don't get. There are times when you feel that these Trotskyists are not in a garage somewhere in the middle of Lima, they might as well be on the moon, in the sense of what they're discussing. The device which is used, the external conflict, I think conceals a desire to discuss contemporary politics in Peru, because those are absolutely riveting now, and I think that would have been far more powerful. The one real figure mentioned by Mario in the book is the veteran guerrilla leader, still active politically, Hugo Blanco – someone I happen to know very well, who's very young, like Alejandro Mayta. So my overall judgement is that it is a very, very powerfully written novel, and very enjoyable; but the overall tone of it I found extremely cynical, compared to his own previous writing.

Mario Vargas Llosa: Well, I have used, of course, as raw material for Mayta, my own experiences at the university, when I was a militant for a year in a very small party which had replaced the Communist Party of Peru after the great repression in 1952. And in '53 and '54, I was in a very, very small organization – just a group. And I have had always the memories of this extraordinary, intense activity, which was at the same time quite useless, because we were totally isolated, just a group of students; we hadn't any kind of contact with the masses, with the workers. The discussions, the political discussions in the book, I suppose are written with the memory of the kind of discussions that we had in these small cells in which we were organized. But most important for me when I was writing this book was what the Trotskyists represented for us at that time. At that time, from a Stalinist perspective, the *great* enemy, the black beast, you know, was – even before American imperialism, before the Nazis and the fascists – were the Trotskyists! And if we were very few in Peru, the Trotskyists were practically nothing – they were three or four, you know – and they were the great enemy: we were absolutely convinced that they were with the police, that they were foreign agents, and we tried to divine what they were doing, to detect their conspiracies . . . And all this in a regime that was a military dictatorship. And what we did was something in many cases very idealistic – very courageous also – and at the same time totally useless, because we were lost in an abstract world of ideological schemes practically without roots in the real society, in the real reality that we were living under. I suppose I have used a lot of these personal experiences in writing the book.

On the other hand, my first idea of the novel was totally different from what it is now. My first idea was to try to reconstruct in a fiction something that had happened in Peru – not in '58, as in the book, but in '62: a revolutionary attempt by a very small group of people, just a few adults and I think ten or twelve schoolboys, in a small city in the central Andes. I was in Paris when this happened, and I remember my amazement, that this had actually taken place in Peru. At that time, everybody was talking about revolution – particularly the Latin Americans in Paris were dreaming about new Cubas in Latin America; but when this actually happened in Peru I was very surprised, and also very moved, you know. It was an absolute revolutionary attempt, because it lasted just a few hours. And I was very excited by the idea of trying to write a fiction recreating what has happened there – how it was possible for a handful of people in such conditions to rebel in this way, to think that it was possible to make a revolution in this way. Well, that was my first idea of the novel. And I suppose it would have been a kind of realistic novel of political adventure, or something similar. That was in '62. Since then, many things happened in my country; many things happened to myself politically; many of my political ideas changed a lot; my own relationship with my own country went through a lot of different stages. And when I started writing the novel, what was happening in Peru changed my idea for the novel. I think it was in 1981. I started first interviewing people who participated in that revolutionary attempt, or witnesses of the event, and I discovered immediately the contradictions, the extraordinarily different versions. In some cases these distortions were obviously deliberate – people had changed the past in order to justify the present, or to justify their own roles in the event. But in other cases it was quite obvious that they didn't know that they were changing the past, that they were really introducing fiction into history, because their memories had been changing, transforming reality more or less as a novelist does; and I was very intrigued with this process of transformation of history in order to justify the present – you know, how the present can transform, deform the past.

And at the same time, when I started to write the novel, I became very worried about the political events in Peru. We had re-established democracy and civilian government: the militaries were out after twelve years of dictatorship. And the elections had been very popular – I think the *immense* majority of Peruvians were in favour of the democratic regime. And at that precise moment, terrorism started in Peru – a new political group, the Shining Path, it started practically the first day of the new regime, with terrorist actions, and they hung dogs from lamp-posts in Lima – that was the beginning . . . And immediately, of course, this started a process of political violence – police first, and then army repression – and the atmosphere of the country, little by little, started to deteriorate, and violence, little by little, increased, took a kind of hold on the city. And it was obvious that this violence would grow and grow, and would start to destroy and corrupt the democratic institutions that we'd been so happy to . . . well, I was very worried and anxious with this. I think the idea of an apocalyptic parable – can I say that? – an apocalyptic parable, which is what I've tried to do with this book, came from this psychological state of mind. It's difficult to try to explain exactly, but I think that what I wanted to do was, first, to tell in a fiction how fiction can be not only a literary process in which you fabricate using raw materials taken from history, from living experience – a myth, a legend, something that is different from the real experience; but also, how fiction infects other fields of experience; how fiction, for instance, is deeply rooted in political activity; how fiction can be the main stimulus for political action, and particularly in radical groups, groups which are convinced that reality can be totally transformed. What is the relationship between fiction and ideology, for instance? Ideology is, or can be, a branch, a manifestation, of this appetite or necessity of fiction that seems so deeply rooted in human life – particularly in countries with utopian traditions as strong as those we have in Latin America. And on the other hand, in this apocalyptic parable, what I wanted to describe – not as an intellectual discourse, but as fiction, in a story – is the mischievous way in which violence takes a society in its fist. What Mayta and his comrades do in the book is something very heroic; no doubt about it, Mayta is a very generous man, his idea of society is a very idealistic one: he is against injustice, he has rebelled against society because of the terrible inequalities – social, economic, cultural; so he's a very positive, driven man. And he accepts, at a given moment, that the only possible way to change this, is by violence. Well, if you look at Peru over the last thirty years, what you see is how these heroic, idealistic and generous values, little by little, once it gets started and becomes established as the rules of the political game in a society, things start to deteriorate systematically. This violence gradually becomes ever less heroic and less idealistic, and more and more blind, turning into something genuinely uncontrollable – ideologically and morally. And that is why I present this kind of apocalyptic vision of a country destroyed by foreign interventions – I wanted to follow the process down to its final consequences. Emphasizing the fiction that is behind it all. It is true that the narrator is rather passive – he's totally passive; he's trying to write a fiction: he's trying to emphasize that to dream, to invent, to write fiction, has a place, even in a society whose essential social problems are so visible. Because in countries like Peru, countries like ours in Latin America, to write fictions, or to write poetry, or to paint a painting, is something that has a meaning, it's something that is morally and historically justified; it's not something useless or ridiculous. Well, I am sure it is not, because I am doing it, you know, although the anguish is still there, and out of this I have also introduced these kinds of anecdotes about the narrator in the novel. So, as you can see, many different kinds of projects and goals were mixed and changing when I was writing the book. What is the final outcome? I think a reader and a critic can probably perceive it better than myself.

TA: From what Mario has said, the book and the violence in the book, and his attitude to that, has been very largely shaped by the clashes between Sendero Luminoso and the state; and that's perfectly understandable. But even within the history of Latin American radicalism, this is rather a strange organization – it still calls itself, I think, a Maoist organization, at a time when Maoism as a political current is virtually dead, both elsewhere in Latin America and certainly in most of Asia, where it was once very powerful. Its politics are, on the face of it, totally crazy, because it does crazy things, I can see that. But from there to draw the conclusion that you do . . .

MVL: But what is my conclusion? I am not sure about my conclusion . . .

TA: What you said is, there's a spiralling violence; but the whole history of Latin America is a history of violence, long before this piddling little group came into existence – the whole history for the last 300 years. Indeed, reading about this Cuban–Bolivian expeditionary force against the Americans, I found myself wondering whether it wasn't a sort of modern equivalent of what has happened in Peru's *own* past, of the conflict between Bolívar and San Martín on the one hand, and between their forces and the Spaniards on the other. So violence is not new; one can't just treat it as something separate, and say, there is violence, and here we are. Because, if you live in Latin America and many other parts of the world, it's not enough to say that the radical groups develop a fiction: they do, some of them do, I grant you that. But, you know, the most fictional character, in some senses, who constructs lie after lie after lie in the Americas today lives in the White House. He is a *real* character, but the way in which he constructs what he regards as his political approach is based on far more fictions, and notions of rewriting history – it's all done fairly systematically; and this power actually rules large parts of Latin America today. Pinochet, unfortunately, is not a fictional character. Somoza was not a fictional character in Nicaragua, where the FSLN had to organize to overthrow him. How else do you overthrow a military dictator, in a country, say, like Nicaragua, which was backed by the United States with money and arms for decades – decades of torture, repression, daily violence. So that's a very real problem. Peru, in that sense, is somewhat exceptional at the present moment; but even in Peru today, the state has utilized the existence of this group to carry out *unbelievable* repression even by Peruvian standards, if you look back at the last thirty or forty years. And it's not just the army. It's also the political party of the centre or the right – APRA, whose gangs go into villages and kill people: communal graves are discovered. So it is horrible – we can't just wash our hands of the thing.

JW: Let's deal a bit with something that Tariq brought up earlier about cynicism – the ending.

MVL: On cynicism, yes, I think the narrator is a bit cynical with his reader at the end, when he reveals that he has been lying – that he has been describing attitudes of Mayta which were totally invented by himself. He is cynical because he exposes his narrative tricks, narrative devices. But I don't think he's cynical in his vision of Mayta, of the society and the problem that he tries to describe – no, he's more paralyzed, don't you think? He's paralyzed by what he sees, what he discovers; and he recognizes that his fiction is a very distorted vision of the historical material that he uses. But that's what a novel *is* – that's the kind of vision that a novel can provide about any kind of historical reality. Is that cynical? I don't know. Perhaps out of this lie, this distortion that the novel, or literature in general, provides of our reality, a fruit comes – a very difficult kind of fruit, you know, because it's a fruit that is not historical, not sociological, certainly not ideological; but it's a fruit in the sense that it expresses a very living experience. Yes, and this, I agree . . .

JW: And in that sense, you are also justifying the role of the novelist? Because Mayta himself couldn't remember really what had happened. So that what really happened is the novel itself; so you've turned it upside-down in that sense?

123

MVL: Well, I think a novel is a very useful complement to history, because not even the most strict and rigorous history can render the total experience. There is something that is lacking in a historical approach, no? And I think this march that history cannot embrace probably comes more easily to fiction.

Question from the floor: *My question is addressed to Tariq Ali. One of your main criticisms in the review of the book was the fact of his cynicism and his lack of interest in a political conscience for Peru. I know Latin American politics are very interesting, but why is it that with the exception of people like Borges, Latin American writers are expected to write with a political conscience? Why can't they just write fiction or whatever takes their interest? It's like he's sort of betraying his country's politics.*

TA: No, that's not my criticism. I mean, I am a great believer in the theory that there are lots of very right-wing people who write very brilliant novels and very brilliant poems, which goes without saying, and that doesn't bother me. But I'm not sure about the view that great literature transcends *all* politics – that's arguable; maybe it does, maybe it doesn't; some certainly does. But the two aren't as totally unrelated as people sometimes think. But *this* novel *is* about politics. Which is why I found it very riveting, you know – much more so than many other novels one reads, because it's about a very interesting part of recent political life and activity. And I constantly felt that I wanted the narrator to engage much more with some of the things he was describing – not from the left, necessarily, but from *some* position, and this he carefully avoided doing, for reasons which he's explained. That's the only point I was making. It isn't a political demand, it's a literary demand.

Q: *It feels a bit like the argument that someone like Sartre, who is the other person I could think of who devoted a series of novels, to, among other things, political activity; the arguments he was having with the Left, with the Communist Party in particular, who wanted a more engaged hero; and when I hear you talk like that, I have those echoes. What I wanted to ask Mario was whether when you hear what Tariq says – which is pretty strong stuff, basically – do you find that that is an example of the morality of the Left? Or do you just say, well, fiction works one way and politics another . . . Is that a political discourse he's making to you, or a literary discourse?*

MVL: Well, I think he has made a combination of both; and it seemed a very civilized political discourse to me. [LAUGHTER] This, unfortunately, is not the political discourse that the extreme Left used to have in Latin America; and when I have to discuss with radicals from Latin America, the level on which the discussion is placed is very different, no? We are very passionate people, as you know, very romantic people, and so we are easily intolerant towards any kind of criticism or opposition, and this has been our great, great problem, for many centuries. But I think your question was very interesting. I don't think a writer has the obligation to commit himself to write about politics; but in Latin America, I would say that a writer has a *moral* obligation to do it. I don't think in England, or in France, or in Italy, it's the same. But in countries like Peru, or Chile, or Colombia, if you are a writer, you are a privileged person – you are a *very* privileged person, in that you know how to write, you know how to read, in countries where many people don't. On the other hand, as a writer, you have a kind of audience; you are respected, even by your enemies, and the reason why the dictatorships are so brutal with writers is because they are afraid of writers – maybe naively, they think that writers have power – that what they do, what they say, what they write is dangerous, because it can change things; and that's why they put them in prison, or send them to asylums. And I think this is true, because in Latin America, as in Europe during the romantic era, the writer is considered a person that has answers not only for literary problems, but for the problems that people have. And that is the reason why a writer is continually asked to make statements about politics, about ethics, even about very trivial things, because a writer is regarded as much more than just an entertainer. So if this power has been given – maybe for the wrong reasons, maybe out of a very naive idea of what a writer is – in Latin America, he has the moral obligation to try to use this power to change things, to improve things. And of course when he is secluded with his own demons, you know, he is free – he can do what he wants, and I think he must serve his demons. But at the same time I think he must try to use his imagination, his knowledge, his facility with words, to try to improve things – to use this power also in a social, civic way. In this sense, I am not against the people who think that a writer in Latin America should commit himself in one way or another.

1986

A Conversation with Juan Goytisolo

Tariq Ali: There's a great deal of talk at the moment, especially in the German press and German literary magazines, bemoaning the fact that currently we seem to see a decline of writers as critics, writers as intellectuals, writers who intervene in a world outside their own novels; the end of the whole French tradition of intervention as typified by Sartre and Simone de Beauvoir. And one reason adduced for this – I don't accept this view, by the way, I'm just telling you what is very common at the moment in discussions – one reason given for this is that culture has been so trivialized over the last three decades that, basically, serious writers and serious writing has no place in the culture. There is a strong element of truth in that, if you look and see how, for example, fiction and theatre are essentially seen more and more now as commodities; they have been for some time, but this is a trend which became very pronounced in recent years, and the art of criticism also seems to have become either part of the hype, or a settling of old scores – by and large; there are of course honourable exceptions. But in the literary pages, it's either friends doing each other a favour or someone with an axe to grind about a particular writer. Serious novels, serious fiction, is either not reviewed or given a tiny mention. Now, Juan Goytisolo, as far as I'm concerned, whose work I started reading many years ago, is one of those writers who is what the German critics are bemoaning they've lost – in fact, they shouldn't bemoan it, because in their own country they've got Günter Grass, who is never shy of intervening in big issues. And Juan, for me and for many other people – not so much in England, but in Spain, in Latin America, and in the Arab world – is one such writer whose fiction is very exciting because both its content and its form are very, very innovative, and I think Juan will accept that there are long passages in his works, sometimes in his fictional works, which, even if you're totally immersed in them, you can only understand by reading aloud, because the rhythm of the language and the structure of the thought is such that you can only totally grasp its meaning by reading it out aloud as poetry. In addition to the novels, which are published by Serpent's Tail – again, a very innovative new publishing house which brings out fiction that other houses tend to be frightened of – apart from his novels, Juan has also written autobiography, and critical essays. But what has just come out is the *Saracen Chronicles*, a selection – not a collection, a tiny selection of Juan's non-fiction output, where he writes about the past and about the present, and the links between the two, which are always there, even if people prefer not to see them. There's some fantastic material in this book, which I found very, very stimulating. It may surprise those who think that Spanish literature since 1492, or the early fourteenth century, has been very traditional, very conservative. This was not the case, of course, and Juan's book highlights some traditional writers very well known to a literary world, but never properly understood. So, Juan, I'd like to start off by asking you a sort of personal-political question, which is this: What were your feelings as you saw the massive celebrations of 1492 taking place this year on virtually a global level across the Atlantic?

Juan Goytisolo: I wrote in the Spanish press, and I delivered a lecture about this matter, and I established a comparison with another commemoration. Three years ago we had the commemoration of the bicentenary of the French Revolution, and now comes the commemoration of the quincentenary of the discovery of America. And I said that the first one, in spite of the fact that after 1789 there was the Terror and the guillotine and Napoleon and the Napoleonic Wars, and the great calamities brought by these wars, there remains something to be celebrated that is at the same time ecumenical and actual – for instance, the Declaration of the Rights of Man and the Citizen. In the case of the conquest, the discovery and conquest of America, the matter is more complicated, because you cannot talk about the ecumenical value of the conquest – at least, the Indians would refute this kind of argument immediately, because they were the victims of this encounter of two worlds, with the destruction of their world by the new world imposed by the colonizer. It was the same thing after, with the English colonization of India, Australia, New Zealand, the French colonization of Africa, and so on. There are two interpretations to valorize the Spanish conquest of America:

one, the Spaniards were looking for gold, and they exploited the cheap labour, first of Indians, and then of blacks, and they introduced the slave trade. But the Spanish historians, they said that was not the reason – the principal reason was the evangelization, bringing the gospel to the people who lived in darkness. But I ask, is there any actual value to imposing one's own culture, language, religion on others, by force? Obviously not. More intelligent historians said we should try to separate the discovery from the conquest, and it's not a celebration of the conquest, but only the discovery. But I ask also, is it possible to isolate one kind of progress, or very important feat, from the context that produced it? For instance, to celebrate now Gagarin, the first man to go into space, without taking into account the price paid – moral, socially, economically – by the Russian people? There are many examples like this. And if we put the discovery of America in the proper context, we shall look at what was happening in Spain at that moment. For instance, the three caravels instead of beginning the journey of discovery from Cádiz, that was the most important harbour in Spain in this period, sailed from Huelva. Why? Because thousands and thousands of Jews, at this very moment, were being expelled from Cádiz harbour to outside Spain. So it's the year of the expulsion of the Jews, the year of the conquest of Granada but with the promise to respect the freedoms, the cultural freedoms and religious freedoms, of the Moors. And we know very well that this promise was immediately cancelled, and they were obliged to become Christians by force. And it was the creation of the Holy Brotherhood that was the first police organization of the modern state. They condemned the homosexual to be burned; they forbade the importation of books printed outside the country; they expelled also the gypsies, warning if they tried to come back to Spain they would have both ears cut off – things like this. All these things are very similar to the much more contemporary regimes that we know very well in this century. And I ask, what are we commemorating? I don't know. If there was a reflection about that, it would be interesting. Or a commemoration of Las Casas – Las Casas was a bishop, a Catholic bishop, who wrote against the exploitation of Indians. Well, that would be a very good idea. Or even to talk of Blanco White, who at the moment of the independence of the former colonies, was the only Spanish intellectual who stood up for the independence, and even now the establishment considers him a traitor, in spite of the fact that they are always talking about the motherland Spain, and the Latin American countries as her children.

TA: Following on from that, there is another aspect which is ignored, both in Spain itself, but also by people outside Spain, who know very little about it: that the Spanish conquistadors who went and conquered what we now know as Latin America, in many cases were the same people who had participated in bloody battles against the Moors in Spain itself; in other words, the logic of what they did in the cleaning up, the ethnic cleansing in Spain – the kicking out of the Jews, the destruction of the Moors, the monolithic state imposed in Spain by the Catholic church – was a preamble to doing that. And we've seen fascist states in the twentieth century, and Stalinist states, which have operated in the same way. But there are more analogies with our century as well, are there not, Juan: for instance, writers who were forced in the sixteenth century to convert, to become what was known as New Christians, then had to write in a particular way, so that, on the one level, the censor and the church wouldn't be worried, but at the same time, in their writing, there was a subversive message; and the work which you write about at great length, and with some amazing information, was the work of Fernando de Rojas, *The Celestina* – I was wondering whether you'd like to talk about that. When you first read it, what was your impression? How many readings . . . ?

JG: Yes, I was very impressed the first time I read *La Celestina*. *La Celestina* is, after the *Quixote*, for me, the most important literary text, and the most audacious, and the only kind of tragicomedy who could compare without any complex of inferiority with the best Shakespeare – it's unique in Spanish literature. Because afterwards there are Calderón's *autos sacramentales*, or the comedy of Lope de Vega – for me not really very interesting, in spite [of] Calderón's theatrical imagination. But the only literary masterpiece was written by a young man, about twenty-two, twenty-three years old, and it's the most pessimistic, the most terrible vision you could imagine. And I ask myself how it's possible that such a young man, at the very moment when Spain was conquering the whole world, could draw a picture so caustic, so . . . critical – and I should say, for me, it's the first text I know in all Western literature where, plainly, God doesn't exist, in spite of the fact that in the introduction, Rojas talks about the passion of Christ, and the bad Jews, and all kinds of things, to hide his hand. But inside *La Celestina* there is only . . . it's the first document with no principle of God, and when you discover the circumstances of Fernando de Rojas's life, you can understand that. He was Jewish; he lost the fight of his ancestors, but obviously didn't accept the new fight, in spite of being obliged to show externally that he was a Catholic. I establish a comparison with Rimbaud. Rimbaud after he arrived at a point, after it was impossible for him to go ahead. And I think, after *La Celestina*, it was impossible for many reasons – personal and political, or religious ones – for Rojas to write another book. He spent his life in Spain, completely retired, and he only . . . for many reasons, for instance, Stephen Gilman, in his book, *The Spain of Fernando de Rojas*, discovered that his father was burned by the Inquisition. One person of his family, a woman, when she was alone at home, said something like, 'In this world there is no justice, no truth, no God'; and after she heard herself, was terrified at the idea that her neighbour heard her, and might go to the Inquisition to denounce her, and herself went to the Inquisition and accused herself – she said, 'it was only a moment of distraction that made me say that', and the Holy Tribunals obliged her to say some prayers, but she saved her life. But we get an idea of the feelings of those who were terrorized – the converts, the New Christians in this period, and the rejection of the old values so manifest and so violent in *La Celestina*.

TA: And following on from that, of course, is Cervantes – you know, the classic of world literature. You were saying earlier that if Cervantes had been alive, he would never have won the Cervantes Prize. [LAUGHTER] Would you like to elaborate on that?

JG: Because Cervantes was . . . we are now almost 99 per cent certain that Cervantes was a New Christian.

TA: Of Jewish origin?

JG: Certainly – Jewish origin, might be his great-grandfather. Fernando de Rojas, manifestly, was not at all Christian; but Cervantes, he was a very sincere Christian, but he, all his life, had the problem of his origins. For instance, when he was fighting against the Turks in Lepanto, and he was injured and lost his left arm, and spent some years in captivity in Algiers – very interesting years, because they put him in touch with Islamic culture; very important in the book. When he was liberated, he asked to go to America, to make his life in America; but New Christians were not permitted to go to America, and his petition was rejected. And the only post he could get was as tax collector – *recaudador de alcabalas*; and it was a post only for traditional Jews, and later, New Christians; an Old Christian would prefer to starve than be considered Jewish because he was a tax collector, and Cervantes was a tax collector. His wife, Catalina Salazar, belonged to the family of Fernando de Rojas – at this moment no Old Christians married with the New ones. For two centuries, there was a distinction. The problem of purity of blood made a distinction between, if you can understand my anachronism, the seropositive and the seronegative; and obviously the descendants of Jews, of Moriscos, they were seropositive. And this was the real situation of this community. But I always say that people, writers, who are not in the midst of the society but on the margin, they are able to judge the society better than those who are in the midst. And I always think that minorities, they have an acute view, an acute perspective on the society that the others are not able to have. That is the reason that most important writers from the end of the fifteenth century to the beginning of the seventeenth century were of this origin, New Christian. It was the case of Teresa of Avila, Góngora, almost Francisco Delicado – almost . . . Francisco Delicado, he stayed Jewish. . . he escaped from Spain, he went to Italy; but the others . . . Arias Montano, the humanist, Fray Luis de León, Mateo Alemán, and so on.

TA: But, Juan, why is it – I'm genuinely very puzzled – I can understand why it was in the Franco period, but why is it that in the post-Franco period in Spain, the literary–political establishment is still so nervous of admitting most of these things, so they are all very much hidden from history in Spain, including the 700 years of Islamic rule?

JG: The reason is not a political problem, it's a much more profound. For two centuries, the problem of Spain was the relationship with Europe. When Spanish culture was completely destroyed by the national Catholicism at the end of the seventeenth century, and Spain began what I call her 'holidays from history' – *vacaciones históricas* – and, little by little, some Spanish writers discovered that Spain was completely separate from the rest of Europe, and it was the moment when the French said, 'L'Afrique commence aux Pyrénées' – Africa begins at the Pyrenees – and the Spanish took that as an insult. And liberals in the nineteenth century were always obsessed with catching up with Europe, to fill this gap between Spain and Europe, and they tried to refuse all the elements in Spanish history that didn't correspond to the European image. For instance, in this century, historians like Menéndez Pidal or Ortega y Gasset – mythical historians, because there is no scientific basis at all for their lucubrations about Spanish history – they insisted always on the Roman and Visigothic heritage of Spain, at the expense of the Semitic branch; they never spoke about Jews or Muslims; Ortega said the Arabs were not an important ingredient of Spanish culture, but he wrote, for instance, that the blood of people in northern Spain was based on the blood of people in southern Spain – these kinds of things. And this complex persists until now; but now Spaniards feel – I wrote about that – not only newly rich and newly free, but also newly European; they must try to be more European than the Europeans. And it's the country of Europe: if there was a referendum on Maastricht, 90 per cent of the people would vote 'yes'. And I made fun of that, I said, if there was a referendum to change the geographical location of Spain, to put Spain in the place of the Netherlands or Denmark, the majority of people would say yes. And that means that the Spaniards always look to Paris or London, and they took the quickest way to Europe, and they Americanized as the best way for them to become European. Even now, to find out about our past disturbs people who pretend to be Europeans, without understanding that this differential sign is the best contribution of Spain to Western culture, because there's no equivalent in Europe to Ruiz's *Libro de buen amor*, or to *La Celestina*, or to Delicado's *La lozana andaluza*, or to Mudéjar art. It's a fantastic hybrid mix of Arabic elements and Christian ones. And that is the real originality of Spanish culture, as Gaudí, our best architect, discovered very well when he wrote that originality means going to the origins, and he was so influenced by Mudéjar art, and so interested by the Arab Muslim mosques that inspired his magnificent creation. That is the reason. There are some people who are trying to uncover that. The first was the great historian Américo Castro, the first to insist that Spain was born at the time when there were three religions and three cultures, and that this trace is permanent in Spanish history. And many disciples, many historians follow this path. But we are completely in opposition with the establishment.

There is another very important element in the creation of the works I am talking about, in *Saracen Chronicles*. Blanco White was the first to discover that the medieval texts in Spain were much more interesting than the books written after the Renaissance, despite the fact that there are many writers – I think of them as the exceptions of genius – such as St John of the Cross, Cervantes, Góngora and Quevedo. But if you compare a medieval text with one that was written after the arrival of Italian models from the Renaissance and the neoclassical world, there is no possible comparison – the medieval ones are much more modern. And we talked about that the other day – I said that literature has the reasons that chronology ignores. And we can now feel the modernity of texts written six centuries ago, and consider as contemporary almost the whole production of Spanish literature now. And I feel, really, a contemporary of Arcipreste de Hita, or Delicado, or St John of the Cross, who influenced me, but not at all of the establishment, of the writers who for me belong, with very rare exceptions, to another century – and I don't know which one, but not my century; that is my perception. And that is very important. And the reason for this is that in the Middle Ages there were no models – no academy, no pressure to give the literary creation a predetermined shape. Many of the methods I develop in my novels were directly inspired by Delicado, or by Rojas, or by Arcipreste de Hita. In Delicado it's very interesting that the characters of the book know that the writer is writing about them; and I discuss, for instance, *La lozana* – she's a Spanish whore who works in Rome in a Jewish brothel during the Borgia period, and at one moment of the novel she says, Oh, here's this man who is always writing about me – what are you looking for now? And she even pays a compliment to the author – she says, You have beautiful eyes, you author. [LAUGHTER] It's fantastic! On every page you discover something completely modern; all the time you have the impression that there's a movie camera, because you can follow in their conversation the movement of the characters, without description – only the attention to this . . . I don't know . . . gaze? And you pass from the general view to the medium shot to the close-up. It's fascinating. And, really, I find no equivalents except in the case of Cervantes, Góngora, Quevedo, or St John of the Cross in the *soi-disant* golden century.

1992

8

A Note on Kipling . . . and Sartre

The White Man's Kipling

Kipling was, without question, the most gifted writer produced by the Raj. The fact that for a very long time he was the only one does not in any way detract from his stature. His work is very well known in the English-speaking world and continues to excite controversy and dissension amongst critics. The current wave of Kipling mania is simply a product of the expiry of all copyright on his work. Hence the rush to produce rival anthologies and introductions.

If the need is for a dose of preciously written literary appreciation, Craig Raine is on offer from Faber. For a more mundane and totally predictable Rajorama there is, as always, the prolific Mr Charles Allen. Add to this a reprint of Carrington's somewhat uncritical, but worthy biography, an elegant memoir from the slightly repressed pen of the Great Man himself and all that we appear to be lacking is good old English literary criticism.

No reason, however, to despair. Eight new Penguin Classics have just come on to the market, introduced by P. N. Furbank, Daniel Karlin, Sandra Kemp, Hermione Lee, Peter Levi, David Trotter, Paul Driver and Sarah Wintle. One begins to yearn for Kipling as seen by Steve Bell. What distinguished Kipling from those who were to follow him was his intimate knowledge of the country. He was greatly affected by his earliest memories, which were of India and not Britain. His father Lockwood was an extremely intelligent and cultured man, with a passion for the cultural and architectural riches of the sub-continent.

Kipling senior was instrumental in establishing one of the finest museums in the country, on the Mall in Lahore, not far from the Zamzamaor, 'Kim's Gun', as it came to be known. It was this world which attracted Rudyard Kipling from the very beginning. The torment of his early years in England with foster-parents and at public school clearly enforced this feeling.

He found an antidote to the claustrophobia of late Victorian England in the open spaces of India. As he grew older, however, he was to discover the restrictions imposed on White India by the strict political and racial rules enforced by the colonial order.

Kipling's pro-imperialist attitudes were never hidden from view. He was a great admirer of Cecil Rhodes and the civilizing mission of Western imperialism. *The White Man's Burden* was not written to mark some upheaval in India, but to celebrate the American occupation of Cuba and the Philippines. To this Craig Raine adds Kipling's anti-Semitism and anti-Irish prejudices.

In spite of all this Kipling was far too perceptive an observer to ignore the seamier sides of his countrymen in India, and he satirizes them mercilessly in *Plain Tales*. Kipling's now forgotten literary predecessors proved to be total failures because of their instrumentalist approach: an imperial-realism which saw its main task as explaining the merits of Company colonialism to the folks at home. Kipling broke decisively from this tradition. Every instinct in him rebelled against that type of servility. His talents were far too real.

Nonetheless he could never totally breach the boundary walls erected by White India. This was a political rather than an aesthetic choice, but it affected his work. That is why I disagree with Raine's comparison with Chekhov or those made by others with Balzac and Mark Twain. The quality of Kipling's literary output was far too uneven for that, even though there were clear Balzacian strains in some of his work.

As far as White or half-White India was concerned, Kipling crossed the class divide with ease. *Plain Tales* contains a number of stories whose heroes are private soldiers, Mulvaney, Learoyd and Ortheris. Kipling chronicles their daily life, habits and language and does so without any regard for the sensitivities of his fellow-members of the local Club, who lived in blissful ignorance of the conditions in which the lower classes of White India lived out their lives or periods of service. In his capacity to recreate their hopes and fears in their own language, Kipling had no rivals in British India, before or after his recognition as a writer.

But this quality alone was not sufficient to transcend his weaknesses, which were the result of a self-limited ordnance on his own part. This can be seen very clearly in *Kim*, his most evocative novel. Here, we have everything. There is local colour, amazing descriptions of Lahore and bazaar life, an uncanny ability to detect nuances in several Indian dialects and convey these to the English reader, the submerged streams of gossip and intrigue and the delightful relationship of Kim and the Lama.

Yet the real hero of the book is the master-spirit – the white blood in the veins of the half-caste Kim. Add to this the totally uncritical defence of the Empire (amongst the weakest passages of the book, and quite unnecessary) and you have a novel which is flawed.

In a number of short stories Kipling reflects the fantasized fears and repressed desires of many of his fellow Englishmen, mainly products of public schools, when he savagely though ineffectively denounces the intellectual pretensions of the Bengali middle classes – they are, you see, getting too uppity – and counterposes to them the rustic Punjabi farmer whose 'strongly marked features glowed with russet bronze' or whose 'beard and moustache, streaked with gray, swept from bold cliffs of brow and cheek in the large sweeps one sees drawn by Michelangelo . . .' This is combined with an idealization of the 'manly virtues' of the Pathan tribesman, whose strong physique and cult of violence was greatly admired by Kipling and Anglo-Indian civil servants.

These mythologies, it is worth saying, were accepted by the heirs of the British and helped to create an atmosphere which led to the break-up of Pakistan in 1971: a final parting of the ways of Punjabis and Bengalis, beautifully described in Rushdie's *Midnight's Children*.

It is odd that no publisher has so far produced a new edition of Kipling's verse. Some of this was of a very high quality and, often, extremely funny. It found admirers everywhere. One of them, Bertolt Brecht, recycled some of Kipling's poems for his own purposes. But as this extract from 'Caledonian Market' reveals, Brecht remained very critical of the Englishman's overall stance:

'Oh, East is East and West is West!'
Their hireling minstrel cried.
But I observed with interest
Bridges across the great divide
And huge guns trundling East I've seen
And cheerful troops keeping them clean.
Meanwhile, from East to West, back rolled
Tea soaked in blood, war wounded, gold.

And the Widow at Windsor, all dressed in black
Grins, takes the money, stuffs it in her pocket
And gives the wounded a pat on the back
And sends them down to the Caledonian Market.
Their walk may have lost its spring, but they try
To hobble around the stalls and buy
A second-hand wooden leg instead
To match their equally wooden head.

Guardian
January 1987

A Note on Sartre

Jean-Paul Sartre dominated the intellectual life of France for almost five decades. From the late 1930s till his death in 1980 he wrote almost continuously. Philosophy, literary criticism, novels, plays, experimental autobiography, political polemics and countless personal letters to lovers, friends, political leaders. He bitterly opposed France's war against Algeria and Vietnam. Together with Bertrand Russell he sponsored a War Crime Tribunal to charge the United States with war crimes against Vietnam and he remained politically alert almost till the end. When I was temporarily placed under country-arrest by the Pakistani Government in 1976 (not allowed to leave the country and forcibly taken off three planes), the telegram of protest that moved me the most (and annoyed the regime) was one from Sartre and De Beauvoir.

I write all this because a stunning new book is about to appear. Sartre's diaries were written when he was conscripted and called up to serve in Alsace during the Phoney War of 1939–40. They covered nine months and constituted a total of seventeen notebooks. Of these twelve have been 'lost', or so we are told by his literary executors. The remaining five give us an idea of the loss that has been suffered. Sartre's *War Diaries* are staggering even to a long-time fan such as myself. They are funny, accessible, experimental, descriptive and, I feel, will be ranked among his most memorable works.

He wrote them when he was thirty-four and they prefigure virtually *all* his later work. His reflections on Koestler, Gide and Malraux are an amazing exercise in self-illumination. His description of how he read Flaubert's *Sentimental Education* while he was manning the telephone switchboard of his military unit is entertaining in itself, but his uninhibited assault on the book is hilarious.

There are five different varieties of writing in these notebooks: self-portraits, philosophical essays, vivid and funny accounts of military experiences, literary reflections and memorable descriptive prose encompassing, with lyrical sharpness, roads, skies, billets, café menus in the region of Alsace where he was stationed during this period. The net result is a dazzlingly literary performance: a synthesis of his diverse talents.

The following notebook entry gives a flavour of the wide range of this volume. Sartre disputes with Freud the contention that a child regards all holes as a symbolic anus. For him it is 'an object of lust because it is a hole'. He then explains: 'And certainly the arsehole is the most alive of holes, a lyrical hole, which puckers like a brow, which tightens in the way a wounded beast contracts, which finally gapes – conquered and ready to yield up its secrets . . . I have nothing against the Freudians composing hymns to the anus but it remains the case that the cult of the hole is anterior to that of the anus, and that it is applied to a large number of objects . . . I think that the pleasure a child takes in giving enemas (numerous are those who play at doctor to have this pleasure: in my own case, one of my earliest memories is of my grandmother's arms raised to the heavens in a hotel-room in Seelisberg, because she'd just caught me in the middle of giving an enema to a little Swiss girl of my own age) is pre-sexual.'

Sartre was the only person ever to refuse the Nobel Prize for Literature. He had a horror of being institutionalized and loathed the sanctimonious piety of the prize-givers. He also hated the conformism of the English intelligentsia and refused all invitations to lecture at British universities. It will be interesting to observe how London's literary mandarins greet this posthumous offering, superbly translated by Quintin Hoare and edited by him with a loving care which is evidenced in the explanatory footnotes.

Time Out
November 1984

9

LITERATURE AND MARKET REALISM

These are strange times. Capitalism, crippled by its own contradictions –
there are thirty million people out of work in the OECD countries alone
– is nonetheless triumphant. From New York to Beijing, via Moscow
and Vladivostok, you can eat the same junk food, watch the same junk
on television and, increasingly, read the same junk novels. In the newly
marketized counties of Eastern and Central Europe, a book can be
consumed just like a McDonald's hamburger. Indigestion and an excess of
wind are no longer a preserve of the stomach. Just as the rival hamburger
concerns advertise their respective wares, so the giant publishing concerns
of North America and Britain buy authors and exhibit them like cattle.
Potential bestsellers are auctioned by a new breed of literary agent. Such
books need to be sold, and it is at this stage that the hype-merchants enter
the fray and the promotion begins.

Many self-proclaimed postmodern writers have entered the spirit of the
new times. Without any sense of shame or modesty they tout their own work
and pander to a literary culture of consumerism. Why shouldn't they? Hasn't
Lyotard, one of the high priests of postmodernism, declared that capitalism
is an orgasm? Can't you see them quivering with pleasure, those citizens of
Mogadishu or La Paz, as they deconstruct this offering from Paris?

Is it particularly surprising, then, that in the face of today's prevailing
winds many a European or North American novelist has consciously or

subconsciously begun to write in the language of advertising? Mass-market fiction, like the indigestible filler in junk food, is meant to be consumed quickly and then excreted. Don't misunderstand me. Good books, even great books, are still being written and some, believe it or not, are even being read, but in most cases these are the products of writers who either live in marginalized countries or have themselves been marginalized by the dominant culture of a triumphalist West.

More and more one finds oneself re-reading old books, if one wishes to recapture the critical tradition. None of us will have exactly the same old books on our shelves, but as the century reaches its conclusion one turns to them more and more. And what do we find? We may be married to the time in which we live in many different ways. We may regard ourselves as modern or postmodern or whatever else. Lost in an old novel written a century or more ago, one is often startled by the parallels and analogies with our own times. 'Ethnic cleansing' in Bosnia, the revival of anti-Semitism in Germany and Russia, the Gulf war . . . the loud and unbearable noises which pierce our eardrums. Are they not echoes of the Crusades, or of what happened in Spain in the fifteenth and sixteenth centuries? The postmodernists may want to forget history, dismiss it as a set of random incidents, but history refuses to fall silent. Read the novels of Joseph Roth, writing in the thirties, and see how he describes the disintegration of the Austro-Hungarian Empire. Serbs and Croats flit through his pages in the wake of the collapse. The story, alas, is only too familiar.

Historical echoes are very pronounced in literature. Juan Goytisolo has written of how it is difficult to read Cervantes in isolation from the real Spain of that time. The great novel is full of allusions to what had happened and what was happening even as the author was composing his text. Take for example the episode of the Morisco Ricote, the shopkeeper from Sancho's village, expelled from Spain by royal edict because he is a Muslim. The homesick Ricote returns to his country in disguise and Cervantes makes him 'weep for Spain', realizing too late what love of country means. He could easily be a Bosnian, a Kurd, a Palestinian, a Somali, a Sudanese. I will now suggest to you a writer of a different nationality and a later century, the Frenchman Balzac. In what for me is the high point of his Human Comedy novels, *Lost Illusions*, one of Balzac's most demonic characters, Vautrin, speaks thus:

> Well, would you like to know what a politically-minded man finds inscribed above the doorway to this nineteenth century of yours? In 1793 Frenchmen invented popular sovereignty and it ended up in imperial absolutism . . . Napoleon was a Jacobin in 1793; in 1804 he donned the Iron Crown. From 1806 onwards the ferocious champions of 'Equality or Death' acquiesced in the creation of a new nobility, which Louis XVIII was to legitimize. The emigrant aristocracy, which lords it today in its Faubourg Saint-Germain, behaved worse still . . . In France then, in politics as well as ethics, all and sundry reached a goal which gave the lie to their beginnings: their opinions belied their behaviour, or else their behaviour belied their opinions. Logic went by the board, both with the people in power and private individuals. So you no longer have any ethics. Today, with you, success is the ruling motive for all the action you take of whatever kind.

Balzac is telling us that in his world, an unstable world reflecting the old Revolution and the Restoration, the aim of power is no longer determined by any principles. Power is for itself and for its own sake. And if you happen to believe that this is wrong then you are part of the problem. How close this feels to our world today. Change a few sentences and dates and you could describe the former Stalinist bureaucrats turned millionaires in Poland, the Ukraine and Russia. Nor is this addiction to success, measured largely by the size of one's bank balance, restricted to the former Soviet Union or Eastern Europe. It was only a few years ago in Spain that a surreal event occurred: a Bourbon king telling a Socialist government that the level of corruption was far too high. Even as we talk, the leader of the Italian Socialists, Bettino Craxi, is being charged with corruption on a grand scale; and only last week, the Socialist minister of justice in the same country resigned because of his own involvement in the wholesale corruption of Italy's political class.

This is our world, but it is also Balzac's world. It can make us very cynical. It can lead to the view which says that all societies are simply power-stuff. However understandable such a view may be, it is wrong. Demography – the production of persons; economics – the production of goods; cultural systems – the production of meanings, these have not stopped. How can they be halted? Society can never be a simple reflection of any power system. It is the sum of its parts, even if some of them seem invisible. A good storyteller must possess several hundred eyes and ears, to spy and eavesdrop continuously. The result is not always a continuous narrative, but one which compels the reader to think and sometimes to read aloud the writer's words so that the rhythm and flow of the language can help us to understand the true meaning.

A few years ago the English-language translation of the first volume of Abdelrehman Munif's epochal five-volume series, *Cities of Salt*, was published in London by a well-established publishing house. Munif's aim is to depict the transformation of Eastern Arabia during the course of this century from ancient Bedouin homelands to modern Gulf states. The novel went unnoticed on the London literary scene. Naturally. The critics were preoccupied with slender, wistful accounts of middle-class life in New York. A short, lightweight but clever book about a man warming his baby's feeding bottle was the rage at the time. Next season the topic might be the epic narrative of a campus murder, with the asocial individual again furnishing the writer's point of view. Let me be blunt. Munif's work is worth much more than most of the junk being turned out by the publishing houses in Britain and America. Does it worry the author, who has already been deprived of his nationality by the ruling family of Saudi Arabia? Not much. Why? Munif lives in exile in Damascus. But he has the satisfaction of knowing that his books are read throughout the Middle East, that they circulate clandestinely in Saudi Arabia itself where they are read and appreciated. He has a very close relationship with his readership, and that is something which is worth much more to the author than accolades from Western critics.

Why do we write and for whom do we write? Each of us will answer these questions in different ways and with differing emphases. For those, and I count myself amongst them, who refuse to distance themselves from history and world politics, the answer is simple. Writers should not run away from reality. In the face of horrors old and new, we must fight back with our literary fists.

The historical process is discontinuous. Revolutions, wars, counter-revolutions, economic blockades, carpet bombing of recalcitrant liberation movements. It is this which profoundly affects individual psyches and thus saves art from eternal repetition. Even when a revolution atrophies and degenerates into its own opposite, the attempt to straitjacket its writers is rarely successful.

'Socialist Realism' produced a monotone literature devoid of real conflict. Writers who broke the rules were declared 'enemies of the people'. Some were shot in the camps. Other survived by abandoning literature. One of these was a novelist whose work had to wait half a century before being published. Andrey Platonov's novels were regarded as so subversive that they were kept in a special section of the archive which was sealed off and unavailable even to specialists in the field. Platonov wrote in an experiential mode, his style very much influenced by modernism. *The Sea of Youth* was written in 1934 and published in 1986; *The Foundation Pit* was written in 1930 and published in 1987; *Chevengur*, a savage satire, was rejected in 1929 and published in 1988. In Chevengur, a small town with exactly eleven Bolsheviks who have already established communism, Platonov depicted the total bureaucratization of the state machine and saw it as a disaster for the Revolution. It was a cancer. If it was not destroyed in time, it would kill the Revolution. Curiously the writer's attitude to the eleven Bolsheviks is remarkably detached. There are no enemies in Chevengur. There are the victims of history, products of an illiteracy that is centuries old and children of absolutism. Platonov gave up writing. That saved his life. He was given a job – doorman at the Writers' Union Club in Moscow, where he doffed his hat to the writers patronized by the state. Small wonder then that the Writers' Union building is set on fire in Bulgakov's satire *The Master and Margarita*.

Another novelist, Vasily Grossman, belongs to a later period. Born in 1905 in the Ukraine, he studied chemistry and worked in the Donbass mines as a safety engineer. In 1933 he moved to Moscow and was befriended by Maxim Gorky. He published a couple of novels and dozens of short stories. None of these were exceptional. During the Second World War he was a correspondent of the Red Army newspaper in Stalingrad. His mother was killed by the Nazis, an event which made Grossman aware of his Jewish roots. This loyal Communist was shattered by Stalin's postwar anti-Semitic outburst and the purging of Jews from the state apparatus. He broke from orthodoxy and, in the process, wrote a masterpiece, *Life and Fate*. It was closely modelled on Tolstoy's *War and Peace*. The work was finished in 1960, confiscated by the secret police a year later. Grossman wrote to the Politburo demanding the return of the manuscript. Suslov informed him that *Life and Fate* could not be published in the Soviet Union for another two hundred years. Every state which has a monopoly of ideas, fears the written word. Grossman died in 1964 – a broken man.

Life and Fate was published posthumously, first in the West in 1985 and then in Gorbachev's Soviet Union. It is a moving and savage denunciation of Stalinism and fascism. The besieged city of Stalingrad is really a metaphor for the twentieth century. The only people for whom the author reveals a real sympathy are the officers and men in House 6/1, men and women who hate the Commissars. They possess independent minds and a fiercely critical spirit; they are members of former Oppositions destroyed by Stalin.

Even as I speak of all this, it seems dated. After all, that whole edifice has collapsed. Platonov and Grossman. How are they relevant to us today? I think for many writers in the great continents of Asia, Africa and Latin America, the parallels are obvious. It is difficult for a thinking writer to be detached from reality. But even in the West, there are lessons to be learnt. There is a growing tendency to uniformity of thought and style. Trivia reigns supreme and literature becomes a branch of the entertainment industry. Instead of Socialist Realism, we have Market Realism – the difference being that the latter is a self-imposed straitjacket. Market-Realist literature needs to be resisted every bit as strongly as the old Socialist Realism. It demands literature that is treated as a fetishized commodity, self-contained and self-referential. The upmarket commodity fosters a surrogate religion, while downmarket kitsch prevails. But such is the velocity at which commodities circulate that soon all such boundaries are broken down. Instead of indicting the arrogance and corruption of power and wealth, it fawns before the media magnates. At its most brazen it simply celebrates shopping, while in the hands of a bold exponent, such as Tom Wolfe, it turns Balzac upside down, becoming the literary equivalent of that new code called for by the Oxford philosopher, John Gray, when he wrote, 'the successful defence of market capitalism requires a revision in conventional morality in which despised occupations and practices – such as those of the speculator and middlemen – are morally rehabilitated'.

The resistance to Market Realism must be, has to be on the level of ideas, not on the basis of gender or race or class. I am not at all sympathetic to the version of political correctness which denounces the whole of European literature as racist and sexist. The logical corollary of this is to say that anti-racist and anti-sexist works are automatically good. Relativism of this sort dissolves all critical judgement and should not be indulged. Toni Morrison's novel *Beloved* is a great book, not because she is a black woman, but because she is a powerful writer who has written a most moving account of what it must have meant to be a slave. Would a white writer – a person without Morrison's historical memory – have written such a book? I doubt it, but then nor could most black people. Steinbeck wrote about the grape-pickers and the Depression. Faulkner concentrated on the decadence of the White South and the gulf between poor and rich. Morrison has evoked slavery. All three are great writers because they are able to weave a multi-layered narrative, which includes as well as transcends forms of social intuition and political intelligence. As Galvano Della Volpe wisely insisted in his *Critique of Taste*, the aesthetic should neither be reduced to sociology nor counterposed to rationality and politics.

Those of us who were born outside Europe or North America know full well that there is not and there cannot be any Chinese wall between literature and politics. I remember, as a child, being taken to *mushairas* in the town of Lahore in Pakistan. These were public poetry readings, performed not in salons but in the open air, before audiences numbering tens of thousands. Much of the audience was illiterate and the words of the poet meant a great deal. The poets, for their part, understood only too well that their true critics were those assembled before them. As the night wore on poets were cheered and heckled, till in the early hours of the morning we chanted the name of the poet who had pleased us the most and he returned to recite once again. Writing a novel is a lonely task, even more lonely than reading a novel. In that sense it is the polar opposite of a public poetry reading. And yet when I write, I must confess, the image I usually have in front of me is that of the audience in Lahore of which I was once a member. The problem for writers in the West today is that they have no equivalent of such an audience, capable of sharing with them the toil of creation by validating their vital intuitions. Instead, if they are to reach their readers, they must ingratiate themselves with a whole series of professional intermediaries – from agent to editor, publicity person to chat-show host – who will judge their work, usually without having read it, by the canons of Market Realism.

Once they have run that gauntlet they will be in the hands of critics and academic pundits who have many ways of keeping at bay what they find disturbing or unfamiliar. Where the editors and the publishing houses like an established brand name, the critics have their own prescribed genre models. The way this works is instructive. Recently two established writers took a step outside their allotted patch – Brian Moore exploring poverty, resistance, corruption and power in *No Other Life*, a novella based on recent events in Haiti, and Julian Barnes exploring the paradoxes of post-Communism in *The Porcupine*, a novella based on recent events in Bulgaria. It might be thought that these authors would be congratulated for attending to important matters as best they could, but instead they were exposed to a lofty critical barrage. In withering terms it was pointed out that Moore was no Graham Greene and that Barnes was no Milan Kundera. Writers from the first world who write about the third must, it seems, write like Greene; and if they write about Eastern Europe then Kundera or, failing that, Bradbury, set the standard. The havoc caused by free-market economics in the East, or the predicament of popular revolutionary movements in the South, are not fitting material for literature, it seems, because the critics have no comforting models to allow them to exist as such. Does it not occur to these critics that there might be new problems to address? And that writers should be encouraged to tackle these problems, rather than settle for pastiche? But, of course, to do so would be to unsettle the market with its carefully allotted and predictable niches, its conformist messages and comfortable stereotypes. The literary culture of Market Realism is not good for criticism, and that is another reason why it is not good for literature either.

New Left Review
May–June 1993

10

A REFLECTION ON ANTI-SEMITISM AND ZIONISM

Anti-Semitism is a racist ideology directed against the Jews. It has old roots. In his classic work, *The Jewish Question: A Marxist Interpretation*, published posthumously in France in 1946, the Belgian Marxist Abram Leon (active in the resistance during the Second World War, he was captured and executed by the Gestapo in 1944) invented the category of a 'people-class' for the role of the Jews who managed to preserve their linguistic, ethnic and religious characteristics through many centuries without becoming assimilated. This was not unique to the Jews, but could apply just as strongly to many ethnic minorities: diaspora Armenians, Copts, Chinese merchants in South East Asia, Muslims in China, etc. The defining characteristic common to these groups is that they became middlemen in a pre-capitalist world, resented alike by rich and poor. Twentieth-century anti-Semitism, usually instigated from above by priests (Russia, Poland), politicians and intellectuals (Germany, France and, after 1938, Italy), or big business (USA, Britain), played on the fears and insecurity of a deprived population. Hence August Bebel's reference to anti-Semitism as 'the socialism of fools'. The roots of anti-Semitism as of other forms of racism are social, political, ideological and economic. The judeocide of the Second World War, carried out by the political-military-industrial complex of German imperialism, was one of the worst crimes of the twentieth century, but not the only one. The

Belgian massacres in the Congo had led to between ten and twelve million deaths before the First World War. The uniqueness of the judeocide was that it took place in Europe (the heart of Christian civilization), and was carried out systematically – by Germans, Poles, Ukrainians, Lithuanians, French and Italians – as if it were the most normal thing in the world, showing 'the banality of evil', in Hannah Arendt's phrase. Since the end of the Second World War popular anti-Semitism of the old variety declined in Western Europe, restricted largely to remnants of fascist or neo-fascist organizations.

In the Arab world there were well-integrated Jewish minorities in Cairo, Baghdad and Damascus. They did not suffer at the time of the European judeocide. Historically, Muslims and Jews have been much closer to each other than either to Christianity. Even after 1948, when tensions rose between the two communities throughout the Arab east, it was largely Zionist provocations – such as the bombing of Jewish cafés in Baghdad – that helped to drive Arab Jews out of their native countries into Israel.

Non-Jewish Zionism has an old pedigree and permeates European culture. It dates back to the birth of Christian fundamentalist sects of the sixteenth and seventeenth centuries which took the Old Testament literally. Members included Oliver Cromwell and John Milton. Later, for other reasons, Rousseau, Locke and Pascal joined the Zionist bandwagon. There is no such thing as the 'historical rights' of Jews to Palestine. This grotesque myth (already in the seventeenth century, Baruch Spinoza referred to the Old Testament as 'a collection of fairy-tales', denounced the prophets and was excommunicated by the Amsterdam synagogue as a result) ignores real history. Long before the Roman conquest of Judea in 70 CE, a large majority of the Jewish population lived outside Palestine. The native Jews were gradually assimilated into neighbouring groups, such as the Phoenicians and the Philistines. Modern Palestinians are, in most cases,

153

descended from the old Hebrew tribes and genetic science has recently confirmed this, much to the annoyance of Zionists.

Later, and for its own vile reasons, the Third Reich too supported a Jewish homeland. The Introduction to the Nuremberg Laws of 15 September 1935 argues,

> If the Jews had a state of their own in which the bulk of the people were at home, the Jewish question could already be considered solved today, even for the Jews themselves. The ardent Zionists of all people have objected least to the basic ideas of the Nuremberg Laws, because they know that these laws are the only correct solution for the Jewish people.

Many years later, Haim Cohen, a former judge of the Supreme Court of Israel, stated,

> The bitter irony of fate decreed that the same biological and racist argument extended by the Nazis, and which inspired the inflammatory laws of Nuremberg, serve as the basis for the official definition of Jewishness in the bosom of the state of Israel.[1]

Modern Zionism is the ideology of secular Jewish nationalism. It has little to do with Judaism as a religion, and many orthodox Jews to this day have remained hostile to Zionism – like the Hassidic sect which joined a Palestinian march in Washington in April 2002, carrying placards which said: 'ZIONISM SUCKS' and 'SHARON: PALESTINIAN BLOOD IS NOT WATER'. Zionism was born in the nineteenth century as a direct response to the vicious anti-Semitism that pervaded Austria.

The first Jewish immigrants to Palestine arrived in 1882. Many of them were interested only in maintaining a cultural presence. Israel was created

---

1   Quoted in Joseph Badi, *Fundamental Laws of the State of Israel*, New York: Twayne Publishers, 1960, 156.

in 1948 by the British Empire, and sustained by its American successor. It was a European settler-state. Its early leaders proclaimed the myth of a 'A Land without People for a People without Land', thus denying the presence of the Palestinians. Last February, the Zionist historian Benny Morris gave a chilling interview to *Haaretz* (reprinted in English in *New Left Review,* March–April 2004) which admitted the truth. Seven hundred thousand Palestinians had been driven out of their villages by the Zionist army in 1948. There were numerous incidents of rape, among other aggressions. He described it accurately as 'ethnic cleansing', rather than genocide, and went on to defend ethnic cleansing if it were carried out by a superior civilization: he compared it to the killing of native Americans by the European settlers in North America. That too, for Morris, was justified. Anti-Semites and Zionists were agreed on one thing: that Jews were a special race which could not be integrated in European societies, and needed its own large ghetto or homeland. The sheer falsehood of this is proved by current demography. The majority of the world's Jews do not live in Israel, but in Western Europe and North America.

Anti-Zionism was a struggle that began against the Zionist colonization project; intellectuals of Jewish origin played an important part in this campaign, and do so to this day inside Israel itself. Most of my knowledge of Zionism and anti-Zionism comes from the writings and speeches of anti-Zionist Jews: Akiva Orr, Moshe Machover, Haim Hanegbi, Isaac Deutscher, Ygael Gluckstein (Tony Cliff), Ernest Mandel, Maxime Rodinson, Nathan Weinstock, to name but a few. They argued that Zionism and the structures of the Jewish state offered no real future to the Jewish people settled in Israel. All they offered was infinite war.

The campaign against the new 'anti-Semitism' in Europe today is no more than a cynical ploy on the part of the Israeli Government to seal off the Zionist state from any criticism of its regular and consistent brutality against the Palestinians. The daily hits carried out by the IDF have wrecked the towns and villages of Palestine, killing thousands of civilians, especially children; and European citizens are aware of this fact. Criticism of Israel cannot and should not be equated with anti-Semitism. The fact is that Israel is not a weak, defenceless state. It is the strongest state in the region. It possesses real, not imaginary, weapons of mass destruction. It possesses more tanks and bomber jets and pilots than the rest of the Arab world put together. To argue that Israel today is threatened by any Arab country is pure demagogy. It is the occupation that creates the conditions which produce suicide bombers. Even a few staunch Zionists are beginning to realize the truth of this. That is why we know that as long as Palestine remains oppressed, there will be no peace in the region.

The daily suffering of the Palestinians (the latest deaths in Gaza included three young boys) does not excite the liberal conscience of Europe, guilt-ridden (and for good reason) by its past inability to defend the Jews of central Europe against extinction. But the judeocide should not be used as a cover to commit crimes against the Palestinian people. European and American voices should be heard loud and clear on this question. To be intimidated by Zionist blackmail is to become an accomplice of war crimes.

2007

Part Two

DIARIES

11

FIRST TIME IN TRIPOLI

'We've been trying to get you to come and talk here for the last three years,' my host complained as we shook hands at the airport. 'Here' was Tripoli, capital of the Socialist People's Arab Jamahiriya, bathed in mild February sunshine; my host a functionary from the World Centre for the Studies and Researches of the Green Book (the Libyan equivalent of the Little Red Book). 'The lecture is just an excuse,' I told him. 'I'm really here to see Leptis Magna.' We both laughed. He because he thought I was joking and me because I wasn't.

I was billeted at the state-funded Funduq al-Kebir, rebuilt in 1982 on the site of the colonial Grand Hotel. The old place looks much nicer in photographs than its soulless replacement, with its surly receptionists, appalling service and second-rate food (the worst breakfasts ever, and that includes Pyongyang circa 1972).

The hotel overlooks the waterfront and is within walking distance of all the main sights, including the great old mosque-church-mosque, the Ottoman souk and the museum. Close by are the huge marble arcades of the colonial period. Some have a Belle-Epoque charm; others are more reminiscent of grandiose Italian Fascist architecture, such as the railway station in Milan. Above both varieties of arcade are beautiful apartments with baroque plaster mouldings and shuttered windows, which once housed the colonials. Walking through the decaying arcades, crowded with noisy men-only cafés, one gets a glimpse of prewar Italy, far preferable to the imitations of Dallas typical of the cities of the Gulf States.

In a waterfront café with a lively Libyan intellectual, freshly returned from Canada and excited about his plans to launch a weekly newspaper, we notice that most of the young women, including those arm-in-arm with a boyfriend, are hijabed. Very few are worn tight like a nun's cowl; more often they are designer versions, and usually (as is also the case in Cairo) it's what is worn below the neck that attracts attention. It is not unusual to see hijabed women wearing tight-fitting tops and jeans. In such cases a display of hair might well be thought a distraction. But my companion is shocked. 'It was very different when I left for Montreal several years ago,' he said. Only a minority covered their heads and most wore skirts. And at least half the people in this café would have been women.'

Has there been pressure from the state?

'Exactly the opposite,' he said. 'The government doesn't impose any norms in matters of dress. Not now and not under the monarchy.' But Gaddafi is pious, I insist. Why else would he have ordered the uprooting of the wonderful vineyards surrounding Tripoli?' Libya's neighbours, Tunisia, Morocco and Algeria have maintained their vineyards.

'It was a mistake,' my companion declared. 'And our wines were better.'

We discussed his project for a cultural magazine. He was confident that changes were on the way in Libya. The secret police were less visible and had stopped harassing citizens. There were a few hundred political prisoners, mainly in Benghazi, a centre of Salafism crushed fifteen years ago after an insurrection. It was in Benghazi last month that several hundred Islamists stormed the Italian consulate, after a Northern League member of Berlusconi's government was seen wearing a T-shirt with one of the Danish cartoons on it. The minister was sacked the following day and Berlusconi apologized.

The next day I met a chain-smoking freelance journalist in his late fifties. In reality he was a creature of the café and did very little during the day apart from smoke and drink Turkish coffee – a character familiar to readers of Mahfouz's *Cairo Trilogy*. He, too, was slightly puzzled by the rapid growth of the hijab industry. His own wife had taken to wearing one about five years ago. Since she was present, I asked her why. She smiled and shrugged. I explained that I was curious to know whether it was a globalized fashion trend or a reflection of the increase in religiosity.

'Both,' she replied. 'And also the proliferation of cable TV. We can now get everything. Pornography and preachers. The hijab in my case is a response to both.'

After his wife had left, the journalist said more. 'I think it is an increase in religiosity, but in men more than women. Many young women do it to please men and think it will put them on the fast track to marriage.' He told me that a few years before a Moroccan woman had accosted him in a hotel restaurant. She was wearing a hijab and he was taken aback to realize that she was a prostitute. 'If we walk out and get in your car, nobody will think twice because I'm wearing a hijab,' she had told him. 'I could be your sister, a cousin or even your wife. So I wear it to make things easier for you men.'

The two internet cafés in the hotel lobby have young male workers wearing jeans, who greet customers with a friendly 'hi.' There are over a dozen messages waiting for me from various media outlets wanting comments or interviews about the Danish cartoons. Nobody in Libya has mentioned them so far. I have a look at the cartoons: most of them are unfunny and the one of Muhammad as a turbaned terrorist is a provocative and crude stereotype. I reply to the questions of the Swedish liberal daily, *Dagens Nyheter*, but ignore most of the requests.

It took five months of concentrated lobbying in the Muslim world by a travelling imam from Denmark to manufacture this 'anger'. In occupied

Afghanistan about five hundred people joined a demonstration. Were their thoughts on the cartoons, or the ruin and destruction around them? Feeling powerless, they used the cartoons as an excuse to march outside a US military base. The marines opened fire and two young boys died. In Lahore the violence was orchestrated by the Jamaat-i-Islami (London rep: Sir Iqbal Sacranie), who tried to regain the political initiative by getting young men armed with clubs to attack a bank. Perhaps they needed some cash. One cleric who clearly doesn't is Maulana Yousaf Qureshi of Peshawar, who is offering a million dollars and a new car to anyone who kills the cartoonist. The make of car is not specified.

All this is very different from the restraint shown by the Muslim Brotherhood in the Arab world and Western Europe, whose members objected but in a new-found, moderate way. They are seriously interested in power and want the United States to believe they are pretty much the same as Christian Democrats. That this is largely the case can be seen in Turkey, where a pro-EU, pro-NATO Islamist party is in power.

That same night, I switched on Al Jazeera and watched Brother Nasrullah, the charismatic Hizbullah leader in Lebanon, calmly informing a press conference that 'if the faithful had carried out Ayatollah Khomeini's injunction and killed the apostate Rushdie, the Danish newspaper editor would never have dared to publish these cartoons.' It's the simplicity that is frightening here. The religious objection to the cartoons is first that they portray the Prophet of Islam, and second that they do so in caricature, a form of representation 'painful' to all believers. There is nothing in the Qur'an itself that forbids portraits of the Prophet or anyone else. Nothing. There are proto-Judaic injunctions against idolatry, but these refer to the worship of statues depicting gods and goddesses. Islamic tradition, the bulk of which was constructed after Muhammad's death, is contradictory on the matter. As the young religion conquered old empires it was faced with practical problems. Whose image should replace that of the Byzantine or Persian rulers on coins? There are early eighth-century Islamic coins with an image of the Prophet. Even centuries later, in the post-Islamic Turkish and Persian traditions, his image was not taboo.

Back in London as I write this I have in front of me a striking edition of the illustrations to the *Miraj-nameh*, an early medieval Islamic account of the Prophet's ascent to heaven from the Dome of the Rock and the punishments he observed as he passed through hell. Some European scholars maintain that a Latin translation of this work might have given Dante a few ideas. The stunning illustrations in this fifteenth-century copy were exquisitely calligraphed by Malik Bakshi of Herat (now in Afghanistan) in the Uighur script. There are 61 illustrations in all, created with great love for the Prophet. He is depicted with Central Asian features and seen flying to heaven on a magical steed with a woman's head. There are also images of a meeting with Gabriel and Adam, of houris at the gates of Paradise and of winebibbers being punished in hell.

Muhammad insisted he was only the Messenger, a human being, not a divinity, and the main reason later Islamic tradition did not want his image shown was the fear it might be worshipped (like that of Jesus and Mary), when that prerogative belonged to Allah alone. But even in the absence of an image, the Prophet of Islam is worshipped as a virtual divinity, otherwise the reaction of the ultra-orthodox to any perceived insult to him is incomprehensible. Muhammad's son-in-law, Caliph Ali, the posthumous inspirer of the Shi'a faction of Islam and his sons, Hasan and Hussein, are also represented in various religious art forms in Iran and worshipped.

As for religious 'pain', this is, mercifully, an experience denied unbelievers like myself and felt only by divines from various faiths who transmit it to their followers, or by politicians in direct contact with the Holy Spirit: Bush, Blair and Ahmadinejad and, of course, the pope and the grand ayotallah.

There are many believers, probably a majority, who remain unaffected by insults from a right-wing Danish paper.

The next day I'm driven to Leptis Magna, the capital of Rome's African Empire, on a road running alongside an unspoilt coastline, and the satanic cartoons fade from memory. As we turn a corner the columns of Leptis suddenly appear, with the turquoise Mediterranean as their backdrop. The size and scale are astonishing. Like much else on the shores of this sea, the city was founded by Phoenician traders, around 1100 BCE; later it fell to Carthage and was incorporated into the Roman Empire by Tiberius after the defeat of Carthage in the Third Punic War in 146 BCE. It provided Rome with an emperor, Septimus Severus, and the arch commemorating him still stands. The Vandals took Leptis in 439, destroying its walls to prevent Roman resistance. By the time the Arabs arrived in 650, the city had been abandoned, but its stones weren't looted and the city was hidden under the sand, until in 1912 Italian archaeologists uncovered it. I was mostly alone for the three hours I spent at Leptis, apart from a few Libyan families with picnics and some Italian tourists.

Many artefacts from Leptis and Sabratha (an ancient Greek city) are now in the museum in Tripoli, which has a stunning collection of virtually intact statues from the ancient world. But another object in the museum catches my attention. Preserved in a glass case, surrounded by antiquities, is a blue 1960s Volkswagen. This is the car which Gaddafi, then a young army captain, drove around Tripoli, encouraging his fellow officers to follow Nasser and topple the pro-Western monarch, King Idris. Gaddafi has run the country since 1969 without feeling the need to create a single political party. He has declared, *pace* Ibn Khaldun, that tribalism is a curse of the Maghreb and that since political parties are only a modern version of tribes, they are dispensable. This thought and others can be found in the Green Book. For the most part it is a collection of verbose and turgid declamations, with the odd original reflection reflecting the zaniness of the author.

It's difficult to gauge what is really happening in Tripoli. Some things we know. Libya's earnings from oil stand at $36 billion a year. Its annual budget is $10 billion. Its population is nearly six million. Naturally nobody starves. The bazaars are full of food, but the level of education and the health facilities are primitive. Thousands of Libyans cross into Tunisia to get medical treatment. The contrast with Cuba, an island always strapped for cash, is instructive. The Medical University of the Americas in Havana trains and educates hundreds of students from South and North America (mainly Afro-Americans and Hispanics). The level of culture and education is very high. Why not in Libya? The state bureaucracy produces a population in its own image. Isolated, provincial, with more than a touch of brutality, it conditions the population, who in return display fear combined with prudence and cunning. It need not be like this, and the latest turn towards the West is an attempt to join the globalized world. Few in Libya believe that Gaddafi was responsible for the Lockerbie disaster, but in order to end sanctions and shift Libya's political position he admitted guilt and agreed to pay a fortune in compensation. The acceptance of imperial hegemony requires tributes of this sort. Does it also require a hereditary leadership? One of Gaddafi's sons, Saif al-Islam, is being groomed for the succession. Since he's a PhD student at the LSE and enamoured of the neoliberal West, there is little criticism here of the proposed handover. Gaddafi, after all, is no longer the head of a 'rogue state' but a 'great statesman' (in the words of Jack Straw) and has received Blair in his tent. This helps maintain the pretence that he's caved in to London, not Washington. It's simple: Saif wants to privatize everything and turn Libya into a Gulf statelet.

Interestingly, the only institution that works well is the cosmopolitan Islamic University, for foreign students only. The Islamic Call (a state-funded reformist network that runs the University) provides a free education in Islam and trains imams. Invited for lunch by the dean, I found students from all over the world. Africans mingled with Chinese and there was a young woman from Myanmar, a few Vietnamese and Filipinos. There is a large library of 80,000 books (compared to 20,000 in the National Library), many of them digitized. In case too many imams come off the production line, each student is also taught a trade: electricians, plumbers and carpenters are being produced here. On my way out I was shown the bookshop. I asked what was available in translation from English. Three books were put on the counter: Shakespeare's *Comedies*, Daphne du Maurier's *Rebecca* and Frances Hodgson Burnett's *The Secret Garden*.

Ahmad Ibrahim al-Faqih, a novelist I had asked to see, was in town. His autobiographical trilogy (*I Shall Present You with Another City, These Are the Borders of My Kingdom* and *A Tunnel Lit by a Woman*) has won him renown throughout the Arab world. Like many Arab writers inspired by the nationalist wave of the 1960s, he became disaffected after the Arab defeat in the Six-Day War. This is not uncommon. Numerous Arab intellectuals, writers and poets are alienated from both their own societies and the West. Few have embraced religion. Al-Faqih's first novel opens: 'A time has passed and another time is not coming.' The final sentence of the trilogy is: 'A time has passed and another time has not come and will not come.' He told me that he is close to finishing a ten-novel work. 'I've just been appointed ambassador to Romania. As you can imagine there is not much to do there, and so I will have plenty of time to finish it.'

Gaddafi, too, writes short stories. One of them, 'Suicide of an Astronaut', is said to be surreal, but my requests for a copy went unheeded. My own talk was on the current situation in the Middle East. The audience consisted of university students and professors and a fair sample of the local diplomatic corps. As is my wont I denounced both the West and the venality of the Arab regimes. I discussed the grotesqueness of the double standards deployed by the West against Iran on the nuclear reactor issue. I didn't know that the Iranian ambassador was in the audience. Certainly, when I referred to his president as an incorruptible but simple-minded fanatic, I didn't notice anyone walk out.

21 February 2006

12

CARACAS TO COCHABAMBA

The 1960s skyscrapers of Caracas seemed uglier than usual. The Hotel Gran Meliá wasn't very appealing either. The kitsch ceiling in the giant lobby was reminiscent of the Dubai School (why does oil wealth seem to result in such bad architecture?) and I wished I was staying, as I normally do, at the shabby, bare, miserable but atmospheric Hilton. I was in Caracas to speak at a conference on global media networks and to attend a meeting of the advisory board of the Spanish/Portuguese cable news channel Telesur – set up jointly by Venezuela, Argentina, Uruguay, Bolivia, Cuba and now Ecuador. Intended to provide an alternative to the CNN/BBC worldview, the new channel has been a modest success, with between five and six million regular viewers. The privately owned channels devote hours of coverage to US Congressional results or a murder on a US campus: Telesur announces these events briefly and devotes the rest of the bulletin to live coverage from Nicaragua, where elections are taking place, or from Ecuador, where a referendum that will lead to the drafting of a new constitution has been won by the new government.

I first raised the idea of setting up a station to counter the Washington Consensus networks at a public meeting here in 2003. It was seized on quickly, but the name I suggested – Al Bolívar – was firmly rejected. It was inappropriate, I was told, since it would exclude the largest continental state, which had no links to the Liberator. In the event, Brazil excluded itself. 'Why won't you support Telesur?' Chávez asked Lula. 'I don't know,' he replied, shame-faced. The reason was obvious: he didn't want to antagonize the Brazilian media or annoy Washington. But Telesur is starting to attract viewers in his country even so.

The conference centre was packed for Chávez's speech. When we were all seated, he was whisked in and a few pleasantries exchanged. 'You must be happy now that Blair is going,' he said to me. I pointed out that my happiness was somewhat circumscribed by the succession. 'Long live the revolution,' he said, practising his English. Then we settled down for his three-hour address, which was being broadcast live. Occasions like this always make me wish I'd brought a picnic basket. The speech was pretty typical. Some facts (for example, that the increase in oil revenues brought about by charging more royalties amounts to a few billion dollars); homespun philosophy; autobiography; an account of his most recent conversation with Castro, together with a rough estimate of the length of time the two men have spent talking to each other (well over a thousand hours); his pride that the Venezuelan government is funding Danny Glover's film about Toussaint L'Ouverture and the Haitian slave uprising; the horrors of occupied Iraq; a sharp attack on the pope for suggesting in the course of his recent visit to Brazil that the indigenous population had not been badly treated and had willingly embraced Christ.

An impromptu song, which normally indicates that the speech is nearing its end, followed the denunciation of the pope, but this time the speech continued. There was a shortish (30-minute) historical detour, much of it to do with Bolívar and how he had been let down by men in the pay of the local aristocracy/oligarchy: 'The history books at school never taught us about these betrayals.' And then there was a discussion of planetary survival before the speech ended with a slogan borrowed from Cuba in bad times: 'Socialism or Death'. It's a truly awful message. When I pointed out to one of Chávez's aides how threatening this sounds, he explained that the president was in Rosa Luxemburg mode. What he really meant was 'Socialism or Barbarism'. I'm not convinced.

Chávez seemed to be slightly subdued and I wondered whether the audience he was really addressing wasn't the army rank and file. The next day, the former vice-president, José Vicente Rangel, told us that there had been a US-Colombian plot to infiltrate Colombian paramilitaries, including snipers, into Venezuela. The aim, he said, had been to create a national emergency: government members and leaders of the opposition would be assassinated and each side would blame the other. A plot to assassinate Chávez involving three senior army officers was uncovered around the same time. Two of the would-be assassins are in prison; the third reportedly fled to Miami.

Chávez's military studies taught him that the enemy must never be reduced to desperation, since this only makes them stronger. His strategy is to offer escape routes. He and his supporters are not vindictive, and the Western media chorus portraying his regime as authoritarian is wide of the mark. It was in full voice when I was in Caracas. The cause this time was a privately owned TV station (RCTV) whose 20-year licence the government had refused to renew. RCTV, in common with most of the Venezuelan media, was involved in the 2002 coup against Chávez's (democratically elected) government. RCTV mobilized support for the coup, falsified footage to suggest that Chávez supporters were killing people, and when the coup failed didn't show any images of Chávez's triumphant return. A year later they made lengthy appeals to the citizens to topple the government during an opposition-engineered oil strike. Again, they were not alone, but their appeals actively encouraged violence.

Asked by a *Guardian* reporter whether I supported the decision, I said I did. He was shocked: 'But now the opposition is without its TV channel.' I asked whether the opposition in Britain or anywhere else in Europe or America had 'its TV'? Which Western government would tolerate any of this? Thatcher refused to renew Thames TV's franchise, and it had merely shown one critical documentary. Blair sacked Greg Dyke and neutered the BBC. Bush has the luxury of uncritical news channels, and Fox TV as a propaganda network.

I warned against an obsession with the power of the media at the conference. After all, Chávez won six elections despite near universal media opposition. Evo Morales in Bolivia and Rafael Correa in Ecuador also won despite unremitting opposition. And this wasn't true only of South America. The French voted against the European Constitution without the support of a single daily newspaper or TV station.

Four days later I was at another conference – this time 'defending humanity', something I often do – in Cochabamba in Bolivia. I was last there forty years ago as part of a four-man team (the others were Perry Anderson, Robin Blackburn and Ralph Schoenman) sent by Bertrand Russell to attend the trial of Régis Debray in Camiri, not far from where a besieged Che Guevara was fighting to escape the Bolivian army. Debray had been captured while attempting to leave the guerrilla encampment and head home. I had also been asked by the Cubans to photograph every Bolivian army officer in the region. This got me into trouble a few times. On one occasion a colonel, pistol drawn, walked up to me and asked for the film. I gave him a blank roll. 'If you take any more photographs of me,' he said, 'I'll shoot you.' I didn't. These photographs and others (including one of Robin Blackburn having a long shower) were despatched to Havana, where they must still be held in some ageing archive.

Cochabamba was where the US Military Advisory Group, which was supervising the operation to capture and kill Guevara, established its HQ. And it was to Cochabamba that I fled from Camiri in 1967 after being briefly arrested, accused of being a Cuban guerrilla called Pombo, Che's bodyguard and one of those who escaped the encampment and returned safely to Cuba. I holed up there till I could get a flight to La Paz and a connection to Europe via Brazil. Hearing me reminisce with Richard Gott, who was also defending humanity, and who had been the *Guardian*'s chief Latin America correspondent in 1967, a young Telesur journalist from Madrid said: 'God. It's just like listening to Spanish Civil War veterans returning to Spain.'

Bolivia has a large Indian population: 62 per cent describe themselves as indigenous; 35 per cent live on less than a dollar a day. It has a turbulent history: wars, coups, revolutions, the odd guerrilla *foco* and numerous uprisings. There were 157 coups between 1825 and 1982 and 70 presidents, half of whom held office for less than a year. Neoliberal slumber lasted throughout the 1990s, before anti-government protests culminated in the 'water wars'. The government sold the water in Cochabamba to Bechtel, who told people it was illegal to collect rainwater. There were clashes with the army, a young demonstrator was killed and the protesters won. The municipality regained control of the water. Such unrest created the basis for the triumph of Morales and the Movement for Socialism in the elections of 2005. Not only was Morales on the left, he was an Aymara Indian, and his victory ended a century and a half of Creole rule. The rich were furious. Within a few months, a campaign of destabilization centred in the Creole stronghold of Santa Cruz had begun. 'They predicted economic chaos,' Rafael Puente, a former government minister and Jesuit priest, told us. 'They said Bolivia would become another Zimbabwe. They accused Evo of starting a civil war. They exchanged doctored photographs on their cell phones depicting their elected president bleeding from a gunshot wound in the head with the words "Viva Santa Cruz" painted above him in blood.' The government went ahead and carried out its election promises, nationalizing energy resources and taking direct control of operations. The increase in state revenues was to be used to help poor families keep their children at school. The government aimed to reduce poverty by 10 per cent, a modest enough aim, but the Santa Cruz businessmen screamed

'Communism!'. When economic conditions improved, the opposition moved on to Morales's relationship with Chávez. The walls of Santa Cruz were plastered with posters reading 'Evo, Chola de Chávez' (*chola* is the word for 'Indian whore'). When one looks at the newspapers here it is hard to work out which man they hate more.

Richard Gott and I wandered around Cochabamba. The Paris Café on the Plaza 14 de Septiembre was still there, looking much less dilapidated. The Roxy cinema where I watched Lee Marvin and Jane Fonda in *Cat Ballou* has also survived, although it is now an evangelical church. Gott insisted that we visit La Cancha. This is the indigenous market opposite the old railway station, reminiscent of an Arab bazaar with its narrow lanes, and commodities transported by wheelbarrow; among other things it has to offer is the most ravishing assortment of multi-coloured potatoes anywhere in the world. Little has changed since 1967, though the quality seems to have declined a bit. I bought two cheap tin plates painted with flowers, which turned out to have been made in China.

Back at the hotel I was ambushed by a Spanish journalist from *El Mundo*: 'You've described Venezuela, Bolivia, Cuba and Ecuador as an axis of hope. What is your axis of evil in this continent?' I told her that I avoid the terms good and evil because they are religious concepts, but that my axis of despair consists of Brazil, Chile and Mexico. 'Could you please add the Dominican Republic?' asked Scheherazade Vicioso, a feminist poet. 'We're always being ignored.' I did so. Then I asked the reason for her name. Her father, a composer, adored *The Thousand and One Nights*. 'I got off lightly,' she added. 'My brother is called Rainer Maria Rilke.'

I left on an early morning flight. An Indian, his back bent, a brush in each hand, was cleaning the streets. Waiting in Caracas for another plane I flicked through the guest book in the VIP lounge. Two messages summed up the contradictions. The first was from Ahn Jung Gu, the president of Samsung in South America: 'Venezuela is one of the core markets for

Samsung. We will continue to invest here and contribute development to this market.' A few entries later: 'Dear President Chávez and Venezuela. Thank you for the love and hospitality of your people. In love and peace. Cindy Sheehan, USA.'

June 2007

13

LOST ILLUSIONS IN DIYARBAKIR

It was barely light in Istanbul as I stumbled into a taxi and headed for the airport to board a flight for Diyarbakir, the largest Kurdish city in eastern Turkey, not far from the Iraqi border. The plane was full, thanks to a large party of what looked like chattering students with closely shaved heads, whose nervous excitement seemed to indicate they'd never left home before. One of them took the window seat next to my interpreter. It turned out he wasn't a student but a newly conscripted soldier, heading east for more training and his first prolonged experience of barrack-room life, perhaps even of conflict. He couldn't have been more than eighteen; this was his first time on a plane. As we took off he clutched the seat in front of him and looked fearfully out of the window. During the flight he calmed down and marvelled at the views of the mountains and lakes below, but as the plane began its descent he grabbed the seat again. Our safe landing was greeted with laughter by many of the shaven-headed platoon.

Only a few weeks previously, some young soldiers had been killed in clashes with guerrillas belonging to the Kurdistan Workers' Party (PKK). It used to be the case that when Turkish soldiers died in the conflict, their mothers were wheeled on to state television to tell the world how proud they were of the sacrifice. They had more sons at home, they would say, ready and waiting to defend the Fatherland. This time the mothers publicly blamed the government for the deaths of their sons.

Diyarbakir is the de facto capital of the Turkish part of Kurdistan, itself a notional state that extends for some six hundred miles through the mountainous regions of south-eastern Turkey, northern Syria, Iraq and Iran. Turkish Kurdistan is home to more than 14 million Kurds, who make up the vast majority of the region's population; there are another four million Kurds in northern Iraq, some five million in Iran and a million in Syria. The Turkish sector is the largest and strategically the most important: it would be central to a Kurdish state. Hence the paranoia exhibited by the Turkish government and its ill-treatment of the Kurdish population, whose living conditions are much worse than those of the Kurds in Iraq or Iran.

Kurdish language and culture were banned at the foundation of the unitary Turkish Republic in 1923. The repression intensified during the 1970s, and martial law was imposed on the region in 1978, followed by two decades of mass arrests, torture, killings, forced deportations and the destruction of Kurdish villages. The PKK, founded by the student leader Abdullah Öcalan in 1978, began a guerrilla war in 1984, claiming the Kurds' right to self-determination within (this was always stressed) the framework of a democratized and demilitarized Turkish state. By 'democratization' Kurds mean the repeal of laws used to harass minorities or to deny them basic political rights. The constitution, for example, established in 1982, requires a party to get 10 per cent of the vote nationally before it can win parliamentary representation – the highest such threshold in the world. Kurdish nationalists consistently receive a majority of the votes in parts of eastern Turkey, but have no members of parliament. When, in 1994, centre-left Kurdish deputies formed a new party to get over the 10 per cent barrier, they were arrested on charges of aiding the PKK and sentenced to 15 years in jail.

An estimated 200,000 Turkish troops have been permanently deployed in Kurdistan since the early 1990s, and in 1996 and 1998 fierce battles resulted in thousands of Kurdish casualties. By February 1999, when the fugitive Öcalan was captured in Kenya – possibly by the CIA – and handed over to Turkey, more than 30,000 Kurds had been killed and some 3,000 villages burned or destroyed, which resulted in a new exodus to Diyarbakir; the city now has a population of more than a million. At the end of 1999, after heavy American lobbying, the EU extended candidate status to Turkey, with further negotiations conditional on some amelioration, at least, of the Kurdish situation. The pace of reforms accelerated after the election of Recep Tayyip Erdoğan's government in November 2002. In 2004, the Kurdish deputies who had been arrested ten years earlier were finally released, and a Kurdish-language programme was broadcast for the first time on state television. In line with EU cultural heritage provisions, restoration work began on the old palace in Diyarbakir – even while Kurdish prisoners were still being tortured in its cellars.

My host, Melike Coşkun, the director of the Anadolu Cultural Centre, suggested a tour of the walls and the turbot-shaped old town. We picked up Şeyhmus Diken, cultural adviser to the recently elected young pro-PKK mayor. He took us to a mosque that was once a cathedral and before that a pagan temple, where sun-worshippers sacrificed virgins on large stone slabs in the courtyard. It was a Friday during Ramadan and the mosque was filling up. The majority belonging to the dominant Sunni Hanafi school occupied the main room while the Shafi'i prayed in a smaller one.

We then visited three empty Christian churches. The first was Chaldean, built in 300 CE, its brick dome exquisitely held in place by intertwined wooden arches. The second, which was Assyrian, was square, and even older, with Aramaic carvings on the wood and stones. The caretaker lives in rooms attached to the church and grows vegetables in what was once the garden of the bishop's palace. Hens roamed about, occasionally laying eggs beneath the altar. The Armenian church was more recent – sixteenth century – but without a roof. It was a more familiar shape, like a Roman Catholic church, and the priest confirmed that the Armenians who had once worshipped here were Catholics. Şeyhmus began to whisper something to him. I became curious. 'It's nothing,' Şeyhmus said. 'Since my triple bypass the only drink I'm allowed is red wine, and there is a tiny vineyard attached to a monastery in the countryside. I pick up a few bottles from this church. It's good wine.' This was strangely reassuring.

We walked over to the old city walls, first built with black stone more than 2,000 years ago, with layers added by each new conqueror. The crenellated parapets and arched galleries are crumbling; many stones have been looted to repair local houses. From an outpost on the wall, the Tigris is visible as it makes its way south. Şeyhmus told me that he had been imprisoned in the palace cells by the Turkish authorities. 'The next time you come,' he promised, 'this building will be totally restored and we will sip our drinks and watch the Tigris flow.' In a large enclosed space below the wall there was an exhibition of photographs of Diyarbakir in 1911. The images, of a virtually intact medieval city, seemed to have little interest in the people who lived there but concentrated on the buildings. The photographer was Gertrude Bell, who later boasted that she had created modern Iraq on behalf of the British Empire by 'drawing lines in the sand'. These lines, of course, also divided the territory of the Kurdish tribes, which claim an unbroken history in this area, stretching back well before the Christian era.

The first written records come after the Arab Muslim conquest. In the tenth century, the Arab historian Masudi listed the Kurdish mountain tribes in his nine-volume history, *Meadows of Gold*. Like most of the inhabitants of the region they converted to Islam in the seventh and eighth centuries, and were recruited to the Muslim armies. They were rebellious, however, and took part in such uprisings as the Kharijite upheavals of the ninth century. (The Kharijites denounced the hereditary tradition as alien to Islam and demanded an elected caliph. They were crushed.) The Kurds settled around Mosul and took part in the epic slave revolt of the Zanj in southern Mesopotamia in 875. This, too, was defeated. Subsequently Kurdish bands wandered the region as mercenaries. Saladin's family belonged to one such group, whose military skills soon propelled its leaders to power. During the sixteenth-century conflicts between the Ottoman Empire and the Safavid dynasty that ruled Iran, Kurdish tribes fought on both sides. Inter-tribal conflicts made Kurdish unity almost impossible.

When Gertrude Bell visited Diyarbakir in 1911, Muslims (mostly Kurds) constituted 40 per cent of the population. Armenians, Chaldeans and Assyrians, groups that had settled in what is now eastern Turkey well over a thousand years before the Christian era, remained the dominant presence. Istanbul was becoming increasingly unhappy with the idea of such a mixed population, and even before the Young Turks seized power from the sultan in 1909, a defensive nationalist wave had led to clashes between Turks and Armenian groups and small-scale massacres in the east. The Armenians began to be seen as the agents of foreign countries whose aim was to dismember the Ottoman Empire. It's true that various wealthy Armenian (and Greek) factions were only too happy to cosy up to the West during the dying days of the Ottoman Empire, but much of the Armenian population continued to live peacefully with their Muslim neighbours in eastern Anatolia. They spoke Turkish as well as their own language, just as the Kurds did. But Armenian nationalist revolutionaries were beginning to talk of an Armenian state and the communities increasingly divided along political lines. A Kurdish militia was set up by the sultan to cow the Armenians, and then Mehmed Talat, the minister for the interior (who would be assassinated by an Armenian nationalist), decided to get rid of them altogether. The Kurdish irregulars carried out the forced expulsions and massacres of 1915 in which up to a million Armenians died.

Melike told me that her grandmother was Armenian, and that Kurdish families had saved many lives and given refuge to Armenian women and children who had converted to Islam in order to survive. Two years ago Fethiye Çetin, a lawyer and a historian, published a book about her grandmother, who in old age had confessed to Çetin that she wasn't a Muslim, but an Armenian Christian. The book was launched at the cultural centre Melike runs. 'The hall was packed with women who had never been near our centre before,' Melike said. 'After Fethiye had finished so many women wanted to speak and discuss their Armenian roots. It was amazing.' Çetin writes that her grandmother was a 'sword leftover' child, which is how people whose lives had been spared were described: 'I felt my blood freeze. I had heard of this expression before. It hurt to find it being used to describe people like my grandmother. My optimism, which was formed with memories of tea breads, turned to pessimism.'

The political logic of ultra-nationalism proved deadly for both victim and perpetrator. The aim of the Young Turks had been to expel the non-Muslim minorities with a view to laying the foundations of a new and solid unitary state. The exchange of populations with Greece was part of this plan. In 1922 Kemal Atatürk came to power and made the plan a reality, under the slogan 'one state, one citizen and one language'. The language was Latinized, with many words of Arab and Persian origin cast aside very much like the unwanted citizens. Given that virtually the entire population was now Muslim, the secular foundations of the new state were extremely weak, with the military as the only enforcer of the new order. The first blowback came with the 1925 Kurdish uprising. Then, as now, religion could not dissolve other differences. The rebellion lasted several months, and when it was finally put down all hopes for Kurdish autonomy disappeared. The Kurds' culture and language were suppressed. Many migrated to Istanbul and Izmir and other towns, but the Kurdish question would never go away.

I had been invited to give a lecture in Diyarbakir on the Kurdish question and the war in Iraq. Four years ago, while the war was still being plotted in Washington, Noam Chomsky and I were invited to address a public sector trade-union congress in Istanbul. Many of those present were of Kurdish origin. I said then that there would be a war and that the Iraqi Kurds would whole-heartedly collaborate with the US, as they had been doing since the Gulf War, and expressed the hope that Turkish Kurds would resist the temptation to do the same. Afterwards I was confronted by some angry Kurds. How dare I mention them in the same breath as their Iraqi cousins? Was I not aware that the PKK had referred to the tribal chiefs in Iraqi Kurdistan as 'primitive nationalists'? In fact, one of them shouted, Massoud Barzani and Jalal Talabani (currently the president of Iraq) were little better than 'mercenaries and prostitutes'. They had sold themselves successively to the Shah of Iran, Israel, Saddam Hussein, Khomeini and now the Americans. How could I even compare them to the PKK? In 2002 I was only too happy to apologize. I now wish I hadn't.

The PKK didn't share the antiwar sentiment that had engulfed the country in 2003, and pushed the newly elected parliament into forbidding the US from entering Iraq from Turkey. But while Kurdish support for the war was sheepish and shame-faced in Istanbul, no such inhibitions were on display in Diyarbakir. Virtually every question after my talk took Kurdish nationalism as its starting point. That was the only way they could see the war. Developments in northern Iraq, or southern Kurdistan, as they call it in Diyarbakir, have created a half-hope, half-belief, that the Americans might undo what Gertrude Bell and the British did and give the Kurds their own state. I pointed out that America's principal ally in Turkey was the army, not the PKK. 'What some of my people don't understand is that you can be an independent state and still not free, especially now,' one veteran muttered in agreement. But most of the people there were happy with the idea of Iraqi Kurdistan becoming an American-Israeli protectorate. 'Give me a reason, other than imperial conspiracy, why Kurds should defend the borders which have been their prisons,' someone said. The reason seemed clear to me: whatever happened they had to go on living there. If they started killing their neighbours, the neighbours would want revenge. By collaborating with the US, the Iraqi Kurdish leaders in the north are putting the lives of fellow Kurds in Baghdad at risk. It's the same in Turkey. There are nearly two million Kurds in Istanbul, including many rich businessmen integrated in the economy. They can't be ignored.

As I was flying back to Istanbul the PKK announced a unilateral ceasefire. Turkey's moderate Islamist government must be secretly relieved. The PKK decision offers the possibility of genuine reforms and autonomy, but this will happen only if the Turkish army agrees to retire to its barracks. Economic conditions in the Kurdish areas are now desperate: the flow of refugees has not stopped and increasing class polarization is reflected in the growth of political Islam. A Kurdish Hizbullah was formed some years ago (with, so it's said, the help of Turkish military intelligence, which hoped it might weaken the PKK), and the conditions are ripe for its growth. Its first big outing in Diyarbakir was a 10,000-strong demonstration against the Danish cartoons. If things don't change, the movement is bound to grow.

November 2006

14

AL JAZEERA

In Cairo and Abu Dhabi, the two Arab capitals I have visited this year, street and palace are for once in harmony. A pre-emptive strike against Saddam Hussein on the grounds that he might, at some point in the future, authorize the production of nuclear weapons, would be, for the people of the region, a classic display of imperial double standards. They know that the only country which possesses both nuclear and chemical weapons is Israel. Arab public opinion has not been so united for decades. And a cable television station, Al Jazeera ('The Peninsula'), has played a crucial part in both promoting and symbolizing this unity. It has raised mass consciousness in the region, by providing a ruthless analysis of what is wrong with the Arab world.

Unity was the recurring theme of the nationalist period of Arab political history. First there was Nasser and his dream of a united Arab republic. Then defeat in war. Then the laments of exiled poets – Nizar Qabbani from Syria, Mahmoud Darwish from Palestine and Muthaffar al-Nawab from Iraq. The Egyptian diva Um Kalthoum sang their poetry and was revered. Then darkness. The 1991 Gulf War demoralized and atomized the Arab world. Secular dissenters continued to meet in the cafés of Damascus, Baghdad, Beirut and Cairo, but could speak only in whispers. Elsewhere, mosques became the organizing centres for a confessional resistance to the New Order and the Great Satan that underpinned it.

The state media networks continued to broadcast propaganda of the crudest kind; criticism of government was unheard of. Then, in 1996, Al Jazeera arrived. It is, as Mohammed El-Nawawy and Adel Iskandar explain in their new book,[1] a TV news channel that defies taboos and prohibitions. Arab viewers abandoned the state networks overnight and Al Jazeera's newsreaders and talk-show hosts became instant celebrities.

Nothing like this had been witnessed since the early 1960s, when nationalist radio stations in Cairo, Baghdad and Damascus issued daily incitements to listeners to topple every crowned head in the region. The Jordanian king was nearly overthrown and the Saudi monarchy seriously destabilized. In both countries, Western aid helped to crush the nationalist revolts. Al Jazeera has no such ambitions: those running the channel are only too aware that a crowned head, the eccentric Emir of Qatar, provides the funds and the headquarters for their operation. The Emir has also allowed the US to construct the largest military base in the region, which boasts a recently completed 13,000-foot runway to handle heavy bombers. Iraq will no doubt be attacked from this base while on Al Jazeera commentators denounce US aggression.

The idea of a semi-independent Arab TV network was first suggested by BBC World Service journalists, and supported by the Foreign Office. A deal was signed with Orbit Radio and Television Service to provide a news programme in Arabic for Orbit's Middle East channel. But Orbit was Saudi-owned, based in London, and its financiers were unwilling to allow news bulletins critical of the Saudi kingdom. The project collapsed in April 1996 after footage of a public execution in that country was broadcast. The BBC retired hurt and the Arab journalists who had been made redundant began to search for a new

1   Mohammed El-Nawawy and Adel Iskandar, *Al Jazeera: How the Free Arab News Network Scooped the World and Changed the Middle East*, Cambridge, MA: Westview Press, 2002.

home. They were lucky. Their quest coincided with a change of ruler in the tiny state of Qatar.

In 1995, the old emir, a traditionalist, was deposed by his son, Hamad bin Khalifa al-Thani, who promised to modernize the statelet. Starting with a dramatic gesture, he abolished the ministry of information. Learning of the collapse of the BBC venture, he offered the journalists a headquarters in Doha and $140 million to restart operations. Sheikh Hamad's father and grandfather had together owned 452 cars, including some hand-built for them. A TV station must have seemed cheap by comparison, and has given the sheikhdom more visibility and prestige than it has ever had. Encouraged by the response to his action, Hamad allowed women to vote and to stand as candidates against men in the municipal elections of 1999. This was a shot across the Saudi bows and was recognized as such.

Virtually none of the journalists who came to work for the new channel was a local. The Syrian-born Faisal al-Qasim, Al Jazeera's most controversial host and now one of the most respected journalists in the Arab world, studied drama at Hull and spent a decade as the anchor of the BBC's Arabic Service. His show, *The Opposite Direction*, features political debates and confrontations conducted with an intensity rarely seen on Western networks. When I met him in Abu Dhabi he had just finished an interview with the local paper and was fending off other journalists and well-wishers. I asked whether the complaints about his show had started to drop away. 'They never stop,' he replied. 'People can't believe that I choose the guests and the subjects. No authority has ever tried to influence or censor me and I have much more freedom than I ever did at the BBC.'

In the early days, the Qatari Government received at least one official complaint about the channel every day from fellow Arab Governments – 500 in the first year alone. Gaddafi withdrew his ambassador from Qatar after the station broadcast an interview with a Libyan opposition leader; Iraq complained when the channel revealed the amount of money that had been spent on Saddam Hussein's birthday celebrations; Tunisia was angry at having been accused of human rights violations; Iranian newspapers resented 'slurs' against Ayatollah Khomeini; Algeria cut off the electricity in several cities to prevent its citizens from watching a programme that accused its army of complicity in several massacres; Arafat objected to Hamas leaders being interviewed, and Hamas was angered by the appearance of Israeli politicians and generals on *The Opposite Direction*.

The Saudi and Egyptian Governments were enraged at criticisms made by dissidents on Al Jazeera. As loyal allies, both countries have had a relatively good press in the West. Before September 11 it required the death of a Westerner in Saudi Arabia to focus attention on that kingdom, but the furore never lasted long. Over the last decade, the Saudis have spent hundreds of millions of pounds to keep Western and Arab media empires and their employees on-message. Al Jazeera's broadsides were viewed as treachery. Riyadh and Cairo put massive pressure on Qatar to muzzle the station, but the emir ignored the protests and his government denied that the channel was the instrument of Qatari foreign policy.

During its early years, Al Jazeera was warmly welcomed in Washington and Jerusalem. Thomas Friedman, the *New York Times* columnist, celebrated the birth of the station with a bucketful of praise: it marked, he said, the dawn of Arab freedom. Ehud Ya'ari was similarly complimentary two years ago in the *Jerusalem Report*: 'Out of a modest, low-rise prefab, five minutes' drive from the Emir's diwan, the tiny Sheikhdom of Qatar is now producing a commodity much in demand in the Arab world: freedom.' The channel's 'powerful video signals', he continued, 'are gradually changing the cultural and political order in the Middle East'.

What happened last September put a stop to these eulogies, especially after Al Jazeera broadcast interviews with Osama bin Laden and his Egyptian deputy, Ayman al-Zawahiri. The bin Laden interviews were banned on Western TV on the spurious grounds that they might contain coded instructions for future terrorist hits. In fact, it was because bin Laden's soft features undermined the portrayal of him as evil incarnate. A senior TV producer in Berlin complained to me last October that his ten-year-old son, after seeing bin Laden on the news, had remarked: 'Papa, he looks like Jesus.'

Qatar now came under very heavy pressure to do something about Al Jazeera. Maureen Quinn, the US ambassador, delivered a strongly worded complaint to the foreign minister. It had little impact. In October, Colin Powell was sent to browbeat the emir, who once again defended the freedom of the press and stressed that the state could not interfere with what he described as a 'private commercial operation'. US officials who met Al Jazeera executives were heard politely and told that the channel would be delighted to interview the American president or his nominees: Condoleezza Rice, Tony Blair and Colin Powell were allowed unlimited time to explain their point of view. The effect of these broadcasts on Arab public opinion was non-existent.

When the bombing of Afghanistan began, Al Jazeera was the only TV network sending out regular reports. And so began its dazzling ascent. Its footage was eagerly sought, bought, carefully edited and shown on CNN, the BBC and every major European network. Then the building in Kabul it was using as a temporary studio was bombed, just as a BBC journalist using its facilities had begun to broadcast a live report. He hit the floor and we witnessed the 'accidental bombing' live on our TV screens. When a Belgrade TV station was targeted by NATO forces in 1999, Clinton and Blair admitted the bombing was deliberate, and justified it on the grounds that 'deliberate misinformation' was being broadcast. Qatar could hardly be categorized as an enemy, and so the spin-doctors were far more careful when it came to explaining the bombing in Kabul: the building was targeted, they claimed, because of 'reports' that it had housed al Qaeda suspects, and they hadn't known that it was Al Jazeera's base.

It is on the second front of the 'war against terror', however, that Al Jazeera's coverage has made the most significant impact. After Israeli tanks entered Nablus earlier this month, the channel broadcast a story about the following incident (the description here comes from LAW, a Palestinian human rights organization):

> Khaled Sif (41), who is married and has four children, received a call on his cellular phone. In order to get a better signal he went to the balcony. The moment he reached the balcony, Israeli forces shot him in the head and killed him. After he heard the shot, Muhammad Faroniya, who is married and has six children, went to the balcony. Israeli forces opened fire and also shot Muhammad Faroniya, wounding him in his chest and abdomen. Mahmoud Faroniya, Muhammad's brother, tried to save his brother, but Israeli forces pointed their guns at him and he was prevented from doing so. Muhammad bled to death. According to eyewitnesses, Israeli forces deliberately left Muhammad Faroniya bleeding for ninety minutes.

The daily coverage on Al Jazeera of stories such as this one stands in contrast to what is shown in Europe, let alone the United States. CNN established its reputation during the Gulf War through the work of its correspondent, Peter Arnett, who remained in Baghdad and whose reports of civilian casualties and the bombing of non-military targets enraged the US, with the result that Western governments are now much more careful to control access to information during times of conflict. They also try hard to stop anyone else covering the stories they are trying to suppress.

Having failed to curb Al Jazeera's influence, however, the US is now going to try to mimic its success. With a war in Iraq seemingly imminent – a war about which the West is profoundly divided, and for which there is no support at all in the Arab world – there are plans to launch a satellite channel in Arabic funded by the US Information Service, to which can be added the expertise of CNN and BBC World. The Israelis have already launched their own version, with little effect. The notion that the Arabs are brainwashed and all that is needed to set them right is regular doses of Bush and Blair is to ignore every reality of the region. But the plot is far advanced.

'What will they name their channel,' I asked Faisal al-Qasim. 'The Empire?'

'No,' he said. 'They have a name for it already. Al-Haqiqat.'

That translates neatly into Russian as 'Pravda'.

August 2002

15

MURDER IN THE FAMILY

If cheating in bed was always settled by the bullet, many of us would be dead. Gerald Martin's new biography of Gabriel García Márquez reveals that *Chronicle of a Death Foretold* was based on the murder of the novelist's friend Cayetano Gentile in Sucre in 1951. He had seduced, deflowered and abandoned Margarita Chica Salas. On her wedding day Margarita's husband was told that she was no longer a virgin. The bride was sent back to her family home. Her brothers then found Gentile and chopped his body into pieces. Márquez blamed the socio-moral dictatorship of the Catholic Church.

But of course it is usually women who are killed for breaking codes of sexual conduct. There have been several recent cases in Britain. Banaz Mahmod, a twenty-year-old of Kurdish origin, was murdered in Surrey at the behest of her father because she'd left an arranged marriage and her father didn't approve of her new boyfriend. Iraq has lately seen a spate of such murders. Last month acid was thrown at three women in Basra who were talking to a male friend. Yet Iraq once had the highest proportion of women integrated into every level of society of any Arab country.

And then there is Pakistan. In 2005 Pervez Musharraf pushed through legislation making honour killing a capital offence, yet official statistics admit to 1,261 honour killings in 2006 and half that number again the following year. The actual figures are probably much higher, since many deaths go unreported. 'Women are considered the property of the males in their family irrespective of their class, ethnic or religious group, and the owner of the property has the right to decide its fate,' Tahira Shahid Khan of Shirkat Gah, a group that campaigns for equal rights for women, reported in 1999. Domestic violence too, according to the Human Rights Commission of Pakistan, is 'considered normal . . . A sample survey showed 82 per cent of women in rural Punjab feared violence resulting from their husbands' displeasure over minor matters; in the most developed urban areas 52 per cent admitted being beaten by their husbands.'

Consider the following. A man dreams his wife has betrayed him. He wakes up and sees her lying next to him. In a fury he kills her. This really happened in Pakistan and the killer escaped punishment. If dreams are to be treated as justification for an honour killing, what woman is safe? Since the police and the judicial system regard murder in the family as a private affair, most cases don't get to court even if they're reported. Society, it's said, needs to protect its foundations. So mostly we rely on the information collected by the Human Rights Commission and on courageous lawyers like Hina Jilani and Asma Jehangir, two sisters both of whom have received numerous death threats.

In 1999, Hina Jilani was in her office with Samia Sarwar, a mother of two from Peshawar seeking a divorce from her husband, when Sarwar's mother burst into the room with two armed men in tow and had her daughter shot dead. In 1989 Samia Sarwar had married a first cousin. For six years he beat her and kicked her. But after he threw her downstairs when she was pregnant with their second child, she went back to her parents' house. The minute she told them she wanted a divorce they threatened to kill her. Yet they were educated and wealthy people.

One widely reported murder this year was that of Tasleem Solangi, the seventeen-year-old daughter of a livestock trader in the Khairpur District of Sind. She wanted to go to university and become a doctor like her uncle, but instead agreed to marry a cousin in order to settle a protracted family dispute over property. Her mother, Zakara Bibi, tried to stop her, but Tasleem was determined. Her father-in-law, Zamir Solangi, came to collect her and swore on the Qur'an that no harm would befall her. A month after the marriage, Zakara had a message from her daughter: 'Please forgive me, mother. I was wrong and you were right. I fear they will kill me.' On 7 March, they did. She was eight months pregnant. The Qur'an-swearer accused her of infidelity and said the baby was not his son's. She went into labour, her child was born and instantly thrown to the dogs. She pleaded for mercy, but the dogs were set on her as well and the terrified girl was then shot dead. On this occasion at least there was an inquiry. Her husband was charged with Tasleem's murder and is currently awaiting trial.

Another case much discussed this year is that of five women in Baluchistan who were buried alive in Baba Kot village, about 250 miles east of Quetta, the Baluch capital. Three of the women were young and wanted to marry men they'd chosen for themselves; two older women were helping them. Three male relatives have been arrested. According to the local police chief, the brother of two of the girls has admitted that he shot three of the women and helped bury them, though they weren't even dead. The trial date is awaited.

Traditionalists have always considered love to be something that brings shame on families: patriarchs should be the ones to decide who is to be married to whom, often for reasons to do with property. If you fall in love, the eighteenth-century Urdu poet Mir Hassan explained (more than once), you will be burned by its fire and perish. That is what happened in the Punjabi city of Wah in late October. Modern Wah has half a million inhabitants and Pakistan's largest ordnance factories, but it was once an idyllic village almost floating on water. The streams and lakes that surrounded it attracted the Mughal emperor Jehangir, who stopped there on his way home from Kashmir, and is said to have exclaimed 'Wah!' or 'Wow!', thus giving the village its name. Before that it had been called Jalalsar after one of my forebears, Sardar Jalal Khan, a leader of the Khattar tribe around 800 years ago. His successors wanted to please the emperor and agreed to the name change. I can't imagine that the decision was taken without a fierce struggle (one faction is said to have been deeply hostile to the arriviste Mughals), but those speaking sweetnesses to power won the day.

Jehangir built a beautiful, domed rest-house in Wah, surrounded on all sides by flowing water. In 1639, his son Shah Jehan supervised the landscaping of beautiful water gardens and pavilions. More than half a century ago, I used to play hide and seek here with my cousins. The pavilions were ruins by then, which made them even more magical on a moonlit night. A cousin swore that the ghosts of the Mughals could be seen in the mist on a winter night, but nobody believed her. The caretaker was extremely sharp-tongued, although when talking to my uncles and aunts, he masked his intelligence in language of exaggerated humility. We were never deceived and threatened to expose him if he gave us a hard time.

Other ghosts lurk there now. A mile and a half from the old village, my youngest maternal uncle, Sardar Ghairat Hyat Khan, built himself a house and moved out of the decaying manor house we'd all shared. My Kashmiri great-grandmother, Ayesha, moved with him. Before she became completely blind she was the best cook in the world and my visits were always rewarding. Shortly before I left Pakistan for Britain I went to say goodbye to her. She said: 'I feel a moustache. Is it really you?' 'No,' I replied, trying to make my voice deeper, 'I am a stranger here, but I was told your bakarkhanis tasted like heaven.' Bakarkhanis are a crumbly, Kashmiri version of the croissant. I've not been to my uncle's house for a long time, but I'm told it's in a state of disrepair and crumbling like the bakarkhanis.

In the last week of October, my uncle's granddaughter, Zainab, barely eighteen years old, was shot dead by her brothers, Inam and Hamza Ahmed. Zainab apparently had a lover and despite repeated warnings refused to stop seeing him. She was on the phone to him in her grandfather's house when her brothers pumped seven bullets into her body. I don't know whether her mother, Ghairat's oldest daughter Roohi, whom I last saw when she was about ten, was part of the plot. Whether or not she was involved, I find it deeply shocking that my uncle allowed the young woman's body to be buried that same day without at least insisting that a First Information Report be lodged at the local police station, let alone demanding an autopsy. Zainab deserved at least that. I am told that Ghairat is old and frail, that he was angry and wanted to ring the police, but was talked out of it by his daughter and other members of his immediate family, who collectively recoiled at having to accept the consequences of what they had witnessed. Perhaps his faith in a just and merciful Allah was not as strong as he used to claim. Whatever the reason, it's unacceptable. The body should be exhumed, the murderers arrested and put on trial, as the law requires.

December 2008

16

THE PIN-UP OF LAHORE

Islamabad remains the official capital, but these days real power in Pakistan is exercised from the Punjabi capital of Lahore. This city, dry, warm and abundant, where I spent the first twenty years of my life and which I still love, is always changing, usually for the worse. The old Mall at its lower end, near Kim's Gun, was once the haunt of bohemians of every sort. Poets, artists, left-wing intellectuals, film directors could be seen at their tables in the Coffee House, cursing the dictator of the day or discussing the merits of blank verse as they dipped their samosas in a mint-chilli compote and sipped tea throughout the month of Ramadan. That was more than thirty years ago. Queen Victoria's statue, which once sat in front of the Punjab Assembly building, has long since gone. Some imaginative soul decided to replace history with fantasy. A giant stone Koran is poised precariously on the plinth where the Queen once sat.

The Mall is Lahore's principal thoroughfare, linking the Civil Lines and cantonment of the old colonial city to the bazaars and monuments of the Mughal Empire. It is choked with cars and taxis moving at five miles an hour. A much-favoured taxi and rickshaw pin-up these days, I noticed, is Osama bin Laden. The State Department's 'most wanted terrorist' is well on his way to becoming a Pakistani hero. Contrary to what outsiders may think, his popularity is not confined to the plebeian sections of the city: many middle-class students are searching for extreme solutions in the guise of religion, and not just in Lahore. This city, more than any other, is an accurate guide to what is going on in the rest of the country, because Pakistan, since the defection of Bangladesh, is really an extended Punjab. The provinces of Sind, Baluchistan and the Frontier are sparsely populated and largely tribal.

The latest excitement in Lahore was the opening of PACE, a large supermarket (whose owners include Imran Khan) in Gulberg, once a spacious residential area, which has now succumbed to the lure of small and big businesses. The entrance to PACE attracted more visitors than the goods on display. Peasants with marvellous moustaches, anointed with mustard-seed oil, came from nearby villages with their entire families and packed the foyer. Adults and children, half-fearful, half-excited, screamed with pleasure as they travelled up and down the new escalators. Rather than Lahore in the epoch of globalization, it could have been a scene from turn-of-the-century Paris, were it not for the noise of loudspeakers in competing mosques compelling one to cease work or conversation and plug one's ears.

Not far from PACE, hidden away in a tiny lane, is one of the new architectural glories of Lahore: the Institute for Women's Studies, a residential postgraduate college for South Asian women. The very idea of such a centre has enraged the Beards. But the director of the Institute, Nighat 'Bunny' Khan, remains unperturbed. I wondered which of the country's top architects were involved.

'None of them,' Bunny replied, her gruff voice tinged with pride. 'We decided to commission a woman, Fawzia Qureshi. She's a senior lecturer in architecture at the National College of Art. This was her first big commission.'

Qureshi has used a tiny plot of land to build a structure on three levels which demonstrates an exemplary management of light and space. The essential purpose of the building – what gives it its special character – is to develop sociability and a sense of community. With its courtyard and terraces and seminar rooms bathed throughout the day in natural light, it is a carefully arranged marriage of modernism and Islamic tradition.

But how long can an Institute for Women's Studies last? In Sind and tribal Baluchistan, women are still killed for bringing 'dishonour' to their families. The writ of the Pakistani state does not extend to these regions; and a woman who refuses to marry a man chosen by her father, or who has an extra-marital affair, is despatched summarily. Everyone knows the identity of the killers but the police remain aloof. The murders are seen as a matter for the family and the village elders. Feminist lawyers and human rights activists have tried for many decades to change things, with some success: this was one area where the previous government was enlightened. But the delicate hand that signed a decree setting up more facilities for women also authorized the arming of the Taliban and the assault on Kabul. The present government is pushing through religious laws designed to make women second-class citizens. Hacks in its employ have already begun to denounce Bunny's Institute as a nest of atheists and Communists. The usual tag in these circumstances would be 'lesbian', but the word, I discovered, does not exist in Urdu or Punjabi. No such inhibitions prevent the use of colourful phrases to describe male homosexuality, incest and bestiality.

The last time I was in Pakistan, more than two years ago, the surface calm was deceptive. As I was lunching with my mother in her favourite Islamabad restaurant, a jovial moustachioed figure came over to greet us from an adjacent table. His wife, Benazir Bhutto, was abroad on a state visit. Senator Asif Zardari, State Minister for Investment, was responsible for entertaining the children in her absence and had brought them out for a special treat. An exchange of pleasantries ensued. I asked how things were proceeding in the country. 'Fine,' he replied with a charming grin. 'All is well.' He should have known better.

Behind closed doors in Islamabad, a palace coup was in motion. Benazir was about to be luxuriously betrayed. Farooq Leghari, the man she had carefully chosen to be President, was preparing to dismiss her government after secret consultations with the Army and the leaders of the opposition. During dinner that same week, an old acquaintance, now a senior civil servant, who is fond of Benazir, was in despair. The president, he said, had sought to defuse the crisis by asking for a special meeting with the prime minister. Benazir, characteristically, turned up with her husband. This annoyed Leghari: one of the subjects he'd wanted to discuss with her was her husband's legendary greed. Despite this, he stayed calm while attempting to convince the First Couple that it was not only their political enemies who were demanding action. The scale of the corruption and the corresponding decay of the Administration had become a national scandal. He was under pressure from the Army and others to move against the Government. In order to resist them, he needed her help. He pleaded with her to discipline her husband and a number of other ministers who were out of control. Zardari, stubborn as always in defence of his own material interests, grinned and taunted the president: nobody in Pakistan, he said, including Leghari, was entirely clean. The threat was obvious: you touch us and we'll expose you.

Leghari felt that the dignity of his office had been insulted. He began to tremble with anger. He suggested that the Minister for Investment leave the room. Benazir nodded, and Zardari walked out. Leghari entreated her again to restrain her husband. She smiled and gave her President a lecture about loyalty, and how much she valued it. The people who were complaining, she told him, were jealous of her husband's business acumen. They were professional whiners, has-beens, rogues resentful at being passed over. She made no concessions.

By Pakistani standards Leghari is an honest, straightforward man. He was Benazir's choice as president only because she thought he lacked ambition and would do her bidding. 'He may not be very bright, but his heart is in the right place,' disappointed contenders were told. Earlier this year,

Leghari told me that this meeting, the last of many, had been decisive. He could no longer tolerate her excesses: if she continued in office, the Army would intervene against democracy for the fourth time in the country's history. Reluctantly, he decided to invoke the Eighth Amendment: a gift to the nation from the late dictator, General Zia-ul-Haq, which gives the president powers to dismiss an elected government. New elections were to be held within 90 days.

Corruption was the main charge levelled against Benazir and Zardari. It was alleged that the couple had used Prime Minister's House to amass a large private fortune – reckoned to be in the region of one billion dollars – and transfer their assets abroad. Immediately after Benazir's fall, Zardari was arrested: he still languishes in a Karachi prison, charged with a series of offences for which government lawyers have yet to find proof acceptable even in a Pakistani court, where standards of evidence are exceptionally low. The state has still to find a reliable witness. Zardari's business associates and friends have remained loyal. One of them, the chairman of Pakistan Steel, committed suicide rather than give evidence against his former patron. Some of Benazir's closest supporters – and they exist – insist that her political prestige was squandered by her husband, that he is a fraud, a poseur, a wastrel, a philanderer and much worse. A few weeks ago, addressing a friendly gathering at a seminar in Islamabad, Benazir tried to defend him. He was much misunderstood, she said, but before she could continue, the audience began to shake their heads in disapproval. 'No! No! No!' they shouted. She paused and then said with a sigh: 'I wonder why I always get the same reaction whenever I mention him.'

I don't think Zardari was the only reason for her unpopularity. The People's Party had done little for the poor who were its natural constituency. Most of her ministers, at national and provincial level, were too busy lining their own pockets. Infant mortality figures remained unchanged through the whole of her time in office. Permanently surrounded by cronies and sycophants, Benazir was isolated from her electorate and oblivious to reality. In the General Election that followed her removal from power, the People's Party suffered a humiliating defeat. The Pakistani electorate may be largely illiterate, but its political sophistication has never been in doubt. Disillusioned, apathetic and weary, Benazir's supporters refused to vote for her, but they could not bring themselves to vote for the enemy. The Muslim League won a giant majority (they hold over two thirds of the seats in the National Assembly), but 70 per cent of the electorate stayed indoors.

Lahore has been the home town of the Sharif family, which now rules Pakistan, since 1947. They were blacksmiths in East Punjab (now in India) and sought refuge in the new Muslim homeland. They worked hard. Their foundries prospered. They had no interest in politics. One day in 1972, Benazir's father, Zulfiqar Ali Bhutto, was advised to nationalize the Sharif family enterprise. It was an economically inept decision, but it pleased party loyalists and distracted attention from Bhutto's failure to push through badly-needed land reforms. The landlords, of course, were only too pleased to support half-baked nationalizations of industries large and small. Muhammed Sharif, the family patriarch, became a sworn enemy of Bhutto. When General Zia took over in July 1977, the Sharif clan cheered loudly. When Zia ordered the execution of Bhutto after a rigged trial, the Sharif family gave thanks to Allah for answering their prayers.

Thus the rivalry between Bhutto's daughter, Benazir, and Muhammed's son, Nawaz, has rich antecedents. Nawaz Sharif became a protégé of Zia's and was brought into politics at the dirty end of the Inter-Services Intelligence (ISI), the most powerful institution in the country. Today, he is the elected prime minister of Pakistan. His brother, Shahbaz Sharif, is the chief minister of the Punjab and their Abaji ('dear father') amuses himself in his dotage by sponsoring the appointment of old cronies as ambassadors. He even selects the president of the country. The current incumbent, a bearded simpleton called Rafiq Tarrar, is one of Abaji's factotums. What makes Tarrar dangerous is his sympathy for an extremist Muslim sect, the Ahle-Hadis, which has its own armed wing.

Of the two brothers, Shahbaz is regarded as the more sophisticated politician, and it is now an open secret that Washington would like to swap the brothers round, sending Shahbaz to Prime Minister's House and giving Nawaz his old job in Lahore. The US Embassy has organized a visit to Washington for Shahbaz to meet Sandy Berger at the White House. A swap would make sense, but in order to effect the change, Abaji will have to be won over.

Little has changed since the Sharif brothers won the last election. Corruption, spreading from the top down, is now so extensive that visiting economists from the World Bank and IMF are shocked. Local wits express dismay at the news that Nigeria heads the list of the world's most corrupt countries. 'Even here,' they say, 'we can't quite make it to the top. Why didn't we bribe the agency compiling the statistics?' The elite, led by the politicians, continues to loot the country's wealth. Benazir's gang has had its turn and now it's that of the Brothers Sharif. Less than one per cent of the population pays income tax. The politicians, many of whom are landowners, refuse to countenance a serious agricultural tax. State-owned banks have been forced by successive governments to lend money to politicians, landlords and businessmen, and discouraged from retrieving it. Bad bank loans stand at 200 billion rupees ($£1 = 85$ rupees) – the rough equivalent of 70 per cent of total public revenue. Pakistan will mark the new millennium with a foreign debt of $42 billion and a domestic debt of $70 billion: the combined figure is $50 billion higher than GDP.

While I was there, the Army was asked by the government to take over the Water and Power Development Authority (WAPDA), and ensure that all electricity bills were paid on time. Soldiers arrived at every house to read the meters and discovered ingenious methods being used to slow down the meter, or to steal electricity directly from the supply system by circumventing the WAPDA wires. Interestingly, most of those involved in such schemes could afford to pay their bills: one of them is a wealthy landowner who is also a minister in the Sharif government. Despite the evidence, she continues to plead her innocence and has not, so far, been asked to resign. In some ways this is the most useful thing the Army has done in Pakistan, and if one were convinced that interventions of this kind could reduce corruption and chicanery, one would welcome the Army taking over the Inland Revenue and various other departments of state. But past experience has shown that officers and soldiers soon get the hang of corruption. It's said that Nawaz Sharif, on Abaji's advice, has kept the Army at bay by bribing corps commanders with money-bags containing a crore of rupees (a 'crore' = ten million) for each general. Someone suggested that the corps commanders should now be known as crore commanders.

The country meanwhile continues to rot. A state that has never provided free education or health care can no longer guarantee subsidized wheat, rice or sugar; nor can it protect innocent lives from random killings. Pakistan's largest city, Karachi, has been involved in a virtual civil war for a decade, with Urdu-speaking children of the refugees who trekked to the new homeland from India in 1947 waging war on indigenous Sindis as well as on the government. Several thousand from all sides have died in armed encounters. In these conditions people have to fend for themselves. The suicide rate is soaring, especially among the poor, driven to insanity by their inability to feed their children. In January a transport worker in Hyderabad who had not been paid for two years went to the Press Club, soaked himself in petrol and set himself alight. He left behind a letter:

'I have lost patience. Me and my fellow workers have been protesting the non-payment of our salaries for a long time. But nobody takes any notice. My wife and mother are seriously ill and I have no money for their treatment. My family is starving and I am fed up with quarrels. I don't have the right to live. I am sure the flames of my body will reach the houses of the rich one day.'

It is the abdication of its traditional role by a corrupt and decaying state, combined with the surreal neoliberal economic prescriptions handed down by the politburos of the IMF and World Bank, that has created the space for political Islam. In successive general elections people have voted against hardline religious parties. (The Pakistani electorate casts proportionately fewer votes than the Israeli electorate for religious extremists.) Until now, Islamism has derived its strength from state patronage, rather than popular support. The ascendancy of religious groups is the legacy of General Zia, who received political, military and financial support from the United States and Britain throughout his eleven years as dictator. The West needed Zia to fight the Afghan war against the former Soviet Union. Nothing else mattered. The CIA, for example, turned a blind eye to the sale of heroin to fund the Mujaheddin, and the number of officially registered heroin addicts in Pakistan rose, from 130 in 1977 to 30,000 in 1988.

In the same period, a network of madrassahs (religious boarding schools) was established throughout the country. Initially, most of these were funded by foreign aid from a variety of Islamic sources. Since board and lodging were free, it was not only the children of Afghan refugees who flocked to them: poor peasant families were only too happy to donate a son to the madrassah. It would be one mouth fewer to feed at home, and the boy would be educated: as they saw it, he might find a job in the city, or, if he was really lucky, in one of the Gulf States.

These schools, however, had no interest in education in a secular sense: what they provided was a new kind of 'religious scholarship'. Together with verses from the Koran (to be learned by rote), the children were taught to banish all doubts. The only truth was divine truth and the only code of conduct was to be found in the Koran and the Hadith. Virtue lay in unthinking obedience. Anyone who rebelled against the imam rebelled against Allah. The madrassahs had a single function: they were nurseries designed to produce fanatics. The primers, for example, stated that the Urdu letter *jeem* stood for 'jihad'; *tay* for *tope* ('cannon'); *kaaf* for 'Kalashnikov' and *khay* for *khoon* ('blood'). The older pupils were instructed in the use of sophisticated hand weapons and taught how to make and plant bombs. ISI agents provided training and supervision. They also observed the development of the more promising students, or *taliban*, who were picked out and sent for more specialized training at secret army camps, the better to fight the holy war against the unbelievers in Afghanistan.

Pakistan's oldest Islamic party, the Jamaat-i-Islami, grew in influence during the Zia years. Its leaders assumed that they would run the madrassahs. The party has always prided itself on its cadre organization, based on the Leninist model of small cells, and has shunned mass membership – although this may have been because it, in turn, was shunned by the masses. With the advent of the madrassahs, its leaders thought their time had come – the students, they believed, were all potential recruits – but they were to be disappointed. Since dollars were freely available thanks to the war, different Islamic factions emerged and began to compete with each other for mastery in the schools and a division of the spoils. The ISI became the arbiter of intra-religious disputes and favoured some groups against others.

For a time the Afghan war consumed the energies of the rival religious groupings. After the first, Cold War version was over, the Pakistani state refused to accept a coalition government in Afghanistan. It was Benazir Bhutto's government that unleashed the Taliban, backed by Pakistan Army commando units, in an attempt to take Kabul. The US, fearful of Iranian influence in the region, supported the decision. The dragon seeds sown in 2,500 madrassahs produced a crop of 225,000 fanatics ready to kill and die for their faith when ordered to do so by their religious leaders. General Naseerullah Babar, Pakistan's minister for the interior, confided to friends that the only solution to the Taliban menace inside Pakistan was to give the extremists their own country and this, he said, was what he had decided to do. The argument was disingenuous at the time, but in the light of what has happened over the last two years, he deserves to be tried as a war criminal.

With the Cold War at an end, the militant Islamic groups had served their purpose and, unsurprisingly, the US no longer felt the need to supply them with funds and weaponry. Overnight they became violently anti-American and began to dream of revenge. Pakistan's political and military leaders, who had served the US loyally and continuously from 1951 onwards, also felt humiliated by Washington's indifference. 'Pakistan was the condom the Americans needed to enter Afghanistan,' a retired general told me. 'We've served our purpose and they think we can be just be flushed down the toilet.'

The Pakistan Army – one of the Pentagon's spoilt brats in Asia – was loath to see the country relegated to the status of Kuwait. That was the meaning of last year's nuclear tantrum. It had the desired effect: Pakistan is back on the 'B list' of countries in the US State Department. On 29 November, Foreign Minister Sartaj Aziz attempted to soothe Western opinion. 'I see no possibility of an accidental nuclear war between Pakistan and India. Pakistan has an effective control and command system.' This is pure nonsense, but even if it were true, imagine what would happen if the Taliban took over the Pakistan Army. Every political leader in Pakistan is aware of the danger. Nawaz Sharif is trying to pre-empt political Islam by stealing some of its clothes, but this is a tactic that rarely works.

The irony of the present situation is that religion in the Punjab was always a relaxed affair. The old tradition of Sufi mysticism, with its emphasis on individual communion with the creator and its hostility to preachers, had deep roots in the countryside. But the annual festivals at the tombs of the Sufi saints, during which the participants sang, danced, drank, inhaled bhang and fornicated to their hearts' content, as they had done for centuries, were forbidden when General Zia placed the country under martial law. In their place came a peculiarly non-Punjabi form of religious extremism, approved by Washington, funded by Saudi petro-dollars and carefully nourished by Zia.

Ninety per cent of Pakistan's Muslims are Sunnis. The rest are mainly Shi'as. The Sunnis themselves are divided into two major schools of thought. The Deobandis represent orthodoxy. The Barelvis believe in a more synthetic Islam, defined and changed by local conditions. For many years their disputes were literary, or took the form of public debates. No longer. Every faction now lays absolute claim to Islam. Disputes are no longer settled by discussion, but by machine-guns and massacres. Some Deobandi factions want Shi'ism declared a heresy and the Shi'as physically eliminated. A war between the sects has been raging for nearly three years. The Sunni Sipah-e-Sahaba (Soldiers of the First Four Caliphs) have attacked Shi'a mosques in the heart of Lahore and massacred the faithful at prayer. The Shi'as have responded in kind. They formed the Sipah-e-Muhammad (Soldiers of Muhammad), got Iranian backing and began to exact a gruesome revenge. Several hundred people have died in these intra-Muslim massacres, mainly Shi'as.

In January this year, an armed Taliban faction seized a group of villages in the Hangu district of Pakistan's North-West Frontier. They declared the area to be under 'Islamic law' and promptly organized the public destruction of TV sets and dish antennae in the village of Zargari. This was followed by the burning of 3,000 'obscene' video and audio cassettes in the small square in Lukki. There is something comical in this hostility to television – it reminds me of a Situationist spectacle in the sixties – but humour is not something associated with the Taliban. 'The hands and feet of thieves will be chopped off and all criminals brought to justice in accordance with Islamic laws', the leader of the movement, Hussain Jalali, announced after the burning of the TV sets.

Jalali's aim is to extend the Afghan experience to Pakistan. 'What can we do?' a supporter of the Sharif brothers asked me, wringing his hands in despair. 'These bastards are all armed!' I pointed out that some of the bastards were being armed by the government to create mayhem in neighbouring Kashmir, and that our bloated Army was also armed. Why wasn't it asked to disarm these groups? Here the conversation ended. For it is no secret that religious extremists have penetrated the Army at every level. What distinguishes the new extremists from the old-style religious groups is that they want to seize power, and for that they need the Army.

Ahle-Hadis, one of the most virulent groups, is a creation of the ISI. It wants to see the Saudi model implanted in Pakistan, but without the monarchy. It has supporters and mosques everywhere, including Britain and the US, whose aim is to supply cadres and money for the worldwide jihad. This group is drawn from the most orthodox of the Sunni sects; it doesn't have a mass following, but it does have Rafiq Tarrar's support, and government ministers grace its meetings. Its sub-office is at 5 Chamberlaine Road in Lahore. I was tempted to go and interview them, but the sight of thirty heavily-armed guards made me change my mind. The group's armed wing, Lashkar-e-Tayyaba (Soldiers of Medina), could not exist without the patronage of the Army. It has a membership of 50,000 militants and is the leading participant in the jihad to 'liberate' Indian Kashmir. Its 'soldiers' are trained by the Army at eight special camps in Azad (Pakistani-controlled) Kashmir, funded by Saudi Arabia and the Pakistan government. The movement recruits teenagers from poor families for the holy war, and has lost several hundred members in Kashmir. The government pays 50,000 rupees (about £600) for each corpse returned from the battlefield: 15,000 go to the family of the 'martyr' and the rest helps to fund the organization.

The Harkat ul-Ansar (Volunteers Movement), once funded by the US and backed by the ISI, was declared a terrorist organization by the State Department last year, and promptly changed its name to Harkatul Mujahn. Its fighters were among the most dedicated Taliban and it has shifted its training camps from the Punjab to Afghanistan. Osama bin Laden is its leader. He continues to maintain close contacts with the ISI and his supporters have warned the government that any attempt to abduct him or ban his organization would lead to an immediate civil war in Pakistan. They boast that the Army will never agree to be used against them because it contains too many of their supporters.

Both these groups want to take over Pakistan, but not in harness. Each dreams of an Islamic Federation, which will impose a Pax Talibana stretching from Lahore to Samarkand, but avoiding the 'Heretics' Republic of Iran'. For all their incoherence and senseless rage, their message is attractive to those who yearn for some semblance of order in their lives. If the fanatics promise to feed them and educate their (male) children, they are prepared to forgo the delights of CNN and BBC World.

The alternative to an Islamic Federation is to mend the breach with India. The recent visit to Lahore of the Indian prime minister, Atal Vajpayee, was welcomed by business interests and an otherwise critical press. There is a great deal of talk about a new permanent settlement: an EU-style arrangement incorporating India, Pakistan, Bangladesh and Sri Lanka, an opening of the frontiers and a no-war pact between India and Pakistan. This is undoubtedly the most rational solution on offer, but it would necessitate the disarming of the Lashkar-e-Tayyaba and other groups. The Indian Prime Minister demanded that this be done as a gesture of goodwill. 'Disarm us if you can,' the Lashkar-e-Tayyaba retorted. 'If you do, we will have to do now what we were planning to do in two years' time. It's up to you.' It is this desire for a head-on clash, whatever its probable outcome, that distinguishes the new wave of Islamic militants in Pakistan. Mercifully, they still constitute a minority in the country, but all that could change if nothing else does.

April 1999

17

ANYONE FOR GULLI-DANDA?

The cricket matches I grew up with in the Indian sub-continent during the forties and fifties lasted five days. The players were dressed in immaculate white or off-white flannels, the ball was dark red and the spectators were well-dressed and sedate. It was no different in the West Indies: English cricket was everywhere the model. Our heroes were the great English batsmen and bowlers of the time. There were great Australians, too, but, we joked, they were only Englishmen twice removed – once from prison and once from England.

I always envied the apparently carefree life of the street children who played cricket the whole day long during the idyllic winter months from November till March. One year, when my parents were abroad, I bunked off school for a week to play with the street teams. It was bliss, even though I wasn't very good and knew the only reason I had been allowed to play was that I had a new cricket ball – then, as now, a rare luxury.

When the street kids weren't playing cricket, they played a game known as gulli-danda, using branches hacked off roadside trees or stray pieces of wood discarded by the shopkeepers. The gulli is a small wooden stake with pointed ends. When you lay it flat, the pointed ends rise slightly above the ground. The danda is a medium-sized stick with which you hit one end of the stake so that it jumps up in the air. As it comes down to about shoulder-level, you strike it really hard with the stick to make it go as far as possible. This isn't as easy as it sounds: timing and eye-hand coordination are critical and you need a lot of practice to become an expert player. As they approached their teens, the more gifted gulli-danda players graduated effortlessly to cricket.

They shone in the matches between rival street-teams, usually played on dusty patches of earth and to a fixed over limit, though the teams were always bowled out before the overs were up. A number of these street cricketers could have gone far, but in the newly independent sub-continent the colonial mode persisted as much in cricket as in the officers' mess and the gymkhana clubs, where civil servants gathered every evening for scotch and political gossip, just as the British had done.

In the first decades after Independence, cricket became more popular, but without any change in its character. Old habits were not easily displaced and at the top level the game remained polite, dominated by the middle and upper classes who still deferred to English ways. Ordinary people were confined to playing in the streets and shouting bawdy comments from the stands during a test match. In the lunch interval of the first tests in Pakistan, there was a display by military bands. The sight of young, hairy-legged Punjabis and Pathans dressed in kilts and playing bagpipes greatly amused English journalists, though we took them for granted. Even now the sound of bagpipes reminds me of the first cricket matches I watched from the Victorian pavilion in the lush green field of the Lawrence Gardens (now the Jinnah Gardens), where Majid Khan's father (and Imran Khan's uncle), the stern-faced Dr Jehangir Khan, used to open the innings, and where, in a crucial test match between India and Pakistan in the fifties, our most exciting batsman, Maqsood, was dismissed one run short of his century. I also remember the nostalgia when the Indian team arrived in Lahore. For my parents' generation, it was a small, temporary, reversal of the ethnic cleansing that had accompanied Partition. In those days the Indian team was greeted warmly by the crowd.

Until fairly recently, test umpires belonged to the country hosting the match and their role in deciding the outcome of a game was often critical. On one occasion in Peshawar in the fifties, when a partisan Pakistani umpire, Idris Beg, raised his finger every time the captain, A. H. Kardar, appealed for lbw (leg-before-wicket), the visiting English team, who'd been drinking after the match, decided on a public-school-style punishment: Idris Beg was captured, debagged and dunked in a swimming pool. British umpires used to be accused of bias tinged with racism by visiting teams from the West Indies and the sub-continent. I once tried to explain the rules of cricket to a young Chinese Communist, a former Red Guard who had become disillusioned and fled to Hong Kong, where, to his amazement, he discovered that some of the local Chinese, including a supporter of the fledgling Democracy Movement, played the game. He listened intently, asked questions, and then fell silent. I assumed he was bored but I was wrong. 'Could you explain something to me?' he asked with a frown. 'Who selects the umpires?' He had grasped at once that a partial umpire could turn the game. It was thanks to Imran Khan, and despite fierce objections from the English, that the principle of neutral umpires in test matches was eventually accepted by the authorities.

The history of cricket is the history of the former colonies overtaking their imperial masters. Cricket, C. L. R. James said, is a metaphor for the Empire: one way of undermining the colonists was to beat them at their favourite game. It was this that fuelled the rise of Australian, West Indian and subcontinental cricket, and, later, mass participation in the game. In the thirties, English sensibilities were offended by the Australians, Don Bradman especially. By the sixties, it was the turn of the West Indies' fast bowlers. They were too fast, too hostile and bowled too many bouncers. Could it be, the fogeys whispered to each other in the Long Room at Lord's, that the blacks had a special gene which enabled them to bowl so fast? Something had to be done, and the white knights of cricket imposed a rule which made it illegal to bowl more than two bouncers an over. They would never get away with that now.

World cricket has changed. The resurgent power is the sub-continent. Cricket is an obsession in India, Pakistan and Sri Lanka. Under Indira Gandhi there was a growth of self-confidence on the part of the underclass in the big towns, and the change of mood had its effect on cricket, which discarded its colonial wardrobe, became more democratic and began to wear the colours of nationalism. In Sri Lanka in the eighties cricket was a release for both the Tamils and the Sinhalese engaged in a debilitating civil war, and it wasn't long before Sri Lanka's incredible batsmen exploded onto the world scene.

The social composition of the Pakistan cricket team began to change after the military dictatorship was toppled in 1969. This process was accelerated when Imran Khan took charge and used his prestige to cut through bureaucracy and cronyism. He encouraged talented young players who had no connections with wealth or with the functionaries in control of the game, and the emergence of players such as Wasim Akram, Waqar Younis and Inzamam-ul-Haq was a direct result. Today, a young boy in a dusty street can see boys slightly older than himself transformed into superstars. The gulli-danda days are over. The kids now play cricket with a tape-ball – an old tennis ball encircled with red insulating tape. The bounce of the tape-ball is unpredictable. Its tendency to deviate as it hits the ground helps to develop batting reflexes and encourages unorthodox styles. The tape-ball forces bowlers to work harder on their wrist technique, since a tennis ball has no seam to make it swing naturally. Ijaz Ahmed, Shahid Afridi, Wasim Akram, Saleem Malik and Yousuf Youhana all grew up playing tape-ball cricket.

These former street players led Pakistan to victory in the 1992 World Cup. Modelled on its football equivalent, this tournament has become the most important event in cricket, easily eclipsing the annual ritual slaughter of the English by the Australians. It also marks the dominance of one-day cricket over the five-day game. The beauty of five-day cricket is that an accomplished team can be beaten by mediocre opponents lucky enough to have a captain with the strategic skills of a chess player. Victory is rarely certain and a drawn match used to be taken as a satisfactory and honourable outcome. When they began, one-day cricket matches with limited overs were regarded as a frivolous side-show, a disruption that had to be tolerated because it drew bigger crowds and more sponsorship money. This was not my mother's view. Monumental impatience had always prevented her from enjoying a five-day match. One-day cricket consumes less time and generates more excitement. Purists were inclined to disagree, but they, too, have been won over by the sheer energy of the fifty-overs game.

Robert Winder's *Hell for Leather* is an account of a trip to India, Pakistan and Sri Lanka in 1996, when these countries were staging the World Cup. Winder found a sub-continent in love with cricket. The contrast with England could not have been more pronounced. His prose, mellifluous when describing South Asian cricket, turns caustic when he writes about his own team. The English manager, Ray Illingworth, is typically graceless and petty, always finding an excuse for the team's churlish behaviour on or off the field. He is slow to appreciate the brilliance of the Sri Lankans. Why, the despairing Winder asked, did England produce so many 'bad-tempered cheese-and-pickle types who played too much, ate too much, drank too much, travelled too much and complained too much. Goodness knows, we had plenty of money, plenty of grounds, plenty of players, plenty of everything. But all these other countries just seemed to have more zip. It didn't seem fair. Boo-hoo.'

England did not do well in the World Cup they hosted last month. The West Indies, too, failed to reach the semi-finals. Theirs was an old team, far too dependent on the triumvirate of Ambrose, Walsh and Lara. How would C. L. R. James have explained this failure? Is West Indian cricket in permanent decline, now that the young have lost interest in Britain? It seems they feel the pull of the United States and aspire to be baseball and basketball stars.

> James: What is it about these tiny little islands in the Caribbean where cricketers seem to grow on trees? They drop like ripe fruit and give us such pleasure. We produce the most amazing batsmen and bowlers with very little effort. I have often thought about this. What is your explanation for this, Vivian?
>
> Richards (smiling): Er, well, yes. I mean. You're right.

I watched this year's World Cup hoping for a repeat of Pakistan's 1992 triumph. The star of the tournament was a Pakistani boy from the streets, Shoaib Akhtar, who bowls at 96 mph. He was discovered by a group of casual onlookers, who alerted Ramiz Raja, a batsman who has played in the national team (and a member, like Imran Khan, of the old Aitchison College cricket elite). Raja went to face Shoaib in the nets. He was scared and impressed and recommended him to Majid Khan and the selectors. Shoaib was given his chance.

The Pakistan team was young, although captained by a veteran, Wasim Akram. It was inexperienced, erratic, petulant, but also very exciting to watch. At the Oval, where they played Zimbabwe, the fans were ebullient, alternately cheerful and critical. Why did Ijaz Ahmed get himself run out so stupidly? Some juicy Punjabi abuse was hurled at the departing batsman's head. Several theories sprang to life around me, each involving a conspiracy of one sort or another. When I suggested that Ijaz might simply have made a mistake, I was told by my good-humoured neighbours that I was naive and didn't know anything about Pakistani cricket. But Pakistan defeated Zimbabwe, which meant that India was out of the World Cup. 'India's going home,' the fans chanted joyously.

But when India beat Pakistan at Old Trafford, angry Pakistan fans had surrounded the team coach and waved tenners at the team to suggest that they had deliberately thrown the match. I was not convinced, but I did begin to wonder when they lost to Bangladesh. The fans had no doubts. It was all about money, filthy money from the betting syndicates in Bombay, Karachi and Dubai. Bangladesh's victory, I was told, had been bought by Bangladeshi businessmen, desperate to give their fledgling team a boost. The celebrations in Dhaka were phenomenal. History, politics and sport had merged and a large banner proclaimed: 'Pakistan's second defeat: 1971 & 1999'.

It is rare for a whole team to be bought: usually, a single player is sent detailed instructions. He must bowl three no-balls in his third over, for example, or make sure he is out after scoring sixteen runs, or some other agreed variant. Buying a few players is known as 'spread-betting'. The effect is to demoralize the entire team. Some players have families who can barely afford one meal a day. What do they do if a syndicate makes them an offer of 30 lakh rupees (nearly half a million pounds) for bowling several bad overs in a given match? And if the offer has come through a senior player who might victimize them if they refuse, the choice is simple.

In the Lahore High Court, a one-man tribunal consisting of Justice Malik Mohammed Qayyum is considering whether some members of the national team are corrupt. The tribunal was established last year at the request of the Pakistan Cricket Board and its chief, Majid Khan. The tribunal made extensive inquiries and took sworn evidence from players such as Rashid Latif, a former wicket-keeper in the Pakistan team. Disgusted by the scale of the corruption, Latif had secretly taped conversations between leading players. A decision was delayed, probably under government pressure. In public Justice Malik said that he did not wish to damage the team until the World Cup was over. There were strong indications that all would be forgiven if Pakistan won the Cup.

But they did not win. The final against Australia was a sad, one-sided match. Having unwisely decided to bat, Pakistan collapsed. Its top-order batsmen could not resist the Australian attack. The middle order crumbled. Shane Warne may have looked unplayable, but Pakistan's batsmen didn't try very hard. The demoralized bowlers, feeling the game was in any case lost, failed to retrieve the situation. Wasim Akram said that they were outplayed and there was nothing more to it. I think, on this occasion, he was telling the truth, but very few people in Pakistan agree with me. The news of the defeat brought angry crowds onto the streets of the major cities (the recent clashes with India over Kashmir have failed to produce comparable shows of feeling). Unable to accept that this Pakistan team could lose to anyone, the crowds assumed the worst. For them the real victors were not Australia, but the betting syndicates.

When Wasim Akram became successful in the mid-nineties, his brother decided to become a bookie. A mid-life decision to change professions was greeted with cynicism by the Pakistani public. After the World Cup, Wasim's house in Lahore was stoned. There were demands for him to be tried by a military tribunal. 'We'll hang you when you return, you fat motherfucker,' the fans chanted outside star batsman Inzamam's bungalow in Multan as they smashed all its windows. The team delayed its departure from London for a few days in the hope that their security could be guaranteed. When they finally landed at Karachi airport, a thousand armed policemen were waiting to protect them from the wrath of several thousand fans chanting 'Hang Wasim!' Inzamam's brother was allowed into the VIP lounge to collect him. They emerged to find that their brand-new car had been set on fire. Wasim's mother issued a statement accepting that some punishment might be necessary if her son were found guilty of any misdemeanours, but pleading for him not to be hanged. When Pakistan was beaten by India in Bangalore in 1996, it was said that Wasim Akram had failed to play in the match, not because he was ill, but on the instructions of a betting syndicate. Fans kidnapped his father and held him hostage for a few days. Perhaps that is why this time his mother decided to launch a pre-emptive strike.

The tribunal is now active again, and Prime Minister Nawaz Sharif – no slouch himself when it comes to making a bit on the side – has said that his tame Accountability Commission (a body formally set up to deal with corruption, which in reality settles accounts with political enemies and intimidates Pakistan's press barons) will also investigate the allegations against the team, though it is unlikely that Wasim Akram will be found guilty and sent to prison. Pakistani intelligence agents, deputed to keep an eye on the team during the World Cup, have reported visits to casinos and bars in the evenings. Had the team beaten Australia, they could have fornicated, gambled, drunk whisky and taken all the drugs they wanted. They would have been revered by the Pakistani people, who feel that cricket players, unlike politicians, are of their own kind. And their sins would have been washed clean by the obligatory stopover at Mecca on their way home.

July 1999

18

CRICKET AND MONEY

The BBC's decision to stop showing cricket in the late 1980s was brought about by a combination of the cricket establishment's greed, misplaced sporting priorities on the part of public broadcasters and, according to some, strong pressure from Margaret Thatcher, who was determined to help Rupert Murdoch build up his television empire. Within a few years there was no live cricket left on terrestrial television. Numerous addicts, myself included, were forced to admit defeat, sign the document of surrender to Sky and offer our collective shilling to Murdoch. It is now impossible to watch live cricket without subscribing to Sky. The cricket season is now global; it has neither a beginning nor an end, which can be severely disruptive of the rest of one's life. If you want to watch matches between South Asian teams, you have to pay an additional fee to Zee TV (India) and ARY (Pakistan). The creation of the Indian Premier League (IPL) last year, and the extravaganza that accompanied it, forced cricket fanatics to buy a temporary subscription to Setanta Sports. Watching cricket is now more expensive than the BBC licence fee.

Yet all this is trivial compared to the big changes that have taken place since the turn of the century. For many years after the end of empire, the Marylebone Cricket Club (MCC), together with the wild colonial boys in Australia and, for a time, white South Africa, dominated the international scene. The Brits made the key decisions and went unchallenged. The

West Indies have too many fast bowlers who are difficult to bat against? Change the law: restrict the bouncers to one an over. Pakistan's seamers can reverse-swing an old ball? They must be cheating: turn the cameras on them and watch every move. So it went on, with the help of a few umpires who found it difficult to rise above ancient prejudices. Mike Marqusee was harsh but accurate when he wrote in *Anyone but England* (1994) that 'the hypocrisy of the English takes root early in cricket, and is one of the things that makes English cricket English – the way it lies about itself to itself.'

In 1956 an MCC team visiting Pakistan, and not doing at all well, were incensed by a series of lbw (leg-before-wicket) decisions awarded to Pakistan's star bowler by the Pakistani umpire Idris Beg. Back at their hotel after the game, as *Time* magazine reported, the English players drowned their sorrows and decided to hunt Beg down. When they found him, they invited him back to their hotel for 'a little private party'. Beg declined, so the players took him anyway – according to Beg – dislocating one of his arms in the process. At the hotel, Beg recounted later, the cricketers doused him with water and forced him to swig some whisky. Not until a team of Pakistani cricketers heard about Beg's ordeal and descended on the party was he rescued from his hosts. (An uncle of mine, who often umpired first-class matches and had observed Beg's behaviour at first hand, told us that 'Beg was a disgrace. Every time Kardar, Pakistan's captain, appealed he raised his finger.')

The next day Beg turned up with his arm in a sling. The MCC dismissed the night's adventure: 'Just banter, old boy. Pure banter.' But Pakistani students paraded in the streets shouting: 'MCC, go back! Long live Idris Beg!' Police searched spectators for weapons, and stood guard over the visiting Brits during play. The English press cheered on. Imagine if it had happened to an English umpire at the hands of the Pakistani team. Many years later, in the 1980s, when one of India's great batsmen, Sunil Gavaskar, declared that it was no big deal playing at Lord's and that he wasn't interested in MCC membership, his remarks were greeted with shock. (I was delighted.)

The ICC had been set up in 1909, as the Imperial Cricket Conference, when South Africa was admitted to test match status and challenged the Anglo–Australian duopoly. It governed by consensus: there would be a discussion, and at the end of it the English chairman got his way. In 1964 the ICC became the International Cricket Conference, but until 1989, the president of the MCC was still automatically made chairman.

By the 1990s the balance of power had shifted. Sixty per cent of the world's cricketing revenue was by then being generated in South Asia. India has a population of a billion, and cricket is its national sport. The Board of Control for Cricket in India (BCCI), riled by long years of English arrogance and condescension, decided it was time to rid itself of the Raj. By this time they had learned enough tricks of the trade from the old colonial bosses and were ready to declare independence. The nervousness at Lords was captured in Mike Atherton's comments in the *Sunday Telegraph*:

> India are the big beast of cricket and everyone is frightened of both their bark and bite. Their rise to dominance began in 1983 with an unexpected World Cup victory over the mighty West Indies . . . It was a sweeping change to the balance of power but one that took England . . . a long time to appreciate . . . Malcolm Speed, the chief executive of the ICC, found himself in a position much occupied by Kofi Annan and the United Nations in recent years: being bullied by a superpower for whom the notions of international law and collective responsibility have long ceased to have any meaning.

In 1996, after what an Australian cricket official referred to as 'a decidedly ugly ICC meeting', Australia and England considered mounting a counter-coup. What had upset them was that South Africa had jumped ship and sided with India. Graham Halbish, a former CEO of the Australian

Cricket Board, revealed that there had been acute concern that 'India, Pakistan and Sri Lanka, with the unexpected support of South Africa and Zimbabwe, were forming a powerful alliance with the potential to take over international cricket.' In *Run Out* (2003), he described how he was 'given the extraordinary task of drawing up a plan . . . so secret and highly sensitive, that it even had a codename – Project Snow'. It was an attempt to split the ICC, so that Australia, England, New Zealand and the West Indies would play each other but nobody else. Halbish was sure that this 'contingency plan would allow us to keep satisfying our television networks, sponsors and crowds'.

Better heads prevailed; the South Asians made a few cosmetic concessions (such as rotating the chairmanship) and a split was averted. The ICC's function today is straightforward: it determines the rules and structure of world cricket and makes decisions that are binding on its members. I thought of Project Snow as I watched the England and Wales Cricket Board (ECB) notables led by its chairman, Giles Clarke, and flanked by English cricketing legends (all Sky employees), lining up to greet Sir Allen Stanford's helicopter as it landed on the nursery ground at Lord's in 2007. The Texas-born, Caribbean-based billionaire (as he was described before we learned that much of his capital was fictitious) was greeted like a monarch. The fantasist from the Antiguan St John's was not in a mood for compromise and proceeded to describe the test cricket played in St John's Wood as 'boring'. The future, as far as he was concerned, lay with 'Twenty20', the shortest version of the game, and no doubt with the rah-rah girls imported from Ukraine and elsewhere whom he thought necessary to enliven proceedings.

In Twenty20, each team plays only one innings, batting for a maximum of twenty overs; the game is completed in about two and a half hours. The IPL is already a massive popular success; the global broadcasting rights alone will earn the BCCI $1 billion over the next ten years. It was felt by some in the English cricketing establishment that a rival competition was badly needed; after all, Twenty20 started out as an English innovation. The plan was simple: to set up a Twenty20 super-series to rival the IPL, which had paraded virtually every non-English cricketing star in several Indian cities before huge and cheering crowds. It would be supervised by the ECB and funded by the Stanford millions.

England's star player, Kevin Pietersen, was signed up as a Stanford ambassador, and appeared happy enough in news photographs. (Now he informs the media that he was always dubious and regarded Stanford as a 'sleazebag'.) A hurried exhibition match between England and the West Indies was organized at Stanford's private club in Antigua last November. The players on the winning team were each promised $1 million. The West Indies (playing as the Stanford Superstars) duly won, but five of the players agreed to let Stanford invest the money on their behalf. They were foolish, but not as foolish as the Antiguan government whose economy is closely linked to Stanford's enterprises, or the Venezuelan oligarchs who used the Stanford Bank in Caracas to launder money.

It was only after the US Securities and Exchange Commission accused Stanford of 'massive and ongoing' financial fraud that the ECB decided to break off all links with him. The proposed Twenty20 rival to the IPL lies in ruins. Project Snow was a childish response to the cricket establishment's loss of hegemony: this most recent debacle is the result of thoughtless greed. In a sense it's unfair to single out the ECB. 'Soft-touch regulation' was the order of the day under Thatcher and her ghastly New Labour mimics. Why should the ECB be any different? True, allegations of one kind or another regarding Stanford's business practices had been doing the rounds for a number of years, and in 2007 the Stanford Group Company was fined $20,000 for violating disclosure norms; but nobody really cared. None of it was unusual in the world of fictitious capital laid bare by the current crisis.

Like in the world in which it is played, much has changed in cricket. The cheating – the betting scandals and the disgraced captains: Hansie Cronje, Mohammed Azharuddin, Wasim Akram et al – are the least of it. A bookie, Hanif Cadbury, was murdered in South Africa, where he had fled after testifying before Justice Qayyum's inquiry into match-fixing in Pakistan: he had spilled the beans about the bookies and how the cricketers collaborated with them. Some of this, as John Major revealed in *More Than a Game*, his accomplished history of cricket, is not exactly new. Extensive match-fixing took place in nineteenth-century Britain, when cricket as we now know it was being invented.

What of the onfield changes? Jean-Marie Brohm, a French sociologist, has described all sport as 'a prison of measured time'. Looked at that way, five-day test cricket is the equivalent of a life sentence. And yet test matches can be tenser and more stimulating than any other form of the game, even when they end in a draw – a possibility that is excluded in shorter forms, where a result is vital. It's fogeyish, of course, to say that things were better in the past, but there is a serious argument here. Fifty-overs-a-side one-day cricket can be enjoyable, but Twenty20 is cricket's answer to the penalty shoot-out: its outcome depends too much on luck. The main thrust behind globalized cricket is commercial, and few bother to hide the fact. It is organized by the money-wallahs and TV schedulers: floodlit night matches, played to secure prime-time audiences, are increasingly common.

Then there are the commentators who vie with each other to see who can dumb down the most, competing with mini-skirted dancers hired to do the cancan when a boundary is scored or a six hit into the crowd. Making a fool of oneself when Twenty20 matches are being played is par for the course: I almost forgot to mention that some of the fielding side are fitted with microphones so that they can be interviewed in the course of the game. The message is clear: 'We don't take it seriously and you shouldn't either. We're only trying to inject a bit of fun into the game and get the young more interested' – though this has never been a problem in South Asia or Australia. There is, of course, lots of money to be made. Most cricketers are underpaid, and I'm in favour of their being paid more, not least because it would reduce the influence of the betting mafias on the stars, which has come close to wrecking the game altogether. One reason the public stopped turning up for test matches in some parts of the world was a deep suspicion that the results had already been decided.

Test cricket at its best has the qualities of an exquisitely choreographed ballet. To watch the great spin bowlers – Abdul Qadir, Shane Warne, Muttiah Muralitharan, Anil Kumble – bowl at the same batsman for over an hour, varying each ball till they trap their victim, is to delight in their artistry. It can also be boring and predictable; but so can its abbreviated offspring, for all its frills.

When the IPL circus first began, with Bollywood stars and Indian corporations getting franchises, I feared the worst. The hoopla, the slavish commentary by overpaid pundits and the unending shots of the IPL commissioner, Lalit Modi, preening like an Indian god minus the make-up, all this was truly awful, but the cricket was exciting and I was hooked. The new season, which begins in five weeks, will be a bit different. No Pakistani players are appearing, because the Indians backed out of touring Pakistan after the Mumbai atrocities. The Australian captain, Ricky Ponting, is staying at home to rest and prepare for the Ashes later in the summer. Of the two English players bought in the IPL slave auctions for over £1 million each, Andrew Flintoff is injured – he might not be able to play in the remaining tests against the West Indies, but can't afford to miss the IPL – and Pietersen is sulking, having lost the Stanford dosh. So he'll go to India and pocket the million. Were he still captain of England he would have been better advised to follow Ponting's example, but the ECB determined otherwise.

Will the economic crisis have more long-term effects on the game? Undoubtedly. Stanford and his English chums were brash, but they were not alone. Their rivals in India are now confronting problems of their own. Last year's IPL champions were the underdog Rajasthan Royals, captained by Shane Warne with energy and skill. They have yet to find a sponsor this year, as the insurance giant Bajaj Allianz has pulled out. Other teams are facing similar difficulties. Much of the TV money, including a ten-year deal with Sony-WSG, is still in place, though Sony is not finding it easy to sell advertising for the series, and Big TV and Pepsi have ended their IPL deals. By the end of this year, it's being said, the Bollywood brigade may well pull out from the field, taking their sponsors with them.

Meanwhile the Chinese government has decided that its youngsters should learn how to play cricket, just in case the shorter version becomes an Olympic event. Former test players from South Asia, especially Pakistan, have been hired to go and act as coaches. If cricket were to take off in China, the ICC would be forced to shift its headquarters to Shanghai and the biggest cricketing event of the sporting calendar in 2030 would be the annual India-China test series. Who knows? Chinese helicopters might be provided with a permanent pad at Lord's.

February 2009

19

AFTER LAHORE

The immediate casualty of the terrorist attack on the Sri Lankan cricket team in Lahore in March 2009 will be the future of cricket in Pakistan. A few optimists point out that the Munich massacre didn't bring the 1972 Olympics to a halt. But I doubt whether even Zimbabwe could now be induced to come and play at the Gaddafi Stadium in Lahore. Who can blame them? Pakistan's captain, Younus Khan, who scored a triple century in the Karachi test a few days before the atrocity, is in mourning. 'When I was a boy,' he said,

> I loved watching Imran Khan, Javed Miandad and Wasim Akram playing against great teams from overseas. It is because of them, seeing them play, that I also played the game. But what if no one comes to Pakistan? How will the youngsters know about the game? What will they do? It would be very easy right now for the ICC and the bosses to say there will be no cricket in Pakistan, but the future will not be good if cricket is taken away from my country.

Many from less educated backgrounds would say the same. Cricket is extremely popular in the slums. Pakistan will now play against foreign teams only in foreign countries, every home match now also an away match. Many poor families have no electricity, let alone television sets. No cricket for them.

Who did this and why? Many questions (as with the murder of Benazir Bhutto) will remain unanswered. Who unleashed these monsters and, more important, was any intelligence operative aware of what was being plotted? Pakistan's intelligence-gathering agencies, civilian and military, employ more than a quarter of a million people. Their agents have infiltrated many, if not all, of the armed groups operating in the country. Since these groups were set up by the intelligence agencies in the first place, it would be surprising if, as is sometimes claimed, all the links had been broken. They are and will no doubt long remain the most toxic assets of the state apparatus.

The largest of these groups, Lashkar-e-Tayyaba, denied all responsibility. It would. Its leader, under post-Mumbai house arrest, promised to help track down the culprits. There is speculation that the attack was the work of a breakaway faction, angry that its leaders and activists should have been interrogated at India's behest. Others insist that it was India's revenge for what happened in Mumbai. Averting their eyes from something too painful to acknowledge, Pakistan's TV stations (usually quite good) point a collective finger at India. Kamran Khan, the anchor of a current affairs show on Geo TV, was clear: 'No need to guess. The identity of the terrorists is evident. Also, it is crystal clear where they have come from. Pakistan now should not sit idle. Instead she should highlight the issue at international forums the way India highlighted Mumbai.' Talat Hussain, a rival talk-show host on Aaj TV, went for a junior minister who'd had the temerity to point out that there was no evidence of an Indian hand behind the attack: 'Why are you taking such a soft position?' Hussain asked the minister. 'Is it possible to have a bigger enemy than India?'

There can be no return to normality if things don't change in Pakistan itself. And there are no easy solutions, only problems. First, the military is seriously divided and any escalation of the war in Afghanistan will only exacerbate these divisions, as Obama's advisers know full well. When the US senator Dianne Feinstein blurted out last month that the drones targeting Pakistani villages, or 'terrorist havens', near the Afghan frontier, were being fired from US bases inside Pakistan, there was surprise and anger in the country. The half-hearted denials by a government whose president is himself viewed as a drone convinced nobody. Within days Google Earth images of the bases in Pakistan were circulating widely on the web. There were no further denials.

Since 9/11, personnel from the US Defense Intelligence Agency have had access to Pakistan's nuclear facilities. The US has repeatedly assured Israel that it has installed PALs, or Permissive Action Links, supplemented by a dual-key safety mechanism, in Islamabad's command and control system that make it impossible for any rogue commander to use it without special code authorization from Pakistan's civilian leader (Allah help us). In Pakistan some claim that US experts have inserted a 'dead switch' into the PALs, which freezes the system just like 'stalling a stolen car from a remote position'. The Israelis still aren't satisfied, however, and want Washington to get Pakistan to give up its nuclear weapons – which might be easier if Israel and India were to set an example.

Second, the civilian government is a complete disaster. When I was in Islamabad a few weeks ago, I was given strictly off-the-record details of two sordid transactions involving President's House. If my informants are right, Zardari and his cronies are back to business as usual, making money and spiriting funds abroad. Meanwhile, religious extremism prevails in the Northwest, while a secular mafia rules Karachi, the largest city, where law and order is non-existent. Last month Zardari dissolved the provincial parliament in the Punjab, sacking the Sharif brothers, his political rivals, who are now mobilizing their supporters on the streets and courting arrest. Were this to escalate into clashes with the police and the paramilitaries, the army would probably be compelled to move in. Zardari is now rehabilitating the defeated and discredited Chaudhrys of Gujarat. What of their former patron? General Musharraf is just back from a successful US tour and, like Tony Blair, has been offered a campus sinecure to give him time to brief a ghost-writer and hasten the appearance of his memoirs. Instead, the general, realizing that he is now more popular than Zardari, is campaigning to share power with him. There is talk of a permanent military takeover, with a civilian façade and a new presidential constitution. Domestic chaos might well lead to institutional change designed yet again to ensure that nothing really changes.

The third problem is the United States, which is now seeing the results of its failure to have an exit strategy from Afghanistan. On 25 February Richard Holbrooke showed up at a Brookings Institution event optimistically titled 'Pakistan: Dream Deferred or Denied?' Stephen Cohen, an expert on the Pakistan military and a senior fellow at the institution, painted a grim picture of the situation in Pakistan. The country, he said, was unravelling at a rapid pace and the US could lose control. If Cohen's analysis was accurate, Holbrooke commented there and then, the policy the new administration had agreed on was largely misguided. He promised to be there for the follow-up discussion, but didn't show up. Since this was Washington, nobody cared about the cricket.

March 2009

20

THE NEW EMPIRE LOYALISTS

Exactly one year before the hijackers hit the Pentagon, Chalmers Johnson, a distinguished American academic, staunch supporter of the US during the wars in Korea and Vietnam, and one-time senior analyst for the CIA, tried to alert his fellow-citizens to the dangers that lay ahead. He offered a trenchant critique of his country's post-Cold War imperial policies: 'Blowback,' he prophesied, 'is shorthand for saying that a nation reaps what it sows, even if it does not fully know or understand what it has sown.

'Given its wealth and power, the United States will be a prime recipient in the foreseeable future of all of the more expectable forms of blowback, particularly terrorist attacks against Americans in and out of the armed forces anywhere on earth, including within the United States.'

But whereas Johnson drew on his past, as a senior state-intellectual within the heart of the American establishment, to warn us of the dangers inherent in the imperial pursuit of economic and military domination, former critics of imperialism found themselves trapped by the debris of September 11. Many have now become its most vociferous loyalists. I am not, in this instance, referring to the belligerati – Salman Rushdie, Martin Amis and friends – ever-present in the liberal press on both sides of the Atlantic. They might well shift again. Rushdie's decision to pose for the cover of a French magazine draped in the stars and stripes could be a temporary aberration.

His new-found love for the empire might even turn out to be as short-lived as his conversion to Islam.

What concerns me more is another group: men and women who were once intensely involved in left-wing activities. It has been a short march for some of them: from the outer fringes of radical politics to the antechambers of the state department. Like many converts, they display an aggressive self-confidence. Having honed their polemical and ideological skills within the Left, they now deploy them against their old friends. This is why they have become the useful idiots of the empire. They will be used and dumped. A few, no doubt, hope to travel further and occupy the space vacated by Chalmers Johnson, but they should be warned: there is already a very long queue.

Others still dream of becoming the Somali, Pakistani, Iraqi or Iranian equivalents of the Afghan puppet, Hamid Karzai. They, too, might be disappointed. Only tried and tested agents can be put in power. Most one-time Marxists or Maoists do not yet pass muster. To do so they have to rewrite their entire past and admit they were wrong in ever backing the old enemies of the empire – in Cuba, Vietnam, Angola, Afghanistan or the Arab East. They have, in other words, to pass the David Horowitz test. Horowitz, the son of communists and biographer of the late Isaac Deutscher, underwent the most amazing self-cleansing in post-1970s America. Today he is a leading polemicist of the Right, constantly denouncing liberals as a bridge to the more sinister figures of the Left.

Compared to him, former Trotskyists Christopher Hitchens and Kanan Makiya must still appear as marginal and slightly frivolous figures. They would certainly fail the Horowitz test, but if the stakes are raised and Baghdad is bombed yet again, this time as a prelude to a land invasion, how will our musketeers react? Makiya, recently outed in this paper as 'Iraq's most eminent dissident thinker', declared that: 'September 11 set a whole new standard . . . if you're in the terrorism business you're going to start thinking big, and you're going to need allies. And if you need allies in the terrorism business, you're going to ask Iraq.'

Makiya's capacity to spin extraordinary spirals of assertion, one above another, based on no empirical facts and without any sense of proportion, becomes – through sheer giddiness of fantastical levitation – completely absurd. Not a single US intelligence agency has managed to prove any Iraqi link with September 11. For that reason, in order to justify a war, they have moved on to other issues, such as possession of 'dangerous weapons'. Not even Saddam's old foes in the Arab world believe this nonsense.

Hitchens reacted more thoughtfully at first to the New York and Washington attacks. He insisted that the 'analytical moment' had to be 'indefinitely postponed', but none the less linked the hits to past policies of the US and criticized George Bush for confusing an act of terrorism with an act of war. He soon moved on to denounce those who made similar, but much sharper criticisms, and began to talk of the supposed 'fascist sympathies of the soft left' – Noam Chomsky, Harold Pinter, Gore Vidal, Susan Sontag, Edward Said et al. In recent television appearances he has sounded more like a saloon-bar bore than the fine, critical mind that blew away the haloes surrounding Henry Kissinger, Bill Clinton and Mother Teresa.

What unites the new empire loyalists is an underlying belief that, despite certain flaws, the military and economic power of the US represents the only emancipatory project and, for that reason, has to be supported against all those who challenge its power. A few prefer Clinton-as-Caesar rather than Bush, but recognize this as a self-indulgence. Deep down they know the empire stands above its leaders.

What they forget is that empires always act in their own self-interest. The British empire cleverly exploited the anti-slavery campaigns to colonize Africa, just as Washington uses the humanitarian hand-wringing of NGOs and the bien-pensants to fight its new wars today. September 11 has been used by the American empire to re-map the world. European continental pieties are beginning to irritate Cheney and Rumsfeld. They laugh in Washington when they hear European politicians talk of revitalizing the UN. There are 189 member states of the UN. In 100 of these states there is a US military presence. For UN, read US?

Neoliberal economics, imposed by the IMF mullahs, has reduced countries in every continent to penury and brought their populations to the edge of despair. The social democracy that appeared an attractive option during the cold war no longer exists. The powerlessness of democratic parliaments and the politicians who inhabit them to change anything has discredited democracy. Crony capitalism can survive without it.

At a time when much of the world is beginning to tire of being 'emancipated' by the US, many liberals have been numbed into silence. One of the most attractive aspects of the US has always been the layers of dissent that have flourished beneath the surface. The generals in the Pentagon suffered a far greater blow than September 11 in the 1970s, when tens of thousands of serving and former GIs demonstrated in front of it in their uniforms and medals and declared their hope that the Vietnamese would win. The new empire loyalists, currently helping to snuff out this tradition, are creating the conditions for more blowbacks.

Counterpunch
March 2002

21

HYBRIDITY AND ALL FOOLS DAY

An innovative critique of April Fools Day is, to say the least, problematic. The anguish and antinomy confronting much of English culture clearly manifests itself in the lacunae of this particular *œuvre*: to discuss April within a specific conjuncture poses real problems, of course, within the framework of the contradiction between informative analysis and analytical information. Could the vulgar English obsession with All Fools Day be treated simply as a *lapsus* in a larger epistemological crisis? Or as the late, great Italian Marxist philologist, Sebastiano Timpanaro, posed the problem in his astute critique of Freud's psychopathology: why *exoriare ex nostris ossibus ultor* rather than the original text? It is a good question, whose underlying verisimilitude is incontrovertible and which sharply poses the dichotomy between Kant and Hegel that Marx was grappling with in April 1843 . . .

The origins of April are unclear. Could it be derived from 'aperire', 'to open', or from Aphrilis, itself derived from Aphrodite, the Greek name of Venus from whom 'to open' is also derived? Why? One has to return to treasured days of youth and boyhood for an answer, and for that a Proustian memory is critical. Let's try another possibility. April could have been the Roman imperial response to Ostara, the pagan Saxon goddess who gave Easter a special tingle. Hegel or Kant? Venus or Ostara? To be trapped within this postmodern paradigm is no longer necessary. We now know that Aprilochus was the day of the penis in Byzantium: references to the

235

sport and reconstructed penii can be seen in the Reykjavik Penis Museum, one of the key attractions of Iceland, after which a dip in the snow (which locals refer to as 'April Showers') becomes essential for both gay and straight visitors.

In medieval Egypt, one day was set aside for the populace to elect its own sultan, who would then ride on a donkey to the palace of the real sultan and speak his mind. This was also an April event, and hugely popular. As a special favour the fool playing the sultan was allowed to play with the donkey for one night. This passion for donkeys, itself a direct result of gender segregation, later spread to Persia. In the twentieth century of the Christian era, believers in the Islamic Republic were severely reprimanded by the late Ayatollah Khomeini, shocked on his travels in rural Iran to encounter so many disoriented donkeys. Imagine a donkey's chorus at the Royal Opera House: 'Please Cry for Us Ayatollah'.

[This is an extract from a longer text first submitted to *New Left Review* in April 1977, but rejected on grounds of taste by the Editor, a Mr Robin Blackburn. It was subsequently rejected by *Les Temps Modernes* in Paris, *Kursbuch* in Berlin, and *Rinascita* in Italy. Its first publication in *Drawbridge* (1 April 2006) is a sign that the realm of freedom has at last arrived.]

22

CINEMA IN THE MUSLIM WORLD

It is as difficult to define or classify Islamic cinema as it would be a Christian, Jewish or Buddhist one. The language of cinema has always been universal. Interpretations vary. Censors had different priorities: in 1950s Hollywood a married couple could not share a double bed and had to be clothed. In South Asia, the censor's scissors clipped out kisses from Western films. The birth of commercial and art movies did not remain confined to the West for long.

The Lumière brothers first exhibited moving pictures in Paris in 1896. A year later there was a private showing at the Yildiz palace in Istanbul. The viewers consisted of the Ottoman Sultan or Caliph – the temporal and spiritual leader of Sunni Islam – and a few selected courtiers. In 1898 the Ottoman public was let in on the secret, and there was a screening in the beer hall in Galatasaray Square. During the next decade cinema halls sprouted like wild mushrooms, and audiences in Istanbul and Smyrna flocked to see everything. Cultural repression began soon after the First World War, in 1919: Ahmet Fehim's films were considered politically provocative and censored by the British occupying authorities.

With the birth of post-Ottoman Turkey, the new industry found a staunch supporter in Latifa Usakligil, the feminist wife of Kemal Atatürk (the marriage lasted two years, from 1923–5). Where Istanbul led, Cairo followed. And Bombay was not far behind. Muslim stars dominated the formative years of Bollywood even though, like Jews in Hollywood, many changed their names to appease the dominant Hindu population. Yusuf Khan became Dilip Kumar, Meena Kumari was once Mahajabeen and it was an Afghan woman, Mumtaz Begum, who entranced audiences as Madhubala. Alone among his colleagues in defying convention, the popular comic actor, Badruddin Kazi, mocked the studio bosses by adopting the Christian name of a much-favoured imperial tipple: Johnny Walker.

When Pakistan was carved out of India's rib in 1947, it was assumed by some that Bollywood's Muslim stars would defect to the new state and thus boost the Lahore film industry. But Lollywood did not happen. The Pakistan government decided to help its cinema by banning film imports from India. The result was a disaster. Commercialism stifled creativity. Since nobody could see Indian movies, Pakistani producers shamelessly plagiarized the Bombay original. Nor could Pakistan produce anything that even remotely resembled the work of Satyajit Ray or Mrinal Sen. Then in the late 1950s and 60s, the military rulers sealed off the country from 'subversive' influences. Hollywood reigned supreme.

A decade later, when Pakistan had its first secular, elected, civilian government, women were encouraged to study and seek employment, but the cinema remained heavily veiled. It had little to do with Islam as such, since the same postcolonial rules were in operation in neighbouring India. On-screen kisses were forbidden. Bosoms could heave but had to be carefully covered and, even at the beach, actresses swam fully clothed. Cinema proprietors in Pakistan decided to spice their shows with a 'tota' (strip). In Lahore, touts would parade outside some movie theatres and whisper to bystanders that a 'one-minute strip' was being shown at the late-night performance. The prowling males would pack the show and halfway through some boring movie, a minute or two of porno-flicks would appear on the screen. After this the cinema emptied.

That was a long time ago. Pakistani movies are still awful. A new low point was reached in 1990 with *International Guerrillas*, which glorified jihadi militarism and vilified Salman Rushdie – the equivalent of Hollywood trash depicting Muslims as terrorists. The 'plot' centred on a gang of Islamist Pakistanis who raid the secure facility where Rushdie is being kept safe. Much violence follows, but the evil Rushdie is killed through divine intervention. The film was a box-office flop. More popular were the porn DVDs that are easily available. Their procurers do a roaring under-the-counter trade, particularly in Islamist strongholds like Peshawar and Quetta. Unsurprisingly, a fair proportion of the bearded militants who spend the day painting veils on billboard actresses settle down that same evening to watch some comforting porn.

It's different in Indonesia, the world's most populous Muslim nation, where only last year the censors passed *Arisan*. The film's plot revolves around an architect's eventual coming out as a gay man. The censors passed a movie depicting male homosexuality and featuring a gay kiss, without exciting a backlash from local clerics. Likewise in Tajikistan, where Djamshed Usmonov's latest film, *Angel on the Right*, depicts sexual, social and political frustrations (infidelity, drunkenness, corruption) without any problems. The style of his films, strongly influenced by Soviet film schools, reflects the strengths of that tradition.

It is clerical Iran that has produced the most vibrant and remarkable cinema of today. Not since the French New Wave have auteurs from a single country dominated the art-cinema market. Compelled by circumstances (like their Communist-bloc counterparts of the 1960s) to rely on symbolism and allegory, Iran's film-makers have produced a varied range of high-quality cinema. One reason for this is the rich intellectual tradition in the country, that transcended the kitsch world of the Shah as much as it does bearded puritanism. The novels of Sadegh Hedayet – especially his masterwork *The Blind Owl* – have a Kafkaesque quality: his heroes are intense loners, floundering in a sea of anguish, remote from those who rule the country. Ahmed Shamlu's poetry was more optimistic in tone, but staunchly oppositional. These writers influenced many of Iran's film-makers – before and after Khomeini's triumph.

Abbas Kiarostami, the father of the Iranian New Wave, is a graduate of Tehran University's faculty of fine arts who sees cinema as an art form no different from painting or sculpture. Landscape and architecture are as important as the actors. Each viewing uncovers something new. The end is usually enigmatic. Different interpretations are always possible. In *Taste of Cherry* (1997) a man is trying to commit suicide, but in a calm and dispassionate fashion. When the censors objected, Kiarostami explained that the movie was really about the different choices involved in living out each day. The suicide was incidental. Not exactly my reading of the movie.

The cinematic language and interior destiny of each Iranian film-maker is different, the international influences on them vary from Rossellini to Fellini, Kurosawa to Hou Hsiao-hsien; but there is a strong sense of solidarity. Even the self-contained Makhmalbaf family sees itself as part of a larger community. They view and comment on each other's work, they help each other artistically and politically.

Jafar Panahi's latest film, *Crimson Gold*, illustrates the process. Panahi was on his way to Kiarostami's exhibition of photographs when he heard of a double killing that had taken place that day in an upmarket jewellery store in Tehran. He was so upset that he left the exhibition. Later he and Kiarostami excavated the story behind the incident. Why had a poor, demobilized veteran from the Iran–Iraq war, now turned pizza delivery man, shot a jeweller and then taken his own life? Kiarostami agreed to write the script for Panahi. The result is a neorealist masterpiece, where fragments taken from a raw reality are seen in relation to the overall class structure of contemporary Iran.

Jafar Panahi is, in some ways, Iran's most fearless film-maker. In *The Circle* he depicted the oppression of women with a rare sensitivity. The religious police are back in action in *Crimson Gold*, waiting to pounce on unmarried young women on their way out of a mixed party where we can see them, silhouetted against the window, dancing and enjoying themselves. It is this daily interference in social relations between the sexes that has completely alienated young people from the clerics. Although, as *Crimson Gold* reveals, underlying all this is a society where the divide between rich and poor increases every month.

Kamal Tabrizi's *Marmoulak* (*The Lizard*), released in the UK this week, satirizes the mullahs. A convict (known as 'the Lizard') escapes from a prison hospital disguised as a mullah. He takes the train to a border town where they are expecting a new mullah. The Lizard has watched enough Iranian television to pick up the clerical style, but he becomes an ultra-humanist cleric, encouraging doubt, analysing Tarantino movies, both surprising and delighting his audience. This film slipped past the censors and played to packed cinemas throughout the country. When mullahs began to be addressed publicly as lizards, panic gripped the cultural establishment and the film was rapidly withdrawn.

This independent, critical school of non-conformist Iranian film directors has risen up against falsehood and irrationality, producing a cinema that has no rivals in the West today. And religion? It is visible in many guises in some of these films, but never centre-stage and never official.

Guardian
April 2005

Part Three

FAREWELLS

23

LEOPOLD TREPPER

Tribute to a departed revolutionary

In January 1982, we learnt of the death of a seventy-seven-year-old Pole in Jerusalem. His name was Leopold Trepper. Few will have heard of this old man: maybe some old Indian communists might remember him. Trepper made his reputation when he ran the most effective spy network for Soviet military intelligence during the Second World War: he even had an agent in the highest circles of the Nazi apparatus. The Gestapo characterized Trepper's agents as 'the red orchestra' and referred to the old fox himself as 'the conductor'. The information supplied by Trepper resulted in crushing defeats for the Nazis. It was his network that warned the Soviet high command of the offensive against Stalingrad, and enabled the Red Army to prepare itself for the siege.

Leopold Trepper was born in Nowy Targ, a small town in Poland, in 1904. At the age of ten he saw a 'Russian spy' being arrested. The 'spy' had a 'little red beard and a big cap tilted over his forehead'. The local Jewish shopkeeper who had extended credit to the 'spy' and his wife was the butt of many a village joke till 1918 when one day he received a letter. It said: '*Please accept my apologies for leaving without paying you in 1914, owing to difficult circumstances. The money is enclosed. Vladimir Ilyich Lenin.*' This is Trepper's first political memory. He joined a left-wing Jewish group, much influenced by Marxism and the Russian revolution. In 1923 he participated in the Cracow general strike and was blacklisted by his employers. He left for Palestine, saw the conditions under which the Arabs lived, understood their oppression and moved leftwards.

In 1925 he joined the Palestine Communist Party and became the secretary of its Haifa branch. He was sent for further studies to Moscow where he attended lectures given by Zinoviev, Radek and Bukharin. Bukharin was the most popular lecturer, and Trepper was later to quote Stalin's future victim as saying: 'Every time the students applaud, it brings me closer to my death.' Like many others of his generation, Trepper believed in the idea of world revolution. Like other Polish communists he became a 'spy' to further that cause. It is, after all, not pure coincidence that the three most powerful and intelligent Soviet spies during the thirties were extremely cultured communist revolutionaries. Trepper and Ignace Reiss were Poles, Richard Sorge was a German.

Ignace Reiss saw through Stalinism. He made the fatal mistake of sending a letter to Stalin informing him of this fact, stating that he thought Trotsky was correct, and returning his medals. Stalin did not bother to reply to the letter. He simply ordered Reiss's liquidation: he was shot dead in Switzerland.[1] Sorge was based in Tokyo where he sent back information giving the exact date of the German invasion of the Soviet Union. His report was disregarded. Sorge was desperate for Stalin to believe him and took incredible risks to send more evidence (he had an agent in the Nazi embassy in Tokyo), but was caught. The Japanese offered him in exchange for their agents, but Stalin refused and Sorge was executed.

Trepper's network was finally broken after a major Gestapo offensive. The 'conductor' was arrested, but managed to effect a spectacular escape.

---

1   My novel *Fear of Mirrors* is a fictional reconstruction of the life and death of Ignace Reiss.

On his return to the Soviet Union he was imprisoned by Stalin. His old boss, General Berzin, had been disgraced and executed as a 'Trotskyite' and Trepper saw, for the first time, the ugliness of the Stalinist system. He was subjected to anti-Semitic jibes by his jailers and underwent mental torture of the worst kind.

He was released in 1954 and his family, who had thought him dead, were overjoyed to see him. But Trepper's trials weren't over. He was given permission to return to his native Poland in 1957. He rejoined the Communist Party and participated in the Polish spring, which erupted after the Poznan demonstrations of 1956. Trepper was shaken to discover that Polish nationalism and Catholicism were reproducing anti-Semitism. Having experienced the Gestapo at first hand, he was staggered to find that prejudice existed even after the experiences of the Warsaw ghetto. The heroism of the 'red orchestra' was soon 'discovered' by the Polish and East German press, but Trepper alone noticed the hypocrisy which celebrated his past successes while doing nothing to combat contemporary anti-Semitism.

After the Six-Day War of 1967, the nationalist General Moczar orchestrated a series of supposedly anti-Zionist demonstrations, which brought every anti-Semite onto the streets underneath the slogan 'Send the Kikes back to Dayan'. The old man was hurt that this could take place in a self-proclaimed socialist state. 'I became a communist because I am a Jew', he was to write in his memoirs some years later. 'In my contact with the workers of Dombrova, I had seen the extent of capitalist exploitation. In Marxism, I found the definitive answer to the Jewish question that had obsessed me since childhood. In my judgement only a socialist society could put an end to racism and anti-Semitism.'

Half a century on from this realization, Trepper was to discover that Stalinist Poland was far removed from socialism. For protesting, he was placed under house arrest and prevented from leaving Poland. An outcry from anti-fascists in the West led to his release. He emigrated to Israel, but refused to renounce his past. He merely wanted to die in peace. His gripping and moving autobiography (*The Great Game*, 1977) ends with the following paragraphs which should be his epitaph:

> This century has brought forth two monsters, Fascism and Stalinism, and our ideal has been engulfed in this apocalypse . . . our failure forbids us to give advice, but because history has too much imagination to repeat itself, it remains possible to hope.
>
> I do not regret the commitment of my youth . . . in Denmark in 1973 a young man asked me in a public meeting: 'Haven't you sacrificed your life for nothing?' I said: 'No'.
>
> No, on one condition: that people understand the lesson of my life as a communist and a revolutionary and do not turn themselves over to a deified party. I know that youth will succeed where we have failed, that socialism will triumph, and that it will not have the colour of the Russian tanks that crushed Prague.

1982

24

GUY DEBORD

I drink, therefore . . .

In October 1917, a few days after the triumph of the Russian Revolution, Petrograd was gripped by a surreal saturnalia. Twelve years earlier, Lenin had referred to revolutions as 'festivals of the oppressed and the exploited'. The latter now decided to prove him right. Soldiers and workers drifted through the city, liberated its most renowned wine-shops and occupied the taverns.

Oblivious to all authority, they celebrated the victory by continuous bouts of drinking. Sleep alone could overpower them. This spontaneous initiative triggered a city-wide fever. The crack Preobrazhensky Regiment, on guard duty at the Winter Palace, found itself unable to resist the delights of the Tsar's cellars and its soldiers became completely drunk. Sent in to restore order, the Bolshevik-led Pavlovsky Regiment decided instead to sample the vintages on offer. A desperate High Command despatched the revolutionary leaders of the garrison to inspire an orderly retreat. They, too, succumbed.

Ultimately, a Finnish regiment led by anarcho-syndicalists threatened to dynamite the wine cellars and shoot looters on sight. Only then did the wave of inebriety recede, marking the end of Dionysian festivities, but also disproving the notion that refined tastes were a preserve of the bourgeoisie. Had that particular reel of history been reversed and replayed in the early 1960s, it seems likely that the artistic avant-gardes who campaigned against bourgeois boredom in the twentieth century – Surrealist left-overs, members of the Letterist International and the First and Second Situationist Internationals, many of whom make an appearance in Andrew Hussey's engaging book on Guy Debord – would have been on the side of the wine-loving Bolshevik soldiery rather than the spoilsport anarchist Finns.[1] Debord was the founding father of the Situationist International, the last politico-cultural avant-garde of the twentieth century.

As *The Game of War* reveals, one aspect of avant-garde existence in Paris during the 1950s and 60s was the passion for alcohol. The Surrealists had experimented with opium and hashish. Hardcore Situationists photographed each other consuming vast amounts of drink. Debord himself provided a literary and a theoretical justification. He often quoted Cervantes's remark that 'under a poor cloak you commonly find a good drinker'. A French government poster with the slogan 'Alcohol Kills Slowly' was defaced by Debord, in an early example of *détournement* (de/re-contextualization), with the reply: 'We don't give a fuck. We've got the time.' More importantly, consuming large quantities of alcohol was essential to loosen the self in order to lead a truly authentic existence.

As the small group of cultural insurrectionists, tanks filled to the brim, drifted in a gentle *dérive* through the maze of the Left Bank, they saw aspects of the city that had escaped them when sober. Psychogeographical drift, as they dubbed this experience, required the fuel of alcohol. In London a century earlier, Marx and Engels, pub-crawling home up Tottenham Court Road to Haverstock Hill, after a hard day in the British Museum Reading Room, had done so without the benefit of theorization.

---

1 Andrew Hussey, *The Game of War: The life and death of Guy Debord*, London: Cape, 2001.

Guy Debord was born in 1931. His father had moved from the Limousin region to Paris as a student of pharmacy. His beautiful mother was the daughter of Neapolitan immigrants who had prospered in the twentieth arrondissement. He was three when his father died. His mother was twenty-three. Not unnaturally, she was more interested in rebuilding her life than in eternal widowhood. Her own mother stepped in and took charge of the household and of Guy, adored and spoilt him, while encouraging his early belief that he was something special.

When Debord was eight, the family abandoned Paris and moved to Nice, just as France was about to be occupied by the Third Reich. From Nice they moved to Pau, where Debord went to secondary school in 1942. It was the same school in which the poet Isidore Ducasse had studied in the 1860s; this left its mark on Debord. The interest was enhanced when he discovered, some years later, that Ducasse had been a favourite of the Surrealists. A couple of hostile stepfathers had made the boy emotionally and intellectually self-dependent from an early age. The example of Ducasse's life, and coming of age in Occupied France, helped Debord develop a hostility to authority. This increased over the years and remained steadfast until his death in 1994.

Hussey provides memorable descriptions of Debord's social and cultural milieu. These are illustrated by mini-narratives, pen-portraits and a series of entertaining vignettes involving lovers, comrades, fellow-artists, friends, ex-friends, ex-comrades, enemies new and old, publishers old and new. He seems to have interviewed virtually everyone still alive who was once associated with Debord. All this is stitched together in crisp and fluent prose. *The Game of War* will be a useful addition to the growing literature on the Situationist project and the theories advocated by its principal architect.

Guy Debord lived life to the full. This was also true of his political philosophy and shaped the activities of those who followed him, usually a couple of dozen cultural revolutionaries, equally contemptuous of culture and of all forms of organization. If any of them strayed from the agreed line, they were unceremoniously expelled and treated as enemies. As Hussey reveals, it was not a life without contradictions. Debord may have loathed Sartre, but his own philosophy could only be described as an ultra-leftist version of existentialism, wholeheartedly individualist in its preoccupations. One of these was an early interest in Surrealism and, in particular, the work of Lautréamont (the pen name of Ducasse) and Georges Bataille.

André Breton and the Surrealists had turned to politics with their 1925 manifestos against the colonial war in Morocco, and Breton himself had attempted to define an anti-Stalinist politics for the Left via a loose alliance with the exiled Trotsky. In the Second Manifesto of Surrealism (1930), Breton wrote of 'the pure young people who refuse to knuckle down' in the lycées, workshops, seminaries, barracks and streets. It was to them that he addressed this manifesto, in order to 'defend Surrealism against the accusation that it is, after all, no more than an intellectual pastime like any other'. In 1960, just before his death, he called for resistance against the Algerian War, but it was not enough for the alienated young bohemians on the Left Bank. They wanted more than words. The Romanian poet Isidore Isou and a handful of followers decided to call themselves 'Letterists' and to practise a form of revolutionary Surrealism. The aim was to arouse French youth from its slumber.

The Letterists saw themselves as representing both continuity and a break with the Surrealist past. France in the 1950s was going through a sour, suffocating and dreary period. The Letterists caught a glimpse of a hazy but radiant future. The first public Letterist deed was to disrupt the Easter Mass at Notre-Dame in 1950. Michel Mourre, dressed as a Dominican monk, walked to the altar and read the sermon drafted by the Letterist poet, Serge Berna. This proclaimed 'the Catholic Church as being the running sore on the decomposed body of the West'. The guards rushed the altar with drawn swords, but not before Mourre had announced 'the death of God'.

The Surrealists, born out of a passionate hatred of Catholicism, had dreamt of such a deed. The Letterists carried it out. The scandal shocked France and gained global notoriety.

When Debord first encountered the Letterists at the Cannes Film Festival in 1951, the *affaire Notre-Dame* was fresh in his mind. He joined the group in disrupting the Festival. This ensured that Isou's film, *Treatise on Slime and Eternity* – 'an aural collage of guttural sound poetry and random noise' – was screened. A bemused and irritated Jean Cocteau pushed through a new Prix de l'Avant-Garde and awarded it to Isou. The intervention was accordingly considered a 'success'.

Soon afterwards, Debord moved to Paris and began to participate in Letterist binges. Within months, he had decided that his mentor Isou was an insufficiently intransigent narcissist. In league with the Belgian surrealist Gil Wolman, Debord organized a secret micro-faction (the Letterist International) and planned a new provocation. Unlike Notre-Dame, this would *épater la gauche*. The opportunity arose when Charlie Chaplin, harassed by McCarthyism in the United States, arrived in Europe for the premiere of *Limelight*. The predominantly Communist-led French Left had organized a massive reception to welcome Charlot to Paris. Debord's group decided to disrupt the event. The Letterist International distributed a pamphlet denouncing Chaplin as 'a fascist insect' whose films amounted to little more than 'emotional blackmail'. Their saccharine images discouraged working-class rebellion and the actor's trademark rattan cane was 'the night-stick of the cop'. The effect was minimal, but the real aim, a public break with Isou, was achieved. A *débordement* (outflanking) had taken place.

The Situationist International (SI) was formed by eight people after a congress in a small village on the Ligurian coast in the summer of 1957. Debord was joined by the Danish artist Asger Jorn, representing the 'Experimental Laboratory'. The London Psychogeographical Committee was represented by its only member, Ralph Rumney. A few months later, the SI had members in all the major Western European countries and Algeria. Most of them were painters. A magazine appeared explaining the aims of the new organization. Central among these was the 'constructed situation', a moment carefully and deliberately planned as an interplay between events and the urban environment. As Debord became more politically engaged, there were predictable rows, followed by the inevitable expulsions. The artists, led by Jorn's younger brother, split and set up the Second Situationist International. Relations between the two groups were not cordial.

By the time he came to write *La Société du spectacle* in 1967, Debord's position was impregnable. All 'rivals' had been removed. He could relax and think. The exquisitely crafted book was a theorization of advanced capitalism. The 'spectacle' was not a reference to the media, but to the entire ensemble of social, political and cultural relations under capitalism, a world in which alienated lives were subjugated by lies. Written under the influence of Saint-Just, Hegel, Marx, Lukács, Breton, the Socialisme ou Barbarie group and alcohol, *The Society of the Spectacle* is structured in the form of dense, illuminating aphorisms on the state of the world. It is (as Anselm Jappe pointed out in his thought-provoking intellectual biography of Debord in 1993) 'in essence a continuation of the work of Marx and Hegel and . . . its importance inheres for the most part precisely in this fact'. In addition, *The Society of the Spectacle*, composed almost entirely of quotations from the old masters blended in a provocative synthesis, is a masterpiece of *détournement*.

Those who have dragged Debord down to the status of a postmodern icon must surely be ignorant of this work. Of all the revolutionary groupuscules who acquired a prominence after the magnificent turbulence of 1968, the Situationists were the most outrageous, and the funniest. Their brilliant epigrams on the walls of Paris ('Commodities are the opium of the people', 'Beneath the cobblestones, the beach', 'I take my desires for reality because

I believe in the reality of my desires', 'Society is a plastic flower', and so on), excitedly copied by journalists and transmitted to the rest of the world, disturbed the bourgeois and the traditional leftist alike.

Hostile to Leninist–Trotskyist notions of a vanguard party, Debord believed in a system of workers' councils. Twenty years later, in *Comments on the Society of the Spectacle*, Debord remained intransigent, but lucid. A defeat had to be registered. The spectacle dominated all: 'The precious advantage which the spectacle has acquired through the outlawing of history, from having driven the recent past into hiding, and from having made everyone forget the spirit of history within society, is above all the ability to cover its own tracks, to conceal the very progress of its recent world conquests.' Debord had disbanded the Situationist International in 1972. He did not like admirers, and feared that many of them would transform Situationism into the petty consumerist ideology of executives who enjoy bottling their own wine, just before 'touching down at Kathmandu'. His body ravaged by alcohol, Debord committed suicide in 1994. Had he been alive today, he might have seen Kathmandu in a new context. I wonder whether Crown Prince Dipendra, who dressed up as a commando, constructed a situation and virtually wiped out the Nepalese monarchy, had ever come across an old Situationist text in the library at Eton?

August 2001

25

MEMORIES OF DEREK JARMAN

It was almost ten years ago. I was producing films and documentaries for Bandung Productions and Channel 4 was still interested in ideas. Not all the commissioning editors had yet become the grasping, meddlesome opportunists of today. I suggested to Gwyn Pritchard, then in charge of Education (now head of Welsh-language BBC in Cardiff) that he should commission a set of four films on philosophy: chamber epics constructed around the lives and ideas of Socrates, Spinoza, Locke and Wittgenstein. He agreed to four scripts on the spot, warning me that budgets were small in his department and that I could not exceed £200,000 per film.

By the time all the other scripts were written and approved, we had already filmed *Spinoza* with Henry Goodman in the title role. Gwyn had moved on. His successor, Karen Brown, was also enthusiastic but, for some reason, not keen on Socrates and so the old Greek fell by the wayside. She asked who was going to direct *Wittgenstein*? I was still thinking. *Spinoza* had been beautifully filmed by Chris Spencer, but the style was naturalistic. *Wittgenstein* needed to be different, slightly surreal.

On an impulse I rang Derek Jarman in Dungeness. I had never met him before, but had greatly admired two of his films – *Caravaggio* and *Edward II* – from afar. After speaking to him that morning I went out and bought a copy of *Modern Nature* from a local bookshop. I read most of it in the office for the rest of the day and finished it the next morning. To my surprise I had enjoyed it enormously. He was much more than a filmmaker or a gay saint.

I know the date I made the call, because Jarman recorded it in his diary. It was 19 May 1992. His enthusiasm surprised me. He told me that he had always wanted to make a film on the philosopher, but had never got beyond the title – *Loony Ludwig*. I sent him Terry Eagleton's script, which was definitely not *Loony Ludwig*.

He read it and rang me back the next day. He liked it and wanted to make the film. A week later I drove to Dungeness and found Prospect Cottage by the sea. The garden was, as had been claimed by every visitor, a work of art, but my enjoyment was restrained by the knowledge that we were overlooked by a giant nuclear reactor. It was then that his illness really hit me.

Nobody else I know would deliberately choose to live so close to a nuclear reactor. Derek no longer cared. AIDS would carry him off sooner rather than later, and he enjoyed living on the edge. He grinned as he told me that it was so lovely to swim on a deserted beach. 'In the summer I often run out of the cottage naked and straight into the sea. It's radioactive all right. Friends have tested it with Geiger counters. Sometimes the reactor ODs and the whole place lights up. It's really sensational, you know what I mean?' I did.

We spent most of the day discussing Wittgenstein. He knew exactly what he wanted. No Merchant–Ivory nonsense. No English Heritage atrocities. Apart from aesthetics, we simply did not have the money to make that sort of a film. It would have to be austere, in keeping with the philosophy. Wittgenstein would record his life in front of black drapes straight into the camera. As he notes in his diaries, *Smiling in Slow Motion*, 'the visualization must mirror the work – no competition from objects.' He was sure he would make it work. He asked which of his films I had seen and liked. I named them. He laughed. After a pause I confessed that *Sebastiane* had, alas, not succeeded in keeping me awake. It was sweet lemonade, whereas *Caravaggio* and *Edward II* were much stronger stuff.

'Why did you make *Sebastiane*?' I asked him.

The reply was instant.

'There was only one real reason. To show a hard-on on the screen.'

We discussed production details and it was the only time on that occasion he mentioned his illness.

'You'd better put an extra director in the budget. The insurers will insist on it. His name is Ken Butler, and he shot the two best scenes in *Edward II* when I had to go into hospital.'

He looked so well that day that it was difficult to imagine him in hospital. As I was about to leave, I suggested to him that with *Wittgenstein* he should shock his fans.

'What do you mean? What do you mean?'

'Not a single bum or willie. Let the audience have withdrawal symptoms.'

He laughed.

'It's a deal. It'll make a change.'

And so it came about that the only sex in *Wittgenstein* is one fairly chaste kiss on the lips exchanged between Wittgenstein and his lover Johnnie. Today the ratings-driven controllers of our TV channels, were they to take such an idea seriously, would insist on maximum bum/willie exposure.

We talked on the phone over the next few days and then I returned to Dungeness, this time by train. We went, as he records, to have lunch in the pub at Lydd and talked about everything. There was no God and no afterlife. He was prepared for blindness and death. It did not frighten him. He said something which has always stayed with me: 'If you want nothing, hope for nothing and fear nothing, you can never be an artist.'

He hated the monarchy, and savaged the honours system. He was very angry with Ian McKellen for accepting a knighthood and entering No. 10

Downing Street. I was amused to see the following entry in his diary. This is the voice I remember so well:

Vivienne Westwood accepts an OBE, dipsy bitch. The silly season's with us: our punk friends accept their little medals of betrayal, sit in their vacuous salons and destroy the creative – like the woodworm in my dresser, which I will paint with insecticide tomorrow. I would love to place a man-sized insectocutor, lit with royal-blue, to burn up this clothes-moth and her like.

I had seen a reference in *Modern Nature* to a trip he made to Pakistan, and questioned him about it.

It emerged that his father had been a senior air-force officer in India and had been seconded to help establish the Pakistan Air Force after independence in 1947. Throughout the fifties, Derek had spent part of the summer holidays in the Himalayan foothills in Northern Pakistan. The Air Force ran a special holiday resort in Kalabagh, two miles north of Nathiagali where my family spent every summer to escape the heat of the plains.

Those were idyllic months. As teenagers I and my friends climbed mountains, went for twenty-mile walks, played tennis and mooned constantly over girls, trying desperately to draw them into our fantasies. There was a freedom in the mountains untouched in those days by urban inhibitions. The thought that a young Jarman had been only a few miles away amused both of us. He had not discovered his sexuality at the time, and roared when I told him that homosexuality in that part of Pakistan was very pronounced. The more snobby locals traced it back to the Greek generals and soldiers who stayed behind after Alexander's conquests.

'If you'd shown the slightest interest, Derek,' I told him, 'there would have been a queue outside your cottage.'

As we began preparations to film *Wittgenstein* he moved into the Bandung offices in Kentish Town, with Ken Butler at his side. Scripts were rewritten. Actors were auditioned. Most of them were people he'd worked with before, and there was always a very special place in his heart for Tilda Swinton. 'If only she'd been a boy,' he would mutter wistfully. Those were joyous days. We were short of money. The British Film Institute helped out, but not enough. Derek was enraged. 'They've just given X a million! A million to make crap, and we can't even get a few hundred thousand.' He asked me to ring a Japanese producer who was 'always good for fifty thousand or so'. Takashi did not let us down. Yet still there wasn't enough to make a film that could be shown on the big screen. In order to make it happen people worked for Derek virtually free, including Sandy Powell who designed the stunning costumes.

During the actual filming we were all amazed. His energy was staggering. He drew on all his reserves and worked twelve hours a day for two whole weeks. Ken Butler was never needed, although his presence cheered us all. Throughout this period, Arif, Bandung's in-house cameraman, recorded Jarman in action. There are fifteen hours of tape. I watched some of them for the first time to refresh my memory. It was as I remembered. The zest for life dominates.

After the film was finished, we stayed in touch. I went to the preview of *Blue*, laughing to myself as sundry celebrities whispered to each other in bewilderment. They couldn't believe that all they were getting was a blue screen and a voice-over. Over lunch at a greasy-spoon Chinese in Soho's Lisle Street, he discussed *The Raft of the Medusa*: he wanted to make a film based on the Géricault painting. It would be a film about death, and the people on the raft would be AIDS victims. He wanted me to get the commission. I rang George Faber at the BBC, who agreed at once. A script was begun. We used to meet and talk. A new biography of J. Edgar Hoover had just appeared which revealed that he had always been a homosexual and a secret transvestite. We laughed uncontrollably. I suggested that the *Raft* might take a surreal turn. We should have a limo surrounded by G-men entering the studio; Hoover in a stunning red frock steps out and orders his cops to arrest the director. I thought it might lighten the mood.

Some months later I got a letter from the St Petersburg Film Festival. They wanted to show *Wittgenstein*, and were inviting Derek and me to introduce the film. I informed them that he was dead and I did not wish to travel alone.

June 2000

26

ABDELREHMAN MUNIF

Abdelrehman Munif, who died, after a protracted illness, in his Damascus exile, was one of the most gifted Arab novelists of the twentieth century. Together with Naguib Mahfouz, he succeeded in transforming the literary landscape of the Arab world by making the novel central to its cultural and political concerns, just as it had been in Europe during most of the nineteenth century.

Born in Amman in 1933 to a Saudi trader and an Iraqi mother, Munif spent his first decade in that city. Despite the defeat of the Ottoman Empire, this was still a world dominated by cities, a world where frontiers were porous and Arab families and trade moved comfortably from Jerusalem to Cairo to Baghdad to Damascus and beyond. All these territories (with the exception of Damascus and Beirut) were under the control of the British Empire. The lines had been drawn in the sand, but no barbed wire or armed guards policed them. Abdelrehman Munif attended primary school in Amman, a secondary school in Baghdad and the university in Cairo. Later he would recall the Amman of his childhood in a delightful memoir, *Story of a City: A Childhood in Amman* (London 1996), in which he described school life in the mid-forties:

> Sometimes, the names of the cities in other Arab countries were confused with one another or not easily remembered, but the hands of all the

students would shoot up when the teacher asked who could name five cities in Palestine. Competing voices drowned each other out: Jerusalem, Jaffa, Haifa, Gaza, Lydda, Ramlah, Acre, Safad, Ramallah, Hebron . . . Palestine was more than just a land and a people. In the mind of every Arab it is a constellation of meanings, symbols and connotations which have accumulated and filtered down through several generations.

And the names of the old towns of Palestine continued to reverberate in Munif's own head. He could never forget the Palestinian refugees whose anguish he had glimpsed in his early teens. Only a few months ago, he referred to Ariel Sharon as the biggest abomination in the Arab East.

Throughout his teenage years he would spend the summer holidays on the Peninsula, with his Saudi family. It was here that he heard countless stories, and spoke with the Bedouins and the oil-merchants and the nouveau-riche emirs who would later populate his fictions. Like the bulk of his generation he was shattered by the Palestinian catastrophe of 1948, and became a staunch Arab nationalist. The rise of Nasser in Egypt and the revolutionary wave that swept the Arab world as a result did not pass him by, and he became a secular socialist militant. For his political opposition to the royal family he was stripped of his Saudi nationality in 1963, and fled to Baghdad. Here he obtained work as an economist in the petroleum industry, and came to understand the importance of the liquid gold that lay beneath the sands of Arabia and Mesopotamia. His knowledge of the commodity and the industry was used to devastating effect in his novels.

He started writing fiction in the late seventies, after resigning from the Ba'ath Party leadership in Baghdad and moving to Damascus. His active political life was over. Henceforth his mind would be fully concentrated on writing fiction. He wrote a total of fifteen novels, but it was *Cities of Salt* – a quintet based on the transformation of the Arab peninsula from ancient Bedouin homeland to a hybrid tribal kleptocracy floating on oil – that established his reputation in the Arab world. He depicted the surprise, fear, uneasiness and tension that gripped Saudi Arabia after the discovery of oil, and his portraits of the country's rulers were thinly disguised, causing a great deal of merriment in the Arab street and even the odd palace.

The two M's – Mahfouz and Munif – became the patriarchs of Arab literature. Naguib Mahfouz's Balzacian reconstruction of family life in Cairo, from the beginning of the twentieth century to the rise of Nasser, won him the Nobel.

Many Arab critics (though not Munif himself) felt that it was the Saudi who better merited the award; but his savage and surreal satires of the royal family, their entourage and the oilmen had made him contraband within official culture. His books were banned in Saudi Arabia and elsewhere in the Gulf. But they travelled nonetheless, and were read secretly by many a Peninsula potentate. Munif's genius lay in his ability to impose the intellectual and the popular on characters that were neither.

Three novels of the Saudi quintet were translated into English by Peter Theroux – *Cities of Salt*, *The Trench* and *Variations on Night and Day* – and published by Knopf in New York. But the American critics did not like them, and John Updike famously denounced the books for not being like the fiction he was used to reading. When I told Munif this he chuckled, and his hands gestured in mock-despair. Despite his enormous popularity with ordinary Arab readers and literary critics (the late Edward Said was one of his biggest fans), he was not fêted and celebrated by officialdom. He was proud of this fact.

I met him only once, when he came to London on a rare visit to be interviewed for a documentary I was producing for Channel 4, in the mid-nineties. Why, I asked, had he chosen the title *Cities of Salt* for his masterwork? Here is part of his reply:

> 'Cities of salt' means cities that offer no sustainable existence. When the waters come in, the first waves will dissolve the salt and reduce

these great glass cities to dust. In antiquity, as you know, many cities simply disappeared. It is possible to foresee the downfall of cities that are inhuman. With no means of livelihood they won't survive. Look at us now, and see how the West sees us. The twentieth century is almost over, but when the West looks at us, all they see is oil and petrodollars. Saudi Arabia is still without a Constitution; the people are deprived of elementary rights. Women are treated as third-class citizens. Such a situation produces a desperate citizenry, without a sense of dignity or belonging . . .

Munif was not in the least surprised that the majority of the 9/11 hijackers were Saudi citizens. After all, he had been warning us of what might happen for the previous four decades. His most recent work was a set of essays on Iraq. He had despised Saddam Hussein, and written of the need for social democracy throughout the Arab world, but he was angered by the war and subsequent occupation. His son Yasir, whom I met in the States a few months ago, told me that the recolonization of Iraq had re-ignited his father's old radicalism, and this is obvious in his last essays. The new situation had forced him to put fiction aside and wield his pen as a weapon against local dictators and imperial warmongers alike.

But it is as a novelist that he will be missed the most. He was a storyteller without compare, who enriched the culture of the Arab world as a whole. He was a strong and independent-minded intellectual who refused to bend the knee before either Prince or Colonel. His work and his example inspired younger writers, both men and women, throughout the Maghreb and the Mashriq and, for that reason, I am almost sure we will see his like again.

January 2004

265

27

PRAMOEDYA ANANTA TOER

The death of the writer Pramoedya Ananta Toer is an enormous loss to world literature. He was a leading intellectual of the Indonesian left and a brilliant writer of fiction, always in pursuit of a time that never came. Sometimes he would think he had glimpsed the future and this immediately became magnified and was reflected in his fiction. His passion for radical politics was never hidden.

In 'Diajang menjerah' or 'She Who Gave Up', a short story published in a 1952 collection (*Tjerita dari Blora*, Stories from Blora), he wrote:

> In such times too the rage for politics roared along like a tidal wave, out of control. Each person felt as though she, he could not be truly alive without being political, without debating political questions. In truth, it was as though they could stay alive even without rice. Even schoolteachers, who had all along lived 'neutrally', were infected by the rage for politics – and, so far as they were able, they influenced their pupils with the politics to which they had attached themselves. Each struggled to claim new members for his party. And schools proved to be fertile battlefields for their struggles. Politics! Politics! No different from rice under the Japanese Occupation.

Indonesia, the largest Muslim country in the world, once contained the largest Communist Party outside the actual world of communism. In 1965, the military seized the country and bathed it in blood: at least a million people, mainly Communists and their sympathizers, were massacred. In Bali and elsewhere, the pro-West military leaders worked with Islamist vigilantes to make sure that few were left alive. Twenty years later a writer from a younger generation, Pripit Rochijat Kartawidjaja, recalled the hellish scenes in a lengthy essay:

> Usually the corpses were no longer recognizable as human. Headless. Stomachs torn open. The smell was unimaginable. To make sure they didn't sink, the carcasses were deliberately tied to, or impaled upon, bamboo stakes. And the departure of the corpses from the Kediri region down the Brantas achieved its golden age when bodies were stacked together on rafts over which the PKI [Indonesian Communist Party] banner grandly flew ... Once the purge of Communist elements got under way, clients stopped coming for sexual satisfaction. The reason: most clients – and prostitutes – were too frightened, for, hanging up in front of the whorehouses, there were a lot of male Communist genitals – like bananas hung out for sale.

Toer, born in 1925 in Blora in central Java, was the country's most distinguished novelist and, significantly, published in the United States. His life was spared. The generals dared not execute him, but hoped that the conditions in which he was kept would take care of the problem.

Arrested after the military coup in Jakarta in 1965, he was sent to Buru Island, a tropical gulag where many died of exhaustion, hard labour or starvation. Toer survived. He would later recall how every night, for three thousand and one nights – eight years – he fought against cruelty, disease and creeping insanity by telling stories to his fellow prisoners. It kept hope alive for him and them. As they listened, the prisoners momentarily forgot where they were or who had sentenced them.

He spent twelve years altogether on Buru. It was not his first experience of prison, and this led him to compare present-day conditions with the colonial past. There was no room for doubt. Conditions were qualitatively worse than they had been almost two decades ago when he was incarcerated at the forced labour camp of Bukitduri, from 1947 to 1949. Then he had been actively engaged in the revolutionary struggle against the Dutch after the Second World War.

The Dutch, unlike their postcolonial emulators, had not deprived him of writing implements and this was where he wrote his first novel, *Perburuan* (1950), translated as *The Fugitive* (1975 and 1990) – a 170-page masterpiece superior in composition and content to the fiction of Albert Camus with which Western critics sometimes compared it.

In *Nyanyi sunyi seorang bisu* (1995; *A Mute's Soliloquy*, 1999) – an affecting account of his life in prison – Toer describes, in spare, contained prose, the institutionalized brutality of Suharto's New Order. The old cargo vessel on which he and eight hundred others are being transported to Buru Island reminds him of the coolies on Captain Bontekoe's ship, the kidnapped Chinese on Michener's ship bound for Hawaii . . . and of course the four million Africans loaded onto British and American ships for transport across the Atlantic.

In extreme moments during the colonial period, the threatened, insecure Dutch administrators, aware of the Javanese obsession with cleanliness, used to hurl excrement at the natives, to humiliate and debase them. The New Order prison ship went one better. The prisoners' hold was adjacent to the latrine and during stormy weather the two locations became merged. The prisoners were regularly mistreated and starved so that only the fittest would survive. Toer describes a desperate menu:

Imagine a diet of gutter rats, the mouldy outgrowth on papaya trees and banana plants, and leeches, skewered on palm-leaf ribs prior to eating. Even

J. P., one of our most well-educated prisoners, found himself reduced to eating cicak, though he always broke off the lizard's toe pads first. He'd become quite an expert at catching them. After amputating the lizard's toes, he would squeeze the unfortunate creature between his thumb and forefinger, shove it to the back of his throat, and swallow it whole. The man's will to defend himself against hunger was a victory in itself.

And all the while the regime sent in preachers and Islamist journalists, to inspect the minds of the inmates and urge them to become Believers:

> I have no doubt that this year, just as in previous years, at the beginning of the fasting month my mates and I will be treated to a lecture by a religious official specially brought in from the free world, on the importance of fasting and controlling one's hunger and desires. Imagine the humour of that!

After fifteen years in his country's prisons, a campaign by Amnesty and other groups in the West helped, in 1979, to secure Toer's release, but it was conditional: until 1992 he was confined to house arrest in Jakarta and forced to report regularly to the police. But his time was his own, and he could write again.

The allegories he had tried out on fellow political prisoners during desperate times developed into a much-acclaimed quartet of novels known as 'Minke's Story' or the 'Buru Quartet'. The first of these, *Bumi manusia* (translated as *This Earth of Mankind*, 1982), was published in 1980 and topped the best-seller list for ten months. The second, too, *Anak semua bangsa* (1980; *A Child of All Nations*, 1984), became a best-seller. Thus thousands of Indonesian citizens chose to welcome 'Pram', their most celebrated dissident, back to literary life.

The novels – part realist, part historical (the succeeding volumes were translated as *Footsteps*, 1990, and *House of Glass*, 1992) – were set in the colonial period. The inspiration was provided by the legendary figure of Tirto Adi Surya, the father of Indonesian nationalist journalism. The scale and depth of the work was such that, for most Indonesian readers forced by the political climate to stifle their own thoughts, the effect was dramatic. Toer was writing about the past, but much of what he wrote resonated with the present. Were Suharto and the New Order a continuation of the colonial regime? In 1981 the books were banned. The publishers were forced to close down. One of them was imprisoned for three months.

Had Pramoedya Ananta Toer been a Soviet dissident, he would have received the Nobel Prize. But his status as a literary master is secure, and (unlike some Latin American contemporaries) he remained unrepentant throughout his life.

> Just as politics cannot be separated from life, life cannot be separated from politics. People who consider themselves to be non-political are no different; they've already been assimilated by the dominant political culture – they just don't notice it any more.

May 2006

28

EDWARD SAID

Thinking of Edward

I think of him often, especially but not only when I read of the sordid deals in which the PLO is engaged with Israel and its US backers. I miss Edward's impetuosity and righteous indignation. He would have had no truck with the shrivelled little Bantustans that the PLO wants to accept. He would have morally destroyed the apologists for such a scheme, along with those intellectual fellow-travellers who think that defending the idea of a secular Palestine means remaining silent on the US–EU embargo on Hamas and who, sapped by years of struggle and the receipt of handsome cheques from some corrupt NGO, are yearning for an accommodation with the enemy on almost any terms. Already in his last writings Edward Said had supported the idea of a single state in Israel-Palestine, and a break with the corruption and bankruptcy of the PLO. He may not have agreed with every dot and comma in Mearsheimer and Walt's magisterial work, *The Israel Lobby*, but he would have loudly applauded its publication for breaking a sacred taboo. His voice is greatly missed in these bad times.

That he was an implacable enemy of the Zionist project and US imperial policies is not in doubt, but he was not a mindless opponent of all things American. He loved New York. It was his home and he knew it and it was no small matter. He would often talk about the city with great passion and humour. His colleagues at Columbia used to refer to his large office as the 'West Bank', and he appreciated the joke. Visiting Britain or France he was both enthusiastic on some levels (French intellectual history, for instance) and detached. He was an inquisitive tourist, a bon vivant who well fitted Edward Gibbon's description of such a person as one who possesses a 'virtue which borders on a vice; the flexible temper which can assimilate itself to every tone of society from the court to the cottage; the happy flow of spirits which can amuse and be amused in every company and situation.' He happily engaged with contemporary ideas, but unlike some of his fans he did not try to compensate for the hollowness of a hole by constructing a hollow dome over it to both frame and enlarge the original. At the same time he was not one of those who feel that the twentieth century had erred in attaching too much importance to intellect and reason, conviction and character. Horrible mistakes had been made by 'our side', crimes had been committed by Western civilization in the Congo and the judeocide of the Second World War which had made Western public opinion, belatedly regretting the genocide, now indifferent to Palestinian suffering. Sometimes, in melancholic mood and feeling more insecure than usual, he would need to be reassured that what he was doing was worthwhile. Posterity's tributes would have pleased him greatly.

The best way to honour his memory is to preserve a fierce independence against despotisms of every variety, regardless of whether they clothe themselves in the uniform of democracy or bludgeon people into submission with a field-marshal's baton.

December 2007

272

Remembering Edward Said

Edward Said was a long-standing friend and comrade. We first met in 1972, at a seminar in New York. Even in those turbulent times, one of the features that distinguished him from the rest of us was his immaculate dress sense: everything was meticulously chosen, down to the socks. It is almost impossible to visualize him any other way. At a conference in his honour in Beirut in 1997, Edward insisted on accompanying Elias Khoury and myself for a swim. As he walked out in his swimming trunks, I asked why the towel did not match. 'When in Rome', he replied, airily; but that evening, as he read an extract from the Arabic manuscript of his memoir *Out of Place*, his attire was faultless. It remained so till the end, throughout his long battle with leukaemia.

Over the last eleven years one had become so used to his illness – the regular hospital stays, the willingness to undergo trials with the latest drugs, the refusal to accept defeat – that one began to think him indestructible. Last year, purely by chance, I met Said's doctor in New York. In response to my questions, he replied that there was no medical explanation for Edward's survival. It was his indomitable spirit as a fighter, his will to live, that had preserved him for so long. Said travelled everywhere. He spoke, as always, of Palestine, but also of the unifying capacities of the three cultures, which he would insist had a great deal in common. The monster was devouring his insides but those who came to hear him could not see the process, and we who knew preferred to forget. When the cursed cancer finally took him the shock was intense.

His quarrel with the political and cultural establishments of the West and the official Arab world is the most important feature of Said's biography. It was the Six-Day War of 1967 that changed his life – prior to that event, he had not been politically engaged. His father, a Palestinian Christian, had emigrated to the United States in 1911, at the age of sixteen, to avoid being drafted by the Ottomans to fight in Bulgaria. He became an American citizen and served, instead, with the US military in France during the First World War. Subsequently he returned to Jerusalem, where Edward was born in 1935. Said never pretended to be a poverty-stricken Palestinian refugee, as some detractors later alleged. The family moved to Cairo, where Wadie Said set up a successful stationery business and Edward was sent to an elite English-language school. His teenage years were lonely, dominated by a Victorian father, in whose eyes the boy required permanent disciplining, and an after-school existence devoid of friends. Novels became a substitute – Defoe, Scott, Kipling, Dickens, Mann. He had been named Edward after the Prince of Wales but, despite his father's monarchism, was despatched for his education not to Britain but to the United States, in 1951. Said would later write of hating his 'puritanical and hypocritical' New England boarding school: it was 'shattering and disorienting'. Until then, he thought he knew exactly who he was, 'moral and physical flaws' and all. In the United States he had to remake himself 'into something the system required'.

Watershed of '67

Nevertheless, he flourished in the Ivy League environment, first at Princeton and then Harvard where, as he later said, he had the privilege to be trained in the German philological tradition of comparative literature. Said began teaching at Columbia in 1963; his first book, on Conrad, was published three years later. When I asked him about it in New York in 1994, in a conversation filmed for Channel 4, he described his early years at Columbia between 1963 and 1967 as a 'Dorian Gray period':

> TA: So one of you was the Comp Lit professor, going about his business, giving his lectures, working with Trilling and the others; yet at

274

the same time, another character was building up inside you – but you kept the two apart?

ES: I had to. There was no place for that other character to be. I had effectively severed my connection with Egypt. Palestine no longer existed. My family lived partly in Egypt and partly in Lebanon. I was a foreigner in both places. I had no interest in the family business, so I was here. Until 1967, I really didn't think about myself as anything other than a person going about his work. I had taken in a few things along the way. I was obsessed with the fact that many of my cultural heroes – Edmund Wilson, Isaiah Berlin, Reinhold Niebuhr – were fanatical Zionists. Not just pro-Israeli: they said the most awful things about the Arabs, in print. But all I could do was note it. Politically, there was no place for me to go. I was in New York when the Six-Day War broke out; and was completely shattered. The world as I had understood it ended at that moment. I had been in the States for years but it was only now that I began to be in touch with other Arabs. By 1970 I was completely immersed in politics and the Palestinian resistance movement.[1]

His 1975 work *Beginnings* – an epic engagement with the problems posed by the 'point of departure', which synthesized the insights of Auerbach, Vico and Freud with a striking reading of the modernist novel – and, above all, *Orientalism*, were the products of this conjuncture. Published in 1978, when Said was already a member of the Palestinian National Council, *Orientalism* combines the polemical vigour of the activist with the passion of the cultural critic. Like all great polemics, it eschews balance. I once told him that, for many South Asians, the problem with the early orientalist British scholars was not their imperialist ideology but, on the contrary, the fact that they were far too politically correct: overawed by the Sanskrit texts they were translating. Said laughed, and insisted that the book was essentially

---

1   This, and following quotes, are from *A Conversation with Edward Said*, a Bandung Films production. The programme was recorded in his Riverside Drive apartment, on a day so humid that Said removed his jacket and tie as the cameras began to roll – creating much merriment in the household.

an attempt to undercut the more fundamental assumptions of the West in relation to the Arab East. The 'discourse' – Foucault was, alas, an important influence – of the Orient, constructed in France and Britain during the two centuries that followed Napoleon's conquest of Egypt, had served both as an instrument of rule and to shore up a European cultural identity, by setting it off against the Arab world.[2] He had deliberately concentrated on the exoticization, vulgarization and distortions of the Middle East and its culture for that reason. To portray imperialist suppositions as a universal truth was a lie, based on skewed and instrumentalist observations that were used in the service of Western domination.

Orientalism spawned a vast academic following. While Said was undoubtedly touched and flattered by the book's success, he was well aware of how it was misused and would often disclaim responsibility for its more monstrous offspring: 'How can anyone accuse me of denouncing "dead white males"? Everyone knows I love Conrad.' He would then go through a list of postmodernist critics, savaging each of them in turn for their stress on identity and hostility to narrative. 'Write it all down', I once told him. 'Why don't you?' came the reply. What we recorded was more restrained:

TA: The 1967 war radicalized you, pushed you in the direction of becoming a Palestinian spokesperson?

ES: Arab, at first, before Palestinian.

TA: And *Orientalism* grew out of that new commitment.

ES: I started to read, methodically, what was being written about the Middle East. It did not correspond to my experience. By

2   Thus Lord Cromer, British consul-general in Egypt for some quarter of a century after 1881: 'The European is a close reasoner; his statements of fact are devoid of any ambiguity; he is a natural logician . . . The mind of the Oriental, on the other hand, like his picturesque streets, is eminently wanting in symmetry . . . He will often break down under the mildest process of cross-examination'. *Orientalism*, London: Penguin Classics, 2003, p. 38.

the early seventies I began to realize that the distortions and misrepresentations were systematic, part of a much larger system of thought that was endemic to the West's whole enterprise of dealing with the Arab world. It confirmed my sense that the study of literature was essentially a historical task, not just an aesthetic one. I still believe in the role of the aesthetic; but the 'kingdom of literature' – 'for its own sake' – is simply wrong. A serious historical investigation must begin from the fact that culture is hopelessly involved in politics. My interest has been in the great canonical literature of the West – read, not as masterpieces that have to be venerated, but as works that have to be grasped in their historical density, so they can resonate. But I also don't think you can do that without liking them; without caring about the books themselves.

Culture and Imperialism, published in 1993, extended the core arguments of *Orientalism* to describe a more general pattern of relationships between the metropolitan West and its overseas territories, beyond that of Europe and the Middle East. Written in a different political period, it attracted some vituperative attacks. There was a celebrated exchange in the *Times Literary Supplement* with Ernest Gellner – who thought Said should give 'at least some expression of gratitude' for imperialism's role as vehicle of modernity – in which neither side took prisoners. Later, when Gellner attempted a reconciliation of sorts, Said was unforgiving; hatred must be pure to be effective and, here as elsewhere, he always gave as good as he got.

But by now, debates on culture had been overshadowed by events in Palestine. When I asked if the year 1917 meant anything to him, he replied without hesitation: 'Yes, the Balfour Declaration'. Said's writings on Palestine have a completely different flavour from anything else he wrote, passionate and biblical in their simplicity. This was his cause. In *The End of the Peace Process*, *Blaming the Victims* and some half-dozen other books, in his *al-Ahram* columns and his essays in *New Left Review* and the *London Review of Books*, the flame that had been ignited in 1967 burned ever brighter. He had helped a generation to understand the real history of Palestine and it was this position, as the true chronicler of his people and their occupied homeland, that won him respect and admiration throughout the world. The Palestinians had become the indirect victims of the European judeocide of the Second World War; but few politicians in the West seemed to care. Said pricked their collective conscience and they did not like him for it.

Anti-Oslo

Two close friends whose advice he had often sought – Ibrahim Abu-Lughod and Eqbal Ahmad – had died within a few years of each other, in 1999 and 2001. Said missed them greatly, but their absence only made him more determined to continue his literary onslaught against the enemy. Though he had served for fourteen years as an independent member on the PNC, and helped to polish and redraft Arafat's address to the UN General Assembly in 1984, he became increasingly critical of the lack of strategic vision that typified most of the Palestinian leadership. Writing in the immediate aftermath of what he termed the 'fashion-show vulgarities' of Arafat and Rabin's handshake on the White House lawn, Said described the Oslo Accords – imposed on the vanquished by the United States and Israel, after the Gulf War of 1991 – as 'an instrument of surrender, a Palestinian Versailles' offering only shrivelled Bantustans in exchange for a series of historic renunciations. Israel, meanwhile, had no reason to let go as long as Washington supplied it with arms and funds.[3] (Arafat's lieutenant Nabil Shaath, echoing *Orientalism*'s more reactionary critics, responded: 'He should stick to literary criticism. After all, Arafat would not deign to

---

3 *London Review of Books*, 21 October 1993.

discuss Shakespeare.') History has vindicated Said's analysis. One of his most scorching attacks on Arafat's leadership, published in 2001 in *New Left Review* and in *al-Ahram*, denounced Oslo as a mere repackaging of the occupation, 'offering a token 18 per cent of the lands seized in 1967 to the corrupt, Vichy-like authority of Arafat, whose mandate has essentially been to police and tax his people on Israel's behalf':

> The Palestinian people deserve better. We have to say clearly that with Arafat and company in command, there is no hope . . . What the Palestinians need are leaders who are really with and of their people, who are actually doing the resisting on the ground, not fat cigar-chomping bureaucrats bent on preserving their business deals and renewing their VIP passes, who have lost all trace of decency or credibility . . . We need a united leadership capable of thinking, planning and taking decisions, rather than grovelling before the Pope or George Bush while the Israelis kill his people with impunity . . . The struggle for liberation from Israeli occupation is where every Palestinian worth anything now stands.[4]

Could Hamas provide a serious alternative? 'This is a protest movement against the occupation', Said told me:

> In my opinion, their ideas about an Islamic state are completely inchoate, unconvincing to anybody who lives there. Nobody takes that aspect of their programme seriously. When you question them, as I have, both on the West Bank and elsewhere: 'What are your economic policies? What are your ideas about power stations, or housing?', they reply: 'Oh, we're thinking about that.' There is no social programme that could be labelled 'Islamic'. I see them as creatures of the moment, for whom Islam is an opportunity to protest against the current stalemate, the mediocrity and bankruptcy of the ruling party. The Palestinian Authority is now hopelessly damaged and lacking in credibility – like the Saudis and Egyptians, a client state for the US.

4 'A People in Need of Leadership', *New Left Review* 2: 11, September–October 2001.

Behind the reiterated Israeli demands that the Authority crack down on Hamas and Islamic Jihad, he detected 'the hope that there will be something resembling a Palestinian civil war, a gleam in the eyes of the Israeli military'. Yet in the final months of his life he could still celebrate the Palestinians' stubborn refusal to accept that they were, as the IDF Chief of Staff had described them, 'a defeated people', and saw signs for a more creative Palestinian politics in the National Political Initiative led by Mustapha Barghouti: 'The vision here is not a manufactured provisional state on 40 per cent of the land, with the refugees abandoned and Jerusalem kept by Israel, but a sovereign territory liberated from military occupation by mass action involving Arabs and Jews wherever possible.'[5]

With his death, the Palestinian nation has lost its most articulate voice in the Northern hemisphere, a world where, by and large, the continuous suffering of the Palestinians is ignored. For official Israelis, they are *untermenschen*; for official Americans, they are all terrorists; for the venal Arab regimes they are a continuing embarrassment. In his last writings, Said vigorously denounced the war on Iraq and its many apologists. He argued for freedom, from violence and from lies. He knew that the dual occupation of Palestine and Iraq had made peace in the region even more remote. His voice is irreplaceable, but his legacy will endure. He has many lives ahead of him.

November 2003

5   *London Review of Books*, 19 June 2003.

29

V. G. KIERNAN

Victor Kiernan, professor emeritus of Modern History at Edinburgh University, who died on 17 February, was an erudite Marxist historian with wide-ranging interests that spanned virtually every continent. His passion for history and radical politics, classical languages and world literature was fairly evenly divided. His interest in languages was developed at home in south Manchester. His father worked for the Manchester Ship Canal as a translator of Spanish and Portuguese, and young Victor picked these up even before getting a scholarship to Manchester Grammar School, where he learnt Greek and Latin. His early love for Horace (his favourite poet) resulted in a late book. He went on to Trinity College, Cambridge where he studied History, imbibed the prevalent anti–fascism and like many others joined the British Communist Party.

Unlike some of his distinguished colleagues (Eric Hobsbawm, Christopher Hill, Rodney Hilton, Edward Thompson) in the Communist Party Historians' Group founded in 1946, Kiernan wrote a great deal on countries and cultures far removed from Britain and Europe. A flavour of the man is evident from the opening paragraphs of a 1989 essay on the monarchy published in the *New Left Review*:

In China an immemorial throne crumbled in 1911; India put its Rajas and Nawabs in the wastepaper-basket as soon as it gained independence in 1947; in Ethiopia the Lion of Judah has lately ceased to roar. Monarchy survives in odd corners of Asia; and in Japan and Britain. In Asia sainthood has often been hereditary, and can yield a comfortable income to remote descendants of holy men; in Europe hereditary monarchy had something of the same numinous character. In both cases a dim sense of an invisible flow of vital forces from generation to generation, linking together the endless series, has been at work. Very primitive feeling may lurk under civilized waistcoats.

Notions derived from age-old magic helped Europe's 'absolute monarchs' to convince taxpayers that a country's entire welfare, even survival, was bound up with its God-sent ruler's. Mughal emperors appeared daily on their balcony so that their subjects could see them and feel satisfied that all was well. Rajput princes would ride in a daily cavalcade through their small capitals, for the same reason. Any practical relevance of the crown to public well-being has long since vanished, but somehow in Britain the existence of a Royal Family seems to convince people in some subliminal way that everything is going to turn out all right for them ... Things of today may have ancient roots; on the other hand antiques are often forgeries, and Royal sentiment in Britain today is largely an artificial product.

His knowledge of India was first-hand. He was there from 1938–46, establishing contacts, organizing study-circles with local Communists and teaching at Aitchison (formerly Chiefs) College – an institution created to educate the Indian nobility along the lines suggested by the late Lord Macaulay. What the students (mostly wooden-headed wastrels) made of Victor has never been revealed, but one or two of the better ones did later embrace radical ideas. It would be nice to think that he was responsible. I can't imagine who else it could have been. The experience taught him a great deal about imperialism, and in a set of stunningly well-written and scholarly books he wrote copiously on the origins and development of the American Empire, the Spanish colonization of South America and on other European empires.

He was by now fluent in Persian and Urdu and had met Allama Muhammad Iqbal and the young Faiz Ahmed Faiz, two of the greatest poets produced by Northern India. Kiernan translated both of them into English, which played no small part in helping to enlarge their audience at a time when imperial languages were totally dominant. His interpretation of Shakespeare is much underrated, but were it put on course-lists it would be a healthy antidote to the embalming.

He had married the dancer and theatrical activist Shanta Gandhi in 1938 in Bombay, but they split up before he left India in 1946. Almost forty years later he married Heather Massey. When I met him soon afterwards he confessed that she had rejuvenated him intellectually. His writings confirmed this view. Throughout his life he stubbornly adhered to Marxist ideas, but without a trace of rigidity or sullenness. He was not one to pander to the latest fashions and despised the postmodernist wave that swept the academy in the 1980s and 90s, rejecting history in favour of trivia. Angered by triumphalist mainstream commentaries proclaiming the virtues of capitalism, he wrote a sharp rebuttal. 'Modern Capitalism and Its Shepherds' was published, again in the *New Left Review*, in October 1990:

> Merchant capital, usurer capital, have been ubiquitous, but they have not by themselves brought about any decisive alteration of the world. It is industrial capital that has led to revolutionary change, and been the highroad to a scientific technology that has transformed agriculture as well as industry, society as well as economy. Industrial capitalism peeped out here and there before the nineteenth century, but on any considerable scale it seems to have been rejected like an alien graft, as something too unnatural to spread far. It has been a strange aberration on the human path, an abrupt mutation. Forces outside economic life were needed to establish it; only very complex, exceptional conditions could engender, or keep alive, the entrepreneurial spirit. There have always been much easier ways of making money than long-term industrial investment, the hard grind of running a factory. J. P. Morgan preferred to sit in a

back parlour on Wall Street smoking cigars and playing solitaire, while money flowed towards him. The English, first to discover the industrial highroad, were soon deserting it for similar parlours in the City, or looking for byways, short cuts and colonial Eldorados.

The current crisis would not have surprised him at all. Fictive capital, I can hear him saying, has no future.

February 2009

INDEX

Fictional characters alphabetized by first name when full name used.

INDEX

INDEX